世界汉语修辞学会

第三辑

GUOJI XIUCIXUE YANJIU

国际修辞学研究

International Rhetoric Studies

陈汝东 主编

高等教育出版社·北京

图书在版编目（C I P）数据

国际修辞学研究．第3辑：汉语、英语／陈汝东主编．-- 北京：高等教育出版社，2015.3
ISBN 978-7-04-041640-4

Ⅰ．①国… Ⅱ．①陈… Ⅲ．①汉语－修辞学－文集－汉、英 Ⅳ．①H15-53

中国版本图书馆CIP数据核字（2015）第015913号

策划编辑 谢 森　　责任编辑 王代军　　封面设计 王 洋　　版式设计 魏 亮
责任校对 孙 悦　　责任印制 刘思涵

出版发行 高等教育出版社
社　　址 北京市西城区德外大街4号
邮政编码 100120
印　　刷 唐山市润丰印务有限公司
开　　本 787mm×1092mm 1/16
印　　张 15.25
字　　数 309千字
购书热线 010-58581118

咨询电话 400-810-0598
网　　址 http://www.hep.edu.cn
　　　　 http://www.hep.com.cn
网上订购 http://www.landraco.com
　　　　 http://www.landraco.com.cn
版　　次 2015年3月第1版
印　　次 2015年3月第1次印刷
定　　价 31.00元

本书如有缺页、倒页、脱页等质量问题，请到所购图书销售部门联系调换

物 料 号 41640-00

Editoral Board

前　言

继往开来，同心同德，繁荣全球修辞学

尊敬的校长阁下，各位来宾、各位同仁、朋友，老师们，同学们，早上好！

今天，在国际同仁特别是韩国同仁的共同努力下，经过两年多的精心筹备，世界汉语修辞学会第三届年会暨修辞学国际学术研讨会胜利开幕了！

出席本届年会的有近百位学者，分别来自美国、德国、韩国、意大利、南非、日本、马来西亚、保加利亚、巴西、墨西哥以及中国大陆、香港和台湾等十多个国家和地区。朋友们，今天我们相聚在美丽的海滨城市仁川，畅谈学术，共享文化，缔结新的友谊。在此，我代表学会和本次会议的组委会向你们表示诚挚热烈的欢迎！

世界汉语修辞学会2007年成立于法国，在韩国注册，秘书处设在中国的北京大学。她是目前世界上最大的汉语修辞学国际学术组织。截至目前，学会吸纳了数十个国家和地区的数百位修辞学及相邻学科的学者。学会先后在中国大陆和香港、日本召开了两届学术年会和四次国际学术会议，并成立了国际修辞传播学会、国际语言传播学会、全球传媒伦理与法制联合会等分会。学会会员已遍及五大洲，实现了修辞学研究上的真正全球化。全球修辞学会的成立，标志着我会发展的一个新的里程碑。

本届年会是我会发展历史上的又一次盛会。出席本次会议的，除了亚洲、非洲、欧洲和北美的学者，还有来自南美洲的学者，国际修辞学大家庭更加壮大。这充分体现了我会和国际修辞学研究的蓬勃态势，也折射出我会强大的凝聚力。相信，本届年会和新成立的全球修辞学会，无疑将进一步推动国际汉语修辞学乃至全球修辞学的发展和繁荣。本次会议的主题是“全球文化融合与冲突中的国际修辞学：东亚与世界”。会议将着力通过多元文化修辞观的综合透视，东西与南北修辞学传统的交融以及跨学科的交叉，铸造国际修辞学发展的全球化趋势。

随着我会学术活动的深入开展，我们对修辞的认识也不断加深。作为一种语言媒介艺术，修辞不仅是演说、劝服、修饰，不仅是美化语言、发现真理，它同时也是一种人类传播秩序和社会秩序，是公共权力和公共秩序建构、社会事务处理、公共政策制定的方式和方法，是一种社会公平、公正的制度体系，是一种人类生活方式，同时也是一种人类文化乃至文明的形态。

修辞学观念的更新，必将带来修辞学研究范式的革命。随着国际修辞学学术交流的深入，世界修辞学正呈现出全球化态势。但是，修辞学研究中的东西隔膜、南北分化，依然存在。在2012年7月初于英国牛津大学召开的“21世纪的修辞学互动论坛”上，我曾倡议，西方修辞学应走出古希腊，走出欧洲，向东，与亚洲修辞文

化交融，向南，与非洲修辞文明对话。亚洲、非洲的修辞学则要向西、向北，与欧洲、美洲接洽，实现修辞学的全球化，建构全球修辞、全球修辞学。

为此，各国学者应从多元文化背景、从全球视角重新审视人类的修辞学传统和未来。这意味着，在数字传播时代，修辞应该且必将成为一种全球秩序，一种普世法则，即通过非武力的修辞手段解决国际争端和冲突，统一全球意志，实现人类共同利益，建构大同世界。全球修辞学会、世界汉语修辞学会无疑是通向这一学术理想的桥梁之一。本届年会的召开，则昭示了修辞学研究全球化的进一步发展。

本次会议的筹备和召开得到了各国学者和组织的大力支持。韩国修辞学会、仁川大学孔子学院、仁川大学中国学研究所等单位，都提供了坚实的物质保障和周到的后勤服务。朴禹洙、金钟甲、罗敏球、安性栽等教授组成的韩国团队，特别是仁川大学孔子学院、中国学研究所的老师和同学们，在会议的筹备及召开中付出了辛勤汗水。在此，我谨代表世界汉语修辞学会向以上单位和个人表示衷心的感谢！

各位同仁、各位朋友，“学术·文化·友谊”是我们学会举办学术活动的宗旨。去年秋天，我们在札幌大学切磋学术，考察日本的北国风情，享受了定山溪的温泉，结下了难忘的友情。今天，老友新朋不远千山万水，再次相聚在美丽的海滨城市——仁川，共享又一场学术盛宴。

“仁川”是一个令人产生无限遐想的名字，她很契合我们学会的宗旨。孔子曾说：“知者乐水，仁者乐山。”今天，来自五湖四海的知者仁人，相聚在“仁川”之畔，研讨修辞之学，温润心志，缔结友谊。国之交在于民相亲，民相亲来自心相知，心相知源自文相通。让我们在短暂的时光中尽情地畅谈学术，相通、相知、相亲，共享“学术·文化·友谊”之乐，共建各国学术交流之桥。

最后，祝各位与会嘉宾、学者在会议期间身体健康，精神愉快！祝大会圆满成功！

谢谢大家！

陈汝东
（［中国］北京大学）

目　录

第五部分 文艺修辞研究 141

第六部分 话语修辞研究 173

第七部分 传统修辞研究 195

第一部分
全球修辞学研究

论修辞学研究的全球化趋势

陈汝东

（［中国］北京大学）

提　要：本文阐述了修辞学研究的全球化态势及其表现形态，剖析了全球修辞、全球修辞学的内涵，分析了其提出的现实和理论依据以及文化背景，阐释了全球修辞学的目标及其建构策略。作者认为，全球修辞是指修辞实践的全球化，它意味着一种全球社会秩序，一种普世法则，一种全球秩序建构的手段和途径，即通过非武力的修辞手段建构全球秩序，通过理性对话处理人类在发展中所面临的共同问题，化解各种国际争端和冲突，统一全球意志，实现人类共同利益，建构大同世界。它既是一种人类共同意志凝聚和灵魂管理的手段与方式，同时也是一种世界秩序和人类文明形态。全球修辞学为世界学术秩序提供了一种新的可能，为世界修辞学研究提供了一种碰撞、融合的新视野。各国学者应具有全球视野和普世情怀，应具有海纳百川的气度，要勇于突破各自的学术传统，实现与其他文化背景中学术传统的平等交流、碰撞与融合。全球修辞学理论体系的建构，既需要多维学科视野，也需要建立全球性的学术组织，奠定新的全球学术交流机制。

关键词：全球修辞；全球修辞学；世界秩序；人类文明

近年来，随着各国修辞学研究的深入，国际学术交流也日益频繁，国际修辞学呈现出融合趋势。“全球修辞”“全球修辞学”逐渐进入修辞学范畴，并有浓缩当前和未来修辞学研究趋势的可能。什么是“全球修辞”“全球修辞学”？它们的内涵是什么？有哪些表现形态？如何进行研究？“全球修辞”“全球修辞学”未来应如何发展？这是值得各国学者研究的问题。本文将对此加以探讨。

一、全球化：国际修辞学研究的新趋势

修辞学领域的“全球化”是一个新概念，它提出的基础是全球化的深入、新媒介技术的普及和国际修辞学研究的不断发展，特别是日益密切和频繁的国际学术交流。下面，让我们来简单回顾一下近些年国际修辞学学术交流的新趋势。

新世纪之前，各大洲之间的修辞学国际学术交流隔阂明显，特别是亚洲、非洲与欧洲之间的学术交流比较欠缺。就中国修辞学的国际交流来说，2000年是一个重要起点。当年7月，笔者邀请美国明尼苏达大学修辞学系的艾伦·葛络斯（Alan Gross）教授来华访问并出席了中国修辞学会在广州召开的年会，这应该是正式访问

中国修辞学界的第一位西方修辞学者。[1] 2006年11月，国际修辞学史学会前会长、美国南加州大学修辞学教授劳伦斯·葛林（Lawrence D. Green）先生应邀来华出席学术会议，并作了题为“全球修辞学史研究”的学术报告。在演讲中，他简述了美国、加拿大、墨西哥、英国、法国、意大利、西班牙、荷兰、德国、丹麦、芬兰、冰岛、挪威、瑞典、波兰、立陶宛、俄罗斯、保加利亚、韩国、日本等国的修辞学研究情况。[2] 这可能是修辞学者首次如此全面地阐述世界修辞学研究的状况。

此后，美国、英国、加拿大、法国、德国、意大利、俄罗斯、丹麦、瑞典、墨西哥、埃及、马来西亚以及日本、韩国等国的许多著名学者先后应邀访问中国修辞学界，比如戴安娜·德豪赛-邦妮（Diane Desrosiers Bonin）、迈克尔·莱夫、施文娟、洛朗·白傲诺、露西娅·蒙德福斯科、大卫·弗兰克（David Frank）、田圣淇、朴禹洙等。2005年7月，国际修辞学史学会正式邀请中国学者陈汝东出席其第15届年会并作报告。此后，各国修辞学会先后多次邀请中国学者出席其学术年会。这些交流活动大大促进了国际修辞学研究的全球化趋势。

2010年之后，亚洲的修辞学国际学术交流迈上了一个新台阶。当年7月在中国香港召开的世界汉语修辞学第二届年会上，来自非洲的修辞学学者菲利普·赛拉兹出现在了学术报告席上。2011年5月和10月，在中国北京大学召开的国际语言传播学前沿论坛和在日本札幌大学召开的国际修辞传播学前沿论坛，汇聚了来自亚洲、非洲、欧洲、美洲的学者。笔者与美国俄勒冈大学罗伯特·柯拉克荣誉学院院长大卫·弗兰克教授、保加利亚索菲亚大学佟卡·亚历山卓娃（Donka Alexandrova）教授，先后阐述了修辞学在全球化中的重要作用，即通过修辞改善国际沟通与合作，解决国际冲突，实现人类和平发展的愿望。[3] 在札幌会议上，我们提出：“各国学者应从各自的学科背景出发，以各自的国别文化建设为基础，共同探讨和建构人类文化发展传播的普遍修辞新秩序，创造人类文化发展、繁荣的新时代。”[4]

国际学术组织的建立和发展也是修辞学全球化的一个重要标志。一方面是成立了许多跨洲国际学术组织，比如国际修辞学史学会、世界汉语修辞学会、欧洲修辞学会等。其中，国际修辞学史学会在原有基础上进一步发展，主动邀请许多亚洲修辞学学者参与，使这个以修辞学史为主要研究对象的学术组织进一步焕发了生命力。更令人瞩目的是，2007年成立于法国的世界汉语修辞学学会，截至目前，该学会吸纳了数十个国家和地区的数百名修辞学学者，先后召开了三届学术年会和四次国际学术会议，并成立了国际修辞传播学会、国际语言传播学会等国际学术组织，

1 当然，在此之前，也有西方学者来华，比如加拿大的高辛勇等，但并没有直接与中国修辞学界进行交流。

2 劳伦斯·葛林：《全球修辞学史研究》，陈汝东译，《江汉大学学报》2007年第1期。

3 《首届国际语言传播学前沿论坛在北京举行》，新华网2011年5月20日。

4 《第二届国际修辞传播学前沿论坛在日本札幌召开》，人民网2011年11月6日；陈汝东：《加强全球修辞传播研究共同促进人类文化发展》，《国际修辞学研究》第二辑，高等教育出版社，2012年10月，第i~iii页。

出席者已遍及亚洲、非洲、欧洲、美洲和大洋洲，实现了修辞学研究真正的全球化。成立于2012年10月的全球修辞学会更是修辞学研究全球化的例证。此外，一些国家的修辞学会的学术活动更加开放，逐渐国际化，比如中国修辞学会、美国修辞学会、韩国修辞学会等等。

学术成果出版与共享上的国际化，也是修辞学研究全球化的重要标志。随着互联网的普及，文献传播的全球化态势也日趋明显。首先是图书出版和流通的全球化，亚马逊等全球化图书销售网络、中国知网等电子数据库，使图书、文献的获取更为便利。其次，各国、各大学的电子书和论文数据库也不断丰富。目前已经出版的期刊或丛书，比如《修辞学》《国际修辞学研究》《非洲修辞学年鉴》等，都刊登了世界各国学者的学术成果，实现了学术成果共享上的全球化。以上表明，国际修辞学研究和交流真正实现了全球学术信息共享，使国际修辞学发展逐步实现或正在实现全球化。

此外，国际修辞学研究上的学科融合也是修辞学研究全球化的态势之一。近些年，修辞学研究逐渐和语言学、哲学、文学以及社会学、心理学等学科进行交叉、融合，特别是与新闻学、传播学进行交叉和融合。这不仅表现在研究方法方面，更重要的是学者的学术背景和知识结构上的交叉与融合。学科跨界成为推动全球修辞学发展繁荣的重要动力，大大推动了修辞学学科空间的拓展，激发了新兴交叉学科的诞生。

二、全球修辞学：一种新的学术视野

修辞学研究的全球化态势必将激发出新的修辞观，它将使人们从人类共同利益和全球秩序角度对修辞的性质、功能进行新的阐释。全球视野中的修辞，不仅是传统意义上的劝服方式、一种知识生产和真理发现的手段和途径，也不仅是一种生活方式和社会秩序，它将成为一种全球秩序、一种普世法则。

在修辞学史上，人类对修辞的阐释就像夜空中的繁星。有修饰观、美辞观、说服观、言语行为观、传播行为观、认知行为观等等，不胜枚举。这其中也有历史与现代、东方与西方的碰撞。在西方的古典修辞学体系中，说服是修辞的核心功能；此外，修辞还被视作生产知识和发现真理的手段和途径。这在20世纪的认知修辞学中体现得更为充分。在西方的三大传统学科——语法、逻辑、修辞中，只有修辞学是可以生产知识的。而在东方，古典修辞学的核心思想却与此大相径庭，其强调的是伦理道德，是“仁”和“礼”，也就是人的内在修养和社会秩序。虽然东西方的修辞学学者在各自的学术思想阐释中并没有达成一致，但事实证明，这两种文明范畴是互补的，尽管它们泾渭分明。知识、真理观体现了社会个体的思想意志，而社会秩序观则体现了宏观的人文意志。在全球视野下，人类的修辞观正面临着融合出新。

我们认为，修辞不仅是说服、论辩、发现真理，同时是“一种人类传播秩序和社会秩序，是公共权力和公共秩序建构、社会事务处理、公共政策制定的方式和方法，是一种社会公平、公正的制度体系，是一种人类生活方式，同时也是一种文化传统和文明形态”，[5] 是一种“人类文化和人类文明的样类”。据此，我们认为，“全球修辞，就是在全球传播时代，人类以全球为语境，运用修辞手段和方法，通过辩论、说服等形式进行信息沟通、情感交流，解决全球冲突，实现意志统一、利益共享的传播行为。”[6]

那么，全球修辞是一种全球社会秩序吗？它在当今的全球数字传播时代具有怎样的意义和价值呢？显然，回答是肯定的。在全球化时代，全球修辞意味着一种全球社会秩序，全球秩序建构的手段和途径，即通过非武力的修辞手段建构全球秩序，通过理性对话解决国际争端和冲突，统一全球意志，实现人类共同利益，建构大同世界。在此意义上，全球修辞也是一种全球性的国际法则，具有普世性。从广泛的修辞范畴来看，战争和武力其实也是一种符号行为，是一种“修辞”，或者说通过非修辞手段而实现修辞回归的手段。在隔阂、分歧、冲突和矛盾不可调和时，也就是说当不可通过调整思想和意志的言说修辞来达到意志上的统一时，人类就诉诸武力和战争，即通过调整四肢的方式来实现意志的调控。其结果是使非理性的一方回到理性的轨道上来。

劳伦斯·葛林教授指出：“在有些国家，修辞学是被作为维系国家统一的途径来研究的。在有些国家，修辞学是被作为构成政府基础的方法来研究的。在有些国家，它赞美一个社会的过去，或者推进一个社会的未来……但是，在西方范围以外，‘修辞学’正在被许多国家奉为文化拯救和通向美好未来的灯塔。”[7] 我们认为，葛林此处所说的“维系国家统一的途径”“构成政府基础的方法”和“文化拯救和通向美好未来的灯塔”，意思与我们所说的修辞学作为社会秩序和社会文明的含义大致相当。

全球修辞的国内事务意义，就是把修辞作为一种社会秩序，通过理性的修辞手段，凝聚和体现公共意志，建构社会权力和权利体系，制定全社会的公共政策，实现全社会的公平与公正。它意味着社会事务必须建立在理性的论辩基础上，而不是建立在权力和权势基础上。每个社会成员都享有平等的言论权利，其公共修辞的内容都可以被公平地纳入社会秩序范畴，无须通过其他途径和手段实现。这也意味着全社会拥有了统一的价值体系。这需要政治、法律和道德上的保障，需要理性的言说者或传播者，同时也需要一个理性的受众社会。

如果说全球修辞意味着一种全球社会秩序，那么什么是全球修辞学呢？我们认为，全球修辞学就是从人类文化和文明视角研究全球修辞规律的新兴交叉学科，它旨在综括人类全球修辞的手段和方法，探讨解决人类共同面临的全球生存与发展问题的修辞战略和对策，揭示全球传播的修辞规律。全球修辞学为修辞学研究的学术秩序提供了一种新的可能，一种世界学术研究碰撞、融合的新视野。

近年来，我们一直致力于国际修辞学研究秩序的建构，先后提出了公共修辞、

---

5 陈汝东：《新兴修辞传播学理论》，北京大学出版社，2011年10月，第178页。

6 陈汝东：《古典与未来：中国修辞学思想的全球意义》，《北京大学报》（哲社版）2013年第5期。

7 劳伦斯·葛林：《全球修辞学史研究》，陈汝东译，《江汉大学学报》2007年第1期。

国家修辞等学术范畴，并引发了许多共鸣。大卫·弗兰克曾指出："首先，我们可以对本土修辞学和全球修辞学进行系统的研究，以揭示它们之间的异同，最终的目标是建构一个基于修辞而不是战争的国际秩序。……其次，比较修辞学的终极目的是建构修辞学的世界同一，使本土修辞学与各国、各地区修辞学群星璀璨，通过修辞消除国际冲突，促进世界人民的相互理解与和平共处。……同理，一个修辞学者也应有双重担当，其研究既属于他的祖国，同时也属于世界。"[8] 他同时认为："中国也具有像古希腊一样悠久的修辞学传统，也有论辩、说服、演说传统。在世界共融环境下，了解中国修辞学已经变得越来越重要，这将有助于增进东西方的学术交流，有助于促进大同世界的建构。"[9]

我们认为，中国古代修辞学思想的核心是"言仁"，即用言说、劝服的方式促进人类理解和关爱。在当今世界，修辞应成为避免和替代暴力和战争的和平手段，给不同文明提供通过道德沟通处理重大问题的机会和途径。[10] 目前"修辞问题不仅是中国问题，也是世界问题，它关系到人类的和平与发展。全世界的修辞学者都应投身和加强对全球修辞秩序和修辞制度的比较研究，以催生出一种能通过修辞来促进世界和平和正义、解决全球普遍问题的传播秩序，从而避免战争和武力"。[11]

三、全球修辞学的建构

在政治、经济、环境和通讯、传播全球化的今天，人类的学术文化研究再囿于东西南北任何一方或一个国家，都已是不可能的，也是不可取的。民族、文化、宗教之间的藩篱、意识形态的隔阂，必须也必然被突破。修辞学研究也是如此。世界修辞学者应具有全球视野，具有普世的情怀，具有海纳百川的气度。中国古语云：泰山不让土壤，故能成其大，河海不择细流，故能就其深。 这应该成为一种国际学术法则。全球修辞学研究应实现不同文化、文明上的平等，没有歧视，没有偏见，无论是东方、西方、南方，还是北方，应一视同仁。

北京大学有一种学术理念，叫作"学术自由，兼容并包"。我们想，这可以用于全球修辞学研究。"时至今日，西方一些学者一直认为东方或中东没有修辞传统。……没有证据表明存在独立于西方的修辞意识。……作为西方的一种意象，东方文化缺乏论辩色彩，情感，直觉和神秘主义是其最重要的文化价值。……亚洲在西方修辞学史中基本不被提及，即使出现，也被当作是无修辞的存在。"[12] 显然，这是一种学术霸权，是一种学术文化上的固执、傲慢与偏见。历史证明，西方学者

---

8 大卫·弗兰克：《问题的修辞和修辞学的问题：建构全球修辞学》，《江淮论坛》2012年第3期。

9 陈汝东：《"国家修辞"成为学术焦点——首届国际语言传播学前沿论坛在北京大学召开》，《中国社会科学报》2011年5月26日，第10版。

10 大卫·弗兰克：编译《北大陈汝东教授应邀出席牛津大学修辞学高峰论坛》，北京大学新闻网 2012年8月21日。

11 《第二届国际修辞传播学前沿论坛在日本札幌召开》，人民网2011年11月6日。

12 大卫·弗兰克：《问题的修辞和修辞学的问题：建构全球修辞学》，《江淮论坛》2012年第3期。

"西方以外没有修辞，没有修辞学"的观点已不攻自破。随着亚洲文明的重新崛起和世界对其修辞学历史的再认识、再发现，特别是经过东亚、南非以及欧洲、美洲国际修辞学者的共同努力，国际修辞学研究已经形成了一个能具有广泛包容性的国际学术大家庭。

但是，全球修辞学的进一步整合发展，必然会存在着国别、民族、宗教和区域文化上的进一步碰撞。2012年7月初，"21世纪的修辞学互动论坛"在英国牛津大学召开。来自英、美、中、加、德、意以及丹麦、澳大利亚等国的20位修辞学学者与会。会上各国学者就21世纪的修辞学研究提出了各自的设想，但是，其核心依然是以西方修辞学尤其是古典修辞学为视角。其中，西方修辞学的领军人物伦敦大学教授布莱恩·维克斯爵士就柏拉图的斐德罗篇发表演讲。在应邀对其演讲进行点评时，笔者指出："对人类古典修辞学思想的阐发应兼顾多元文化背景，应有东西、南北视野，既关注古希腊、古罗马的修辞学传统，还应关照东方的修辞学传统，关注非洲的修辞学传统，特别是东方的儒家修辞学传统。21世纪的修辞学研究应从古希腊走出来，走向英国、德国……，走向亚洲，走向全球；修辞学者应胸怀当下的全球修辞现实，既要从古典文献中汲取营养，同时还应着眼未来的理论创新。"[13]对此，大卫·弗兰克教授指出："西方学者需要从古典传统和现代表达两个层面去认识和发现中国修辞学。"[14] 这在一定程度上反映了欧美学者对东方修辞学学术文化态度的转变，也折射出了全球修辞学研究的东方转向态势。

全球视野下的国际修辞学研究，不仅需要对修辞、修辞学范畴进行重新认识和阐释，还需要对世界各国修辞学研究的对象、目的、范围、理论体系进行新视角下的审视。全球的研究材料，将不再局限于一个国家、一个民族，而是要从全球范围选取。全球网络传播使修辞研究对象的全球化成为可能。全球修辞学理论体系的建构也不应再局限于一种语言、一种文化，而是多种语言、多元文化。当然，除此之外，还需要多维学科视野，需要建立全球性的学术组织，奠定新的全球学术交流机制。

修辞的全球化，无疑是国际政治、经济、文化和传播全球化的结果，而国际修辞学研究的全球化，则是学术交流日趋融合的结果，同时也是各国修辞学者不断努力的结晶。修辞学研究的全球化为修辞、修辞学范畴的重新阐释和创造提供了新的契机，也为各国学者进一步的广泛交流与合作，创造了新的空间。一个崭新的修辞学学术研究的格局正期待更多国际学者的加入，它预示了人类全球修辞学光辉灿烂的前景，同时也预示了人类通过和平手段——全球修辞，实现人类和平的美好未来。

---

13 大卫·弗兰克：《北大陈汝东教授应邀出席牛津大学修辞学高峰论坛》，惠东坡编译，北京大学新闻网 2012年8月21日。

14 大卫·弗兰克：《北大陈汝东教授应邀出席牛津大学修辞学高峰论坛》，惠东坡编译，北京大学新闻网 2012年8月21日。

On Globalizing Trends of Rhetoric Studies

Chen Rudong

(Peking University, China)

Abstract: This paper expounds the globalizing trends of international rhetoric studies and its forms. It also analyzes the connotations of global rhetoric and global rhetoric studies, the practical and theoretical basis and culture background which they are put forward. And then this paper explains the academic goal of global rhetoric studies and the strategies for achieving it. The author thinks that global rhetoric is the globalization of rhetorical practice. It means a global social system, a universal code and approaches to them. Global rhetoric means to defuse international conflicts, to deal with all the developmental problems of human being by rhetorical conversation rather than violence and war, to unify the global public wills, to realize the common interests, to build a Great Unity. Global rhetoric is also a mean and a way for managing human souls and gathering common will of human beings, as well being a world order and one form of human civilization. Global rhetoric offers a new possibility of new vision and academic order for international rhetoric studies. International scholars should take global vision and universal feelings, break through their own academic tradition bravely and treat others equally. The building of global rhetorical theory needs not only multiple disciplinary vision but also new global organization.

Keywords: global rhetoric; world order; human civilization; trend

World Rhetoric in the 21st Century: Conversation Between Sir Brian Vickers and Chen Rudong

David A. Frank

(University of Oregon, USA)

Abstract: The "Rhetoric in the Twenty-First Century: An Interactive Symposium" (3~7 July 2012) hosted a group of international scholars of rhetoric at the University of Oxford. The exchange between Sir Brian Vickers, a leading scholar of rhetoric in the west, and Professor Rudong Chen of Peking University, President of the Global Rhetoric Society of the World, and the leading rhetoric scholar in China, on the trends of international rhetoric studies and purpose and function of rhetoric was a highlight of the Symposium. The dialogue reflects the contrasting and conflicts on cultural perspectives between the West and the East. It attracts the attention of scholars in the field of rhetoric studies. In this article, the author considers the Vickers–Chen exchange and how it contributes to better understanding of Chinese, Western, and cosmopolitan expressions of rhetoric. Toward this goal, the issues raised by the top dialogue of Vickers–Chen illustrate the importance of international academic exchanges on the topic of rhetoric. These exchanges have encouraged Western scholars of rhetoric to abandon the view that there was no rhetorical tradition in China or the East. As Chen revealed in his response to Vickers, Chinese rhetoric can offer a paradigm for education, collaboration, and appreciation of cultural difference. While Chinese and Western rhetorics do differ on important key points, the Vickers–Chen exchange demonstrates that Chinese and Western rhetorics can be brought into harmony through a cosmopolitan comprehension and appreciation of the strengths they both bring to the development of a truly global rhetoric in the 21st century.

Keywords: University of Oxford, Peking University, Brian Vickers, Chen Rudong, global rhetoric

Founded in 1121 CE, the University of Oxford is the oldest English-speaking institution and hosts some of the most prestigious colleges in the world. Founded in 1898, Peking University is considered the most respected institution of higher education in China and is among the elite institutions of higher education in the world. The "Rhetoric in the 21st Century: An Interactive Symposium" (3~7 July 2012), organized by James J. Murphy, Professor Emeritus of English at the University of California-Davis, and Nicholas J. Crowe, of the Centre for Medieval & Renaissance Studies, Oxford, brought scholars from the West and the East, and from Oxford and Peking University to a seminar devoted to debate, dialogue, and discussion on the topic of rhetoric.

The leaders of the seminar selected four keynote speakers to make a provocative argument on the theme of rhetoric in the twenty-first century, including Sir Brian Vickers, Peter Mack, James J. Murphy, and Jennifer Richards. Nineteen delegates were selected from a number of applications. Participants from eight countries attended the seminar. The Interactive Symposium achieved its goals. With scholars representing different rhetorical traditions, assumptions and commonplaces were expressed, challenged, rejected and accepted on the basis of their argumentative power. All the participants and delegates were moved to an agreement that rhetoric could provide a method and mode of thinking for this century. Reflecting a Western bias, Cicero, the Roman, was the most cited rhetorician, with his *De Oratore* the most mentioned rhetorical text.

The high point of the symposium was the exchange between Sir Brian Vickers, a leading scholar of rhetoric in the west, and Professor Rudong Chen of Peking University, President of the Chinese Rhetoric Society of the World, and the leading rhetoric scholar in China, on the purpose and function of rhetoric. My goal in this essay is to describe the exchange between professors Vickers and Chen as it reveals both the present and the future of the study of rhetoric.

Vickers' book *In Defense of Rhetoric* is among the most important English contributions of rhetoric in the twentieth century.[1] In his keynote address, Vickers argued twenty-first-century rhetorical studies would not differ markedly from the rhetoric of preceding centuries. He identified three major areas of research in rhetoric for the twenty-first century: First, Vickers urged scholars to conduct textual analysis of rhetorical commentaries. This analysis would include increasing the number of translations that place texts in their contexts. Vickers offered as examples Virginia Cox and John Oastler Ward's *The Rhetoric of Cicero in Its Medieval and Early-Renaissance Commentary Tradition*, James J. Murphy and Jerry Green's *Renaissance Rhetoric Short-Title Catalogue 1460–1700*, and Gert Ueding, Gregor Kalivoda, and Franz-Hubert Robling's comprehensive seven-volume German survey of rhetoric, *Historisches*

1 Brian Vickers, *In Defence of Rhetoric* (Oxford Clarendon Press ; Oxford University Press, 1988).

Wörterbuch der Rhetorik.[2]

Second, Vickers called for the study of rhetoric as an expression of a social phenomenon. Rhetoric scholars, Vickers continued, should consider how rhetorical theories are handed down by one generation to the next. The study of how rhetoric is taught, he emphasized, should be a focus of sustained study.

Third, rhetoric should be studied as an expression of political activity. Vickers expressed concern about the role played by rhetoric in the political arena: good people and good rhetoric do not always achieve positive results in democracies. Vickers suggested the following questions might guide rhetorical scholars in this century: How does persuasion work? How does persuasion happen? He made a point of lamenting the state of political rhetoric in the United States and Britain to illustrate the obvious need for a better political discourse.

In response to Vickers' keynote address, Professor Chen, one of the two Asian scholars attending the seminar, invited his western audience to consider Chinese rhetoric in both its ancient and modern expressions, considerations that had not appeared in Vickers' keynote address. Persuasion, argumentation, and the discovery of truth in western rhetoric are all important, Chen agreed. However, as Chen observed, Chinese rhetoric embraces "a way of life" "a social system" "a culture" and "a civilization". In ancient China, Chen noted, rhetoric was concerned with morality, ethics, and most importantly, accepted the Confucian emphasis on love. Rhetoric, Chen concluded, serves as an alternative to war and violence, offering civilizations a means to negotiate significant problems through moral communication rather than violence.

Sir Vickers' review of the Western rhetorical tradition was thorough, accurate, but needed professor Chen's insights given the 21st century will not belong to England or the West. Western scholars of rhetoric have yet to fully appreciate the rhetoric offered by the traditions and scholars of Asian rhetorics. Professor Chen, in his response to one of the most influential scholar of rhetoric in the West, modeled how cross-cultural dialogue on rhetoric ought to and can take place. He honored Sir Vickers' by treating him with deference, accurately interpreted what Sir Vickers said, and provided a complement to Vickers' history: the rhetorical traditions and scholarship of China.

Unfortunately, professor Vickers' keynote address did not reflect an understanding nor an appreciation of Asian rhetorical traditions. This tradition is outlined in

2 Virginia Cox and John O. Ward, *The Rhetoric of Cicero in Its Medieval and Early Renaissance Commentary Tradition* (Leiden ; Boston: Brill, 2006); Lawrence D. Green and James Jerome Murphy, *Renaissance Rhetoric Short-Title Catalogue 1460-1700*, 2nd ed. (Aldershot, England ; Burlington, VT: Ashgate, 2006); Gert Ueding, Gregor Kalivoda, and Franz-Hubert Robling, *Historisches Wèorterbuch Der Rhetorik* (Tèubingen: M. Niemeyer, 1992).

professor Chen's "Rhetoric in East Asia: China and Japan," published in *The International Encyclopaedia of Communication.*[3] Here, professor Chen describes the family characteristics of Asian and Chinese rhetoric. Chinese rhetorical thought, he notes, can be traced back to the Spring and Autumn period (770–476 BCE) of Chinese history, preceding birth of Greek rhetorical thought.

In this article, professor Chen highlights four functions served by rhetoric in ancient China: The cultivation of morality, fulfillment of the good life, interpersonal diplomacy through dialogue, and management of society. Rhetorical competence and persuasive behavior were at the center of ancient Chinese society. To be rhetorically competent, professor Chen writes, the speaker in ancient China followed the principles of ritual, humanity, loyalty, and truthfulness. "They also outlined rhetorical the principle of bringing rhetoric into harmony with rhetorical situations through the techniques of 'Wén' (refinement) 'Zhì' (simplicity), 'Dá' (clarity) and 'Qiǎo' (literary grace)." [4]

When professor Chen outlines the functions and principles of ancient Chinese rhetoric, it is clear that they remain relevant to the modern Chinese rhetorical practices. They will, of course, need to account for the rhetorical problems faced by contemporary China. Before ancient Chinese rhetorical principles can inform modern Chinese rhetorical theory, professor Chen is wise to call for a thorough study of modern Chinese national rhetoric. He is currently leading a major project designed to achieve this goal.

Professor Chen also points to modern Chinese texts on rhetoric, which include Wang Dechun and Chen Chen's *Modern Rhetoric*, Zheng Yuanhan's *Speech Stylistics*, Li Yunhan's *Stylistics of Chinese Language*, Wang Xījie's *General Rhetoric*, Liu Huanhui's *Compendium of Rhetoric*, Zhang Lianqiang's studies on the *Theoretical Basis of Rhetoric*, and Rudong Chen's *Introduction to Socio-psychological Rhetoric*, *Chinese Rhetoric for Foreigners*, *Cognitive Rhetoric*, *The Contemporary Rhetoric of Chinese*, and etc. Professor Chen has written more than eight books, published by Peking University Press and other press in China, on the topic of rhetoric and communication.

In these books, he surveys the roles played by language, image, media, visualizations, persuasion, and a host of other topics in the construction of meaning. His books offer Chinese readers a comprehensive overview of rhetoric in its broadest expression. Because he has studied in England and the United States, he can identify where Chinese and Western rhetorics overlap and where they differ. There is no more important problem modern China faces than the problem of rhetoric, Chen argues. These books and articles

---

3 Chen Rudong, "Rhetoric in East Asia: China and Japan", *The International Encyclopedia of Communication*, edited by Wolfgang Donsbach, Blackwell Publishing Ltd. 2008, pp.4228-4231.

4 Ibid.

need to be brought into dialogue with those highlighted by professor Vickers.

Toward the end of bridging Western and Eastern rhetorics, one group of rhetorical scholars at the Oxford conference took the position during the final parliamentary debate that translation ought to be the foundation for the study of rhetoric in the twenty-first century. In arguing their case, the group suggested that translation (*translatio studii*) and the discipline of translation studies could foster the study of rhetoric in a global context. Translation assumes meaning can be communicated across and between cultures. The goal of translating rhetorical texts would be to promote a global rhetorical culture.

A truly global rhetoric would include a broadened understanding of "reason"; a focus on ethics, on audience, and an emphasis on cosmopolitanism, which could serve as touchstones for this approach. Metaphors, the party contended, are in this regard critical in conveying experience and ideas. Translation by definition requires flexibility, ethical recognition of others, and creative responses to texts that may yield multiple meanings. The process of persuasion (rhetoric) itself, the party argued, was rooted in translation, arising first from the soul and mind and proceeding then to its transmission in the verbal, visual or written expressions. If there argument has worth, then rhetorical scholars need to engage in a more robust effort to translate rhetorical texts in Asian languages into English and English rhetorical texts into Asian languages.

Similar to professor Chen's position that rhetoric is the major problem facing China, a second group of scholars argued that rhetoric in the twenty-first century should be described as a cure and not the illin cases where misunderstanding and misinterpretation arise. An ethical rhetoric, they suggest, presumes a responsive posture, and the centrality of audiences to constitute an ethical community. Global audiences and their rhetorics are diverse: an understanding of the history of rhetoric must remain open to reinterpretation, and rooted in the recognition that there are multiple rhetorics.

The Vickers–Chen exchange highlights the need to complement the study of Western rhetorics with those of the east. As such, the exchange teaches us that we should engage in a thorough accounting of local and global rhetorics, seeking out where there are differences and similarities, and following professor Chen's vision of cultivating international exchanges based on rhetoric rather than war. The Oxford conference, and the Vickers–Chen exchange, suggests it is possible and desirable for rhetorical scholars, from different traditions, to engage in the dialogues, disagreements, and discovery necessary to foster a global society founded on the best principles drawn from Cicero and Confucius.

Professor Chen, in a recent paper titled "On Globalizing Trends of Rhetoric Studies", delivered to the Chinese Rhetoric Society of the World, describes how eastern and western rhetorics could fit into a larger global constellation of rhetorics.[5] National rhetorics (those of China and the United States for example) are characterized by the myths and logics that nations use to form their identities and their view of other nations. Chen argues that national rhetorics should be a focus of study. Such study should complement efforts to place national rhetorics in the larger galaxy of global rhetorics. Scholars of rhetoric, Chen suggests, can contribute to an understanding of their own national rhetorics and to a more universal understanding of rhetoric through comparative analysis and comparisons. These comparisons, Chen continues, will lead to collisions and some incompatibilities that can be worked through with rhetoric. Chen's vision is exciting and can help foster the development of a global rhetorical culture.

Scholars who study Chinese national rhetoric would focus on the myths the Chinese people believe are important. Toward this end, identification of Chinese myths, with those that are central to Chinese identity, would be emphasized. The study of Chinese national rhetoric, Chen maintains, will highlight benevolence and a focus on persuasion, rather than violence, as the means of promoting social change. As the oldest civilization in the world, Chen rightly notes that China, like Greece, had a tradition of argumentation, debate, and persuasion; the Chinese do not need to import rhetoric from the West.

The study of Chinese national rhetoric will allow scholars to appreciate how Chinese mythic rhetoric animates Chinese social and international policy. For example, Chinese and American diplomats need to appreciate Chinese myths and how they are communicated. I believe President Obama's selection of John Huntsman as his first ambassador to China reflected a commitment to grounding American foreign policy in an understanding of Chinese culture; Huntsman speaks fluent Mandarin and has a strong command of Chinese history. Although the China and the US have faced conflict during Obama's first term, the Obama administration, operating under the influence of Huntsman, pursued a policy of engagement. Similarly, contemporary Chinese foreign policy seeks to bring China's image into alignment with its role as one of the two leading global powers. Toward this end, Chinese academics are promoting the study of public diplomacy, seeking to develop the "soft power" of persuasion to improve China's image.

Professor Chen has led the effort in China to invigorate the study of rhetoric, seeing that it can promote an understanding of national images. Chen seeks to promote and understanding of "national image building, competence and strategies of national rhetoric, especially the national rhetorical competence of national leader, officials,

5 Chen Rudong, *On Globalizing Trends of Rhetoric Studies*, Paper presented to the Third Biennial Bienienl Conference of the Chinese Rhetoric Society of the World, Incheon University, Korea, October, 2012.

reporter and the public." Chinese leaders, Chen writes, must demonstrate "rhetorical competence" in a global context. Toward this end, Chen and other Chinese scholars of rhetoric define "rhetorical competence" very broadly to include knowledge of both China's myths and those of China's global neighbors. To accomplish this goal, professor Chen and an international group of scholars have created opportunities for Chinese and Western scholars of rhetoric to meet and discuss topics of common interest.

These discussions began in the year 2000 with an American rhetorical scholar visiting China to cultivate relationships with Chinese scholars of rhetoric. Since the year 2000, the study of rhetoric has emerged as an important field in China, with the formation of the Chinese Rhetoric Society of the World in 2007 marking the arrival of Chinese rhetoric on the global academic stage. The society, under the leadership of professor Chen and a host of other Asian scholars, has attracted scholars of rhetoric from around the world to China. Scholars from the United States and the United Kingdom, and Canada, and France, and Germany, and Italy, and Russia, and Denmark Sweden, and Mexico, and Egypt, and Malaysia, as well as Japan, and Korea have attended conferences organized by the Chinese Rhetoric Society of the World.

As an American member of the Chinese Rhetoric Society of the World, I can testify that the Society has helped me better understand Chinese culture and myths as they are expressed through rhetoric. And, I have returned from Society conferences impressed with my Chinese colleagues who study and teach rhetoric. Far too many Americans and scholars of rhetoric are unaware of the Chinese rhetorial tradition. Jerome Murphy, who now know better, wrote in 1972 that there was no evidence of a rhetorical conscience outside the West.[6] This misperception was due to a lack of contact between Chinese and Western scholars of rhetoric and to the entrenched Western belief that Asia is devoid of argumentative reason, that emotion, intuition and mysticism are the most important cultural values in the East. The studies offered by the scholars who are members of the Chinese Rhetoric Society of the World have challenged and replaced these misperceptions with essays demonstrating the presence of argumentative reason in Chinese ancient and modern culture.

The Vickers–Chen exchange is an illustration of progress made in the study of rhetoric, for it invited a juxtaposition of different rhetorical traditions. Such juxtapositions will be the method for global studies of rhetoric, which is the next step professor Chen and other internationally focused scholars of rhetoric would like to take.

The first step, which both Vickers and Chen would endorse, is for scholars interested in global rhetoric to read the foundational global rhetorical texts. Vickers

6 James Jerome Murphy, *A Synoptic History of Classical Rhetoric*, 1st ed., Studies in Speech (New York: Random House, 1972).

would, of course, select the texts of Plato and Cicero; Chen would invite scholars to read the texts of Confucius and those offered by School of Ming. As Vickers observed in his Oxford keynote address, these texts would warrant translation from Greek and English into Chinese, with annotated commentaries designed for a Chinese or Asian audiences. Similarly, Chinese rhetorical texts need to be translated into English, with the assistance of scholars who have some understanding of the Western rhetorical traditions.[7]

Juxtaposition of different rhetorical traditions is not enough, for they only provide comparative descriptions of diverse perspectives on rhetoric. Chen calls for both a "collision" of rhetorical traditions and the possibility, at least on some topics, of a communion. One example of such comparison is my collaboration with WooSoo Park from Republic of Korea to study of the American rhetoric professor Robert Oliver's service as a ghostwriter to Syngman Rhee, the first president of the Republic of Korea. The purpose of this research project is to tell the story of the 18-year collaboration (1942~1960) between Syngman Rhee (1875~1965), the first president of South Korea, and Robert T. Oliver (1909~2000), a professor at the Pennsylvania State University, USA. Park and I consider both the collisions of American and South Korean Cultures in their collaborations and where they agreed.

Chen is right: we cannot leave the study of rhetorical texts and traditions at level of description. We must, as Chen did at Oxford, identify where there are disagreements and incompatibility. The Vickers–Chen exchange at Oxford highlighted a major difference: Vickers' view of rhetoric, derived from Plato, centered on truth and argumentation. Chen's Chinese influenced outlook focused on benevolence and ethics. An extended dialogue between the two scholars, beyond the encounter at Oxford, would have revealed that Chinese rhetoric, as Chen briefly noted in his presentation, does concern truth and persuasion; Vickers would have acknowledged that Greek rhetoric did concern itself with ethics. Regardless, there are differences between the Greek and Chinese systems of rhetoric that need to be acknowledged.

Drawing on argumentative reason, scholars of rhetoric can then deal with these differences through reasoned discourse. In so doing, scholars of rhetoric would be engaging in a truly global rhetoric as citizens of nations concerned with their images, and as citizens of the world, who remain committed to values that transcend nations. Professor Chen in his paper presented to the Chinese Rhetoric Society of the World called for a global society based on rhetoric. This global society would use argument,

7 For examples, see Xing Lu and David A. Frank, "On the Study of Ancient Chinese Rhetoric/Bian," *Western Journal of Communication* 57, no. 4 (1993): 445-63; Xing Lu, *Rhetoric in Ancient China, Fifth to Third Century, B.C.E. : A Comparison with Classical Greek Rhetoric*, Studies in Rhetoric/Communication (Columbia: University of South Carolina Press, 1998).

rather than war and violence, to deal with differences. There are rhetorical texts that may deserve to be foundations for this global society. I would advance Chaïm Perelman and Lucie Olbrechts-Tyteca's *New Rhetoric: A Treatise on Argumentation* as one such text.[8] In the aftermath of World War II and the murder of millions, Perelman and Olbrechts-Tyteca offered rhetoric as a method for humans to deal with difference through reasoned argumentation. They sought to bring reason (logic) into balance with the persuasion of audiences. Like Chen, they believe humans can reason together.

Perelman and Olbrechts-Tyteca also advanced the idea of a "universal audience." This same idea is advanced, although not with these words, by professor Chen. A universal audience stands in relationship with local or national audiences. In calling for a global society founded on rhetoric, professor Chen, like Perelman and Olbrechts-Tyteca, seeks to develop universal principles of justice and peace that can help adjudicated differences of opinion and policy. These principles themselves would be the result of considered persuasion. And, there maybe issues that are not to be open to persuasion, and there may be room for radically different perspectives to co-exist in the same rhetorical constellation.

Professor Chen is seeking to promote a truly rhetorical culture in China and is leading efforts to extend rhetorical thinking, drawing on both western and eastern traditions of rhetoric, through dialogue and contacts with non-Asian scholars. I join him in these efforts. He is right to say that the problem facing China and the world is rhetoric, and rhetoric, as he argues, is also the solution.

---

8 Chaim Perelman and Lucie Olbrechts-Tyteca, *The New Rhetoric: A Treatise on Argumentation* (Notre Dame, [Ind.]: University of Notre Dame Press, 1969); David A. Frank, "A Traumatic Reading of Twentieth-Century Rhetorical Theory: The Belgian Holocaust, Malines, Perelman, and De Man." *Quarterly Journal of Speech* 93(2007): 308-43. See my article that explains how Perelman offered rhetoric as a reasoned alternative to war and violence.

Conflict and Hope: Creating Rhetorical Capabilities

James Crosswhite
(University of Oregon, USA)

Abstract: In the first part of their 1958 Traité de l'argumentation, Chaim Perelman and Lucie Olbrechts-Tyteca describe several conditions that must obtain in order for argumentation to take place, and they gather some of these conditions together under the heading of "The Contact of Minds". These conditions have an important role in that they specify both what is necessary in order for argumentation to be genuine and also the ground on which any particular instance of argumentation can be criticized. I make a case that the conditions for the contact of minds can be best understood as rhetorical capabilities. I draw from current discussions of capabilities in political philosophy and in economics and in the theory of justice to offer a more complicated picture of what realizing these conditions would mean. In the end, these capabilities describe goals both for education in a global context and for human development itself.
Keywords: rhetoric; argumentation; capabilities; the contact of minds

This paper originated in an attempt to address a conference theme: World Rhetoric Studies in a Time of Global-cultural Amalgamation and Conflict. I originally found the theme intimidating, overwhelming. How can one possibly say anything coherent and meaningful and focused about the international study of rhetoric in the context of the unifying and fragmenting effects of contemporary global forces? And how can one possibly do anything of the sort in a short oral presentation—or even an article? The conference was held in Incheon, South Korea. I arrived in Incheon about a month after I had delivered seven lectures on rhetoric at Beihang University in Beijing, mostly to teachers and graduate students, but one to an audience of undergraduate English majors.

I want to introduce this paper by telling you about some students I encountered there, and perhaps explaining why, when I arrived in Incheon, I no longer believed that my original feelings were appropriate.

First, a very bright first-year undergraduate asked a question at the end of a lecture on essential rhetorical skills. He prefaced his in-class question by explaining that he had his own blog and that he had blogged about the China–Japan conflict over the Diaoyu Islands. He had friends in Japan who did not feel as intensely about this conflict as his Chinese friends. He explored the perspectives and arguments on each side in his blog. He explained that he himself was from Nanjing and that he had no illusions about history. Nevertheless, he was shocked when his friends called him a traitor and far worse names. "Why is this?" he asked me. "And what can I do? What do you recommend?" I spoke about *pathos*, about how emotions determine whether and how well we are able to reason about an issue, and I spoke about *kairos*, about how it might not be possible to be reasonable about a controversy at one time but that it might become possible at a later time, in different circumstances—but nothing I could say was as profound as his honest question and the historical and social context in which it was asked. By the way, this same student pursued me afterwards, out of class, asking very sophisticated and penetrating questions about American views of manifest destiny, the idea of providence, and American exceptionalism.

Second, a graduate student spoke up at the end of a lecture in which I had explained rhetoric as an ability to find all the arguments on all sides of an issue. His question: "Wouldn't that be paralyzing?" Probably the best possible question! I thought and spoke my way very slowly through a response, reformulating his question as I spoke: Is it possible to step back from the conflicts before us, to take an interest not in any of the available sides but rather in the process by which all sides receive justice, a process that helps conflict and change take place more peacefully? Is it possible to be motivated not by desire but by compassion? Is it possible to have a passionate commitment to compassion? What kind of passion is this? I found myself developing a long but unambiguously affirmative answer. In this context, certainly, anything else, any wavering or being too sophisticated, would be wrong.

My guides during my weekend excursions in Beijing had been two graduate students who had expressed an interest in rhetoric. The day after this lecture, the young man who asked this question accompanied us on our trip out to Tianjin, challenging me (in the best sense) with questions about rhetoric all along the way.

So I start with these two questions. The brief answer to the first involved, again, an explanation of *pathos* and *kairos*. But the more developed and long-term answer would involve a fuller account of rhetorical capabilities. The answer to the second—the paralysis question—would also involve rhetorical capabilities. Seeing from all sides of a controversy is not paralyzing if we have the right rhetorical capabilities—in this instance, emotional capabilities and capabilities of character—a passion for letting everyone have a say, for seeing from all sides, and a passion for a process of justice. So, in this small way of introducing very smart, very well-informed, contemporary, multilingual Chinese students and teachers to the study of European rhetoric, in English, in a context in which our discussions covered multiple traditions in which modern and traditional and Confucian and Buddhist and Christian and American and European and Chinese and social and economic forces and many other influences all came into play, I had already been thrust into a process of amalgamation that was of course already well under way. So that is one context for thinking about capabilities—and a very motivating one for me.

Here is another context: considering rhetorical capabilities as capabilities for peaceful and creative and productive conflict. The "hope" in the title of my talk is a hope for the cultivation of these capabilities. This is an educational project, a project of formation, of human development, and my task today is to situate rhetoric, as an educational project, in the context of human development. I will activate two parts of the rhetorical tradition in speaking of rhetoric this way. First, the part that is concerned with education and formation, and, second, the part that sees rhetoric as an offshoot or branch of politics—that is, as focused on guiding and conducting conflicts peacefully and settling them justly.

1. The Contact of Minds

In the opening chapters of *The New Rhetoric*, Chaim Perelman and Lucie Olbrechts-Tyteca describe the rhetorical framework (*les cadres*) within which argumentation takes place. Argumentation can take place only within certain bounds. A general requirement is for what *The New Rhetoric* calls "*le contact des esprits*," or the contact of minds: "For there to be argumentation, it is necessary that, at a given moment, an effective community of minds be realized" (*Traité*, 18). A number of conditions must be met for this contact or community to be realized. Here is a list:

1) A common language.
2) Common techniques and media for communication.
3) A reason to argue — a goal to be achieved through argumentation.
4) An agreement on the rules and procedures for how the discourse should take place.
5) A renunciation of coercion and violence and a commitment to appealing to the other person's freedom.

6) A speaker who can give arguments and gain the attention of an audience. (And so agreement on a speaker.)
7) An audience, which will serve as a judge of the arguments. (And so agreement on an audience.)
8) The audience must be receptive to argumentation and must give attention to it.
9) The speaker must attach importance to this audience, and must be capable of getting and keeping its attention.
10) The audience must be willing to change its mind on the basis of the arguments given.

A contact of this kind is necessary because all argumentation develops in relation to an audience and is offered in order to lead an audience to make one choice rather than another, and so a sufficient meeting of minds must occur in order for the deliberation and the choice to be genuine. The accomplishment of any of the conditions I have listed is a matter of degree, and the judges of whether the conditions actually achieved are good enough are, first, the interlocutors (who may not participate if the conditions are judged wanting), and then the audience (which may fail to be convinced because the conditions are not sufficiently realized). And so, these conditions have an important role in that they specify both what is necessary in order for argumentation to have a chance of being genuine and also the grounds on which some particular instance of argumentation can be criticized. Without the symmetry, or fairness, achieved in the realization of these conditions, the argumentative process and its results are not justifiable.

My general claim in this paper is that it is possible and useful to think of these conditions from a different angle as rhetorical capabilities. I will explain two intellectual motives for such an account of rhetorical capabilities. One motive for a capabilities approach comes from a simple reflection on public sphere theory. A second motive comes from the capabilities approach as it has arisen in the theory of justice and in human development thinking.

2. Public Sphere Theory and the Place of Capabilities

Public sphere theory was developed most famously by Jürgen Habermas in *The Structural Transformation of the Public Sphere*. One way of thinking of the origin of rhetoric in the European tradition is to think of it as arising alongside the legal reforms in ancient Greek cities in which citizens would engage in large numbers in direct deliberations about policies and in which they would serve as jurors in large juries, and Habermas mentions this context as a kind of forecast of a public sphere.

In such contexts, there was a stress on symmetries of power, on equality, even though it is almost everywhere assumed that the symmetry is never perfect. The challenge to describe the conditions in which this symmetry holds and the conditions in which asymmetry is so extreme that it de-legitimates the argumentation taking place has been a challenge for democratic theory from the start. The justifiability of the outcome of argumentation is in part a function of the justice of the conditions in which the argumentation takes place. Habermas' notion of a public sphere is related to this effort to describe appropriate conditions, and so is his eventual notion of an ideal speech situation.

According to Habermas, a public sphere is a group of "private persons" assembled to discuss matters of public concern or common interest. He focuses on early modern Europe up to the 18th century, during which time the public sphere functioned as a counter-weight to states with absolute power. The goal was to hold the state accountable to society by way of "openness" or "publicness".

This structure, this sphere, was shaped, according to Habermas, by many conditions that have obvious connections to concerns with justice and equality. Here are a few: Information on state functioning should be available. There should be unrestricted rational discussion of public matters. The public sphere should be open and accessible to all. It should be a place where merely private interests are inadmissible. Inequalities of status must be disregarded. Participants deliberate as peers. True public opinion involves a consensus about the common good. There must be ways of publicizing the deliberations and results that take place. In this list of conditions, Habermas is clearly describing an ideal—an ideal structure of symmetrical relations that will allow the results of argumentation to have true legitimacy.

Habermas' approach has of course come in for criticisms. Some have been eloquently expressed by Nancy Fraser. I will address only two of them here: first, that disregarding social status is not necessary; second, that there should be no restriction to discussing only the common good and not private issues. That is, the essential objection is this: The fact that society is stratified should be reflected in the structure of the public sphere. Members of groups that occupy less powerful strata should be able to represent and pursue their interests as members of those groups.

An acknowledgment of this may be implicit in the fact that the description of a public sphere, like the description of the ideal speech situation, is an ideal. Any real instance of a public sphere will have inequalities that are not disregarded and will have participants who introduce private interests into the discussion. This does not mean that the ideal is not an ideal. It can be, as Habermas has pointed out, a counterfactual ideal—one that allows us to know what we are aiming toward and one that can provide the ground for criticism when real communicative situations stray too far from the ideal—even if the ideal itself can never be fully realized. In any case, "private" interests that are matters of inequality might, with attention, come to be understood to be relevant to the public good.

However, there is a kind of social status, a kind of inequality, that simply cannot be disregarded, even in some ideal condition, because it undermines the very process that defines the public sphere, and this is an inequality in rhetorical capabilities. If one does not have the capability to reason and deliberate and form arguments and to appeal to shared notions of what is good, then others cannot simply disregard this lack of capability or set it aside or put it out of play. Stratified societies stratify not just wealth and health and safety and opportunity and power; they also stratify the rhetorical capabilities that allow people to participate in public life, to deliberate about a common good. The fundamental objection to the ideal of the public sphere may not be so much an objection as a demand—a demand that rhetorical capabilities should be broadly achieved by everyone, all groups, from all social strata.

3. Rhetorical Capabilities and the Contact of Minds

But how might we best conceive of these rhetorical capabilities? And in what context? There is a good answer to this question. We should integrate rhetorical capabilities with the capabilities approach that has taken shape in human development work and in the theory of justice. The capabilities approach makes an effort to shift the focus of policy and development analysis from resources (income and GDP) to capabilities. For the capabilities approach, the question is not something like: How much wealth is available on average? But rather: What are people actually able to be and do? Rather than focusing on averages, it treats each person as a goal and focuses on the ability to choose to be or do something. The capabilities approach is concerned with inequality and justice. It aims to give a clear task to government and public policy, but it is also pluralist—different people make different choices and different nations and cultures and historical periods may emphasize different capabilities.

The approach differentiates between an ability to do or not do—a capability—and the realization of that capability in actual choice and activity—a functioning. The approach focuses on the ability and not the actual choice to use it or not. And capabilities have internal and external dimensions; they are complex. They lie partly within individuals and partly in the external social conditions that are available. Finally, there is a disagreement between the major proponents of the approach, Martha Nussbaum and Amartya Sen, about whether a theory of capabilities should produce a list of the central capabilities. Sen tends to think that such lists should be produced out of the process of making specific comparisons or setting specific goals for some nation or group. Nussbaum believes that such a list is desirable, both for giving concrete guidance to governments and development groups and for providing the right focus for measuring progress in development.

Here are Nussbaum's central capabilities, taken from her book, *Creating Capabilities* (33-34):

1) Life. Being able to live to the end of a human life of normal length; dying prematurely, or before one's life is so reduced as to be not worth living.
2) Bodily Health. Being able to have good health, including reproductive health; to be adequately nourished; to have adequate shelter.
3) Bodily Integrity. Being able to move freely from place to place; to be secure against violent assault, including sexual assault and domestic violence; having opportunities for sexual satisfaction and for choice in matters of reproduction.
4) Senses, Imagination, and Thought. Being able to use the senses, to imagine, think, and reason — and to do these things in a "truly human" way, a way informed and cultivated by an adequate education, including, but by no means limited to, literacy and basic mathematical and scientific training.

Being able to use imagination and thought in connection with experiencing and producing works and events of one's own choice, religious, literary, musical, and so forth. Being able to use one's mind in ways protected by guarantees of freedom of expression with respect to both political and artistic speech, and freedom of religious exercise. Being able to have pleasurable experiences and to avoid non-beneficial pain.

5) Emotions. Being able to have attachments to things and people outside ourselves; to love those who love and care for us, to grieve at their absence; in general, to love, to grieve, to experience longing, gratitude, and justified anger. Not having one's emotional development blighted by fear and anxiety. (Supporting this capability means supporting forms of human association that can be shown to be crucial in their development.)
6) Practical Reason. Being able to form a conception of the good and to engage in critical reflection about the planning of one's life. (This entails protection for the liberty of conscience and religious observance.)
7) Affiliation.
   A. Being able to live with and toward others, to recognize and show concern for other human beings, to engage in various forms of social interaction;

to be able to imagine the situation of another. (Protecting this capability means protecting institutions that constitute and nourish such forms of affiliation, and also protecting the freedom of assembly and political speech.)

B. Having the social bases of self-respect and non-humiliation; being able to be treated as a dignified being whose worth is equal to that of others. This entails provisions of nondiscrimination on the basis of race, sex, sexual orientation, ethnicity, caste, religion, national origin.

8) Other Species. Being able to live with concern for and in relation to animals, plants, and the world of nature.
9) Play. Being able to laugh, to play, to enjoy recreational activities.
10) Control Over One's Environment.
    A. Political. Being able to participate effectively in political choices that govern one's life; having the right of political participation, protections of free speech and association.
    B. Material. Being able to hold property (both land and movable goods), and having property rights on an equal basis with others; having the right to seek employment on an equal basis with others; having the freedom from unwarranted search and seizure. In work, being able to work as a human being, exercising practical reason, and entering into meaningful relationships of mutual recognition with other workers.

Nussbaum and others have noted that two of these, affiliation and practical reasoning, are what have come to be called "fertile functions." That is, when these capabilities are realized in actual functioning, they have a tendency to enhance many of the other capabilities. I believe that an account of rhetorical capabilities can help to explain why this is so and fill out the picture about what practical reasoning and affiliation really amount to because practical reasoning and affiliation are themselves rhetorical capabilities. Rhetorical capabilities produce the ability to engage in argumentation about questions of what is good and how to pursue it—that is, to engage in practical reasoning. They also allow one to engage in practical cooperation and deliberation with others, to achieve a contact of minds, and so affiliate in communities of speech and discourse in which common goods are shared and in which conflicts are resolved by appealing to shared notions of what is good. These functionings are "fertile" because each capability is essentially a capability to choose, and rhetorical capabilities guide choices and thus enhance them. We reasoned about choices, outwardly and inwardly (as Isocrates says), only because we have the power of speech and reasoning.

What might a list of rhetorical capabilities look like? We can start with the conditions for the contact of minds. They describe something like the conditions of equality or justice that others have sought, and they can easily be translated into capabilities:

1) Being able to learn and share a language.
2) Being able to speak or write or sign or design or employ some shared technique that will achieve the openness necessary for argumentation.
3) Being able to recognize or imagine reasons to have a discussion.
4) Being able to formulate and agree on the rules and procedures for how a discussion will proceed.
5) Being able to recognize and refuse coercion and violence and instead appeal to the other person's freedom.
6) Being able to become a speaker and being able to acknowledge others as speakers. Being able to gain the attention of other people and give it to them.
7) Being able to share an audience, to recognize a common judge—being able to grant jurisdiction.
8) Being able to become an audience, to recognize argumentation, to give attention to it, and to judge it.
9) Being able to experience and acknowledge the significance and value of the views of others.
10) Being able to change one's mind—and one's life—when the experience of argumentative transcendence calls for it.

Some of these capabilities have to do with developing something like character or virtues, and others have to do with getting an education of the right kind. Still others probably require practical experience in certain social conditions. In every case, though, they appear to be reasonable goals for development as well as something like conditions for just deliberations that will have justifiable outcomes. That is, when participants in deliberations, or in some version of a public sphere, have these capabilities, above some threshold, then some of the most important inequalities that trouble rhetoric, democracies, and human development in general, will have been addressed. These capabilities are, however, just the beginning; together they make up the general capability of being capable of forming a community of minds, *le contact des esprits*. A more complete list would, if we followed the beginning here, have to take account of not just the framework of argumentation, but also of what The New Rhetoric calls its starting points and its techniques.

If there is to be a rhetorical theory and a broad rhetorical project for our time, one that addresses the needs of a new generation of global citizens, I cannot think of a better place to start than with this notion of the contact of minds.

References

[1] Nussbaum, Martha. *Creating Capabilities*[M]. Cambridge, MA: Harvard University Press, 2011.

[2] Perelman, Chaim & Lucie Olbrechts-Tyteca. *The New Rhetoric: A Treatise on Argumentation*[M]. Notre Dame: University of Notre Dame Press, 1969. (Originally published as *Traité de l'argumentation: La nouvelle rhétorique*[M]. Paris: Presses Universitaires de France, 1958.)

[3] Sen, Amartya. *The Idea of Justice*[M]. Cambridge, MA: Harvard University Press, 2009.

Strategic Communications: A New Field for Rhetoric[1]

Philippe-Joseph Salazar
(University of Cape Town, South Africa)

A recent National Summit on Strategic Communications[2] afforded me the opportunity to observe, as a rhetorician, a field cognate to my current investigation into surveillance and secrecy[3], and this field is called "Stratcomm" or "strategic communications" (plural)[4]. Participants were US generals and admirals, NATO representatives[5], CCOs[6] and diplomats, together with foreign delegations.

Stratcomm was originally invented by military personnel of the USA and NATO, an integrated communications strategy developed after the bombing campaigns of the former Yugoslavia (1995 and 1999), during the War of Afghanistan (since 2001) and, to a certain degree more difficult to identify, during the War of Iraq (2003). It is noticeable how the US Navy and Marine Corps personnel are at the forefront of the field with an intellectual expertise I have already noted elsewhere[7].

While forming a single persuasive strategy tactics developed in the three military contexts mentioned were aimed at persuading four distinct audiences in regard of the appropriateness of these military actions and of the expected combined effect (stability, prosperity, peace etc.). The four rhetorical audiences were the personnel involved (NATO, Allies), local entities or collaborationists, the saved or subjugated populations (in military jargon, "populace") and the international environment, whether in terms of organisational or of media.

This strategy was a sum of methods aimed at establishing an influence applied

1 Research supported by the National Research Foundation of South Africa. Opinions expressed are those of the Author.

2 Organised by Grupp Global Partners LLC, www.strategicsummit.com in Washington.

3 See my "Du Secret d'Etat au Royaume-Uni: Classified, Secrecy and the State in Modern Britain", Centre français de recherche sur le renseignement, TL31, August 2013, http://www.cf2r.org/

4 The abbreviation varies: Stratcom, StratComm, Stratcomm but the fixed part, "communications," remains plural.

5 http://www.aco.nato.int/stratcom.aspx

6 Chief Communications Officers.

7 See my "Patriotisme rhétorique, au cœur de l'Amérique" http://www.lesinfluences.fr/Patriotisme-rhetorique-au-cœur-de.html, and chapter "Onze Novembre à Washington", in my *Paroles de Leaders* (Bourin, 2011).

systematically by an entity that has already taken the power, in order to ensure that this overtaking is so internalised by those who are its targets that the entity in question occupies the entire field of application and completes its initial goal — a control accepted as permissible by its targets with a concomitant, gradual and publicized decrease in coercion.

The teams and the individuals who invented Stratcomm did so by the systematisation and extension of public relations techniques, information services, simple press agencies — all communicational practices that have become outdated and unsuitable for the dimension of the recent conflicts in which the newness (a genocide a one-hour flight away from Venice), the legality (the intervention in Kosovo) or the legitimacy (the War of Iraq) — without counting a return on investment — remain contested and where the political outcomes remain subject to controversy and serve, in the renewal of this form of dispersed guerrilla, to justify jihadist terrorism. In sum, they moved into rhetoric.

Stratcomm, as described here, is recent but is already developed enough for the participants of this conclave to propose a transfer of skills from the military to the societal; namely to consider application to government action, and commercial, financial and industrial action (or "corporate"), and to the work of NGOs and INGOs. We are there, at the heart of an overall rhetorical strategy. Stratcomm wants to use the real (or imagined) gains of a military strategy of persuasion to formulate a general communications strategy applicable to all areas of public affairs.

It is in this that the rhetorician is interested, but I will focus here on the expectations of the military model and not on its transfer to the civil, the governmental or the entrepreneurial.

Stratcomm is above all an "economy" of persuasion: it strategizes rhetorically coercive acts, which are difficult to put in place; punitive measures, which are complicated to manage; material interventions, which are costly and garish and often perceived as an abuse of power, therefore suspicious to the population and international opinion. Stratcomm takes the reins of the brutal takeover, it softens the effect of the control until the power thus established presents itself to target audiences as a natural benefit (e.g. the education of girls in Muslim countries). Stratcomm allows to act on the collective mindset and thus achieves (military) action, giving it "influence" rather than power. It is a rhetorical bringing together of "all available means" (Aristotle, *Rhetoric* 1355b).

The strategy of influence is to transform what is at first a coercive action of A on B, and which B resists actively or passively, in an acceptance by B that A acts in favour of B — naturally. Therefore, Stratcomm converts an action of A on B into "agency" of B, in other words, the transformation of the subjects of a brutal and external action into social agents in the sham of their autonomy. We know the formulae: "The Kosovars have taken control of their destiny." "The Afghan government is in charge of its security." etc. Indeed but, initially, if there is a "destiny" or "security," it is due to an external intervention. The cause, which is external, becomes an internal finality thanks to Stratcomm.

"Agency" as a concept comes from the field of economy: an agent or authorised representative is one who acts on behalf of the principal. In this strategy the "populace" subject to the effects of control by the influence of Stratcomm can be persuaded that it act by itself when it is in reality acting on behalf of the principal — the occupying power. Influence is to make act and disguise this "to make act" as acting.

Now, the term "influence" is the unspoken element. However, by an inevitable return of the repressed during the more relaxed part of questions and answers, two of the participants — a rear admiral in charge of US Navy Information and the director of communications and public diplomacy of the State Department — summarised their thoughts by stating that the whole system "boils down to influence." The Marine went even further in this natural return to the rhetorical foundation of Stratcomm, beyond the effects of scientificity intended by flow charts and flashcards, when he affirmed that "speech-writing craft is essential." He even came to abandon the idea that the role of a Stratcomm specialist is to "advise and counsel" the commander in chief, a traditional rhetorical role of adviser to the prince; in other words: how to influence who in the position of "commanding and controlling" admits that the use of brute force or legitimate authority must be extended by a force of influence, and agrees to put in place the necessary and placatory shams.

But this fundamentally realistic conception, in the Machiavellian sense and therefore exactly political, of the extension of the use of force by the persuasive influence, was never explicitly put on the table. There is a blockage and this blockage deserves scrutiny.

This methodological blockage comes from the fact that all intervening parties — even those who by profession are adept in the manipulation of information — insist repeatedly on this maxim: "Truth First," or more precisely: "We must be the first to convey the truth" (for example in the episode of a US soldier who opened fire on villagers) in order to create a strategy of influence[8].

This statement and this will to be the "first to tell the truth" are curious in two regards: first, from a philosophical point of view, if a truth is "the truth," little does it

8 I quote from my notes the remarkable opening address delivered by General John Allen, former commander in chief of NATO in Afghanistan or ISAF. His intervention was his first "public" speech since having declined his appointment to the supreme command of this organization in Europe and taken early retirement. The text of the speech remains embargoed.

matter whether one is the first or the second to tell it. It is only if one wants to manage an information, i.e. shape its effects — or in short, to be rhetorical — that one insists on holding the advantage in the field of influence. Yet there is no doubt that this primacy displayed of the truth, expressed by general officers whose integrity is certain, operates from a "moral" conviction and that it is the ethical kingpin that "morally" backs, even ennobles, Stratcomm's strategy: it is interesting that it is Hannah Arendt, and not a Stracomm operative, who declared:

"To look upon politics from the perspective of truth means to take one's stand outside the political realm. This standpoint is the standpoint of the truth teller, who forfeits his position — and, with it, the validity of what he has to say — if he tries to interfere directly in human affairs and to speak the language of persuasion or of violence." [9]

However the anti-political "truth teller" position is the one advocated by the sponsors and strategists of influence who claim to stand by truth and by the use of force, whether military, economic or societal; in short, "political."

There is a paradox here, and in my view a danger, that we would call self-defeating, an intellectual suicide. Influence is political by nature, therefore, by nature, amoral.

The paradox is the following: the moral philosophy of rhetoric, as I see it, is amoral and anti-truth, while military communication or intelligence strategists, who are often accused of being liars or manipulators, defend (and believe in) truth and an ethics of language. Yet the foundation upon which the different versions of Stratcomm is : what is an action of influence?

Let us then go back to the *Rhetoric*.

Aristotle makes a fundamental distinction between the two types of actions that articulate a single act of persuasion. Specifically, an act of persuasion is a strategy that activates two tactics: the first tactic is called *kinêsis* and the second is *energeia*. In English: kinetic action and energetic action. If "kinetic" surprises, it is however a standard term in the US military glossary: "kinetic action."

The fundamental distinction made by Aristotle is between these two actions or tactics that together form a strategic action of persuasion, applicable to the action of influence.

Kinêsis: an act is complete when the purpose of the act is attained, that is to say, when the action, the movement that moves it, leads it to its objective (I walk from A to B and I reach B.) In rhetoric, as a technology for seizing or holding power, there is a kinetic action when a target audience accepts the validity of an argument of which it is the target.

9 "Truth and Politics," in *Between Past and Future: Eight Exercises in Political Thought*, Penguin, 1968.

Energeia: an act of persuasion is truly realised when it achieves a complete form that stands out as the right method (even if I do not walk from A to B, I definitely know how to get there.)

In other words, the kinetic action is material (I go from A to B), the energetic action is formal (I understand how to get there, the procedure); and the influential action is both physical and formal (if I go there, I know how to say how I got there; if I do not go, how would I have gone, and how does it work every time.)

Let us now transpose this rhetorical scheme of action to Stratcomm. In the action of public persuasion or strategic influence it is not enough that a tactical action is fulfilled (we take imams to an allied country of moderate Islam, for them to see that Islamic law can operate in compatibility with the democratic rights of women, etc.)[10]. But it is also necessary that, when the specific instance or example for action (that stimulates agency as defined above) is no longer present in the mind of those who have been exposed to it, the generalising energy of the example (a formal procedure) nevertheless still continues. This allows those who have been exposed to a given situation, to transfer and to apply the lesson to other comparable situations (e.g. the rights of children or the humane treatment of animals). In short, the dual action of persuasion must allow for a cognitive transfer: the kinetic action is specific and concrete. The energetic action is generalising and formal. The first tactic has to do with a precise target. The second tactic is a "training" of the minds. The two put together form a strategy of influence.

Stratcomm, as it now stands, comes up against the question of the truth and morality of information management. A disjunction is evident between who defines the policy to be pursued and who is in charge of the control centre where coordination must take place with those who conceive and manage the strategy of influence. A recent book by the North American essayist, Thomas E. Ricks, *The Generals*[11], delivers a merciless indictment on the strategic ineffectiveness of the US military machine[12], echoing the more general condemnation by historian Richard Kohn:

> *Nearly twenty years after the end of the Cold War, the American military, financed by more money than the entire rest of the world spends on its armed forces, failed to defeat insurgencies or fully suppress sectarian civil wars in two crucial countries, each with less than a tenth of the U.S. population, [...] Why such a*

10 Quoted from my notes. Material embargoed.

11 Richard E. Ricks, *The Generals: American Command from World War II to Today*, Penguin, 2013.

12 Here, in other words, the US Army.

disjunction between enormous expenditures and declining capability? [13]

One solution would be found within Stratcomm's effort to raise, through strategies of influence, the degree of effectiveness that exorbitant expenses and expansive force failed to produce. This shows the magnitude that this discipline of control is taking, whether it resolves the theoretical issues that, as a rhetorician and from my vantage point, I believe must be raised.

13 Richard H. Kohn, "Tarnished Brass: Is the US Military Profession in Decline?", *World Affairs*, Spring 2009, http://www.worldaffairsjournal.org/article/tarnished-brass-us-military-profession-decline

第二部分

古典修辞研究

The Aim and the Task of Rhetoric: The Reasons for Its Artistic Nature

Lucia Calboli Montefusco
(The University of Bologna, Italy)

Abstract: As it is well known, already in the antiquity the question, whether rhetoric is or is not an art, has been lively debated by philosophers and rhetoricians. The nub of the problem was the relationship between its aim and its task, i.e. how and why rhetoric can attain persuasion. According to the sophists rhetoric was an art able to create persuasion in the hearers about anything. Plato, on the contrary, denied the artistic nature of rhetoric and only considered it as a practice attaining persuasion by flattering the souls of the hearers with empty words. Aristotle focused differently on the question: keeping the aim of rhetoric distinct from its task, he could consider rhetoric as an art because, as any other art does in its field, it has the task to discover the cause why we can persuade. Since then the discussion continued for centuries. In the Latin world, for example, Cicero and Quintilian devoted to it the greatest attention. Far from being neglected today, the artistic nature of rhetoric has called the attention of several modern scholars, such as Jonathan Barnes, David Roochnik or Brian Vickers. I will carry on this discussion focusing on the change of the connotation of rhetoric according to the different points of view of the ancient authors.

Keywords: rhetoric; reason; artistic nature

What is rhetoric? What for we need it? How can it persuade people? Several answers, as well known, have been given in the past to these questions and lively debates focusing on the nature and the function of rhetoric have been carried on along centuries. Plato, e.g., in his *Gorgias*, puts in the mouths of the interlocutors of the dialogue different opinions about the essence of rhetoric. Right at the beginning, the sophist Polus not only considers rhetoric, professed by his teacher Gorgias, as an art, but even as the best of the arts and says that, as any other art, it has been discovered through experience (*Gorg*. 448 C). Socrates, on his turn, firmly contrasts Gorgias' understanding of rhetoric as the art that gives to men "the ability to persuade with speeches either judges in the law courts or statesmen in the council-chamber or the commons in the Assembly or an audience at any other meeting that may be held on public affair" (*Gorg*. 452 E). According to this understanding, more shortly, rhetoric is indeed nothing else than "a producer of persuasion" (*Gorg*. 453 A πειθοῦς δημιουργός), but this persuasion, as Socrates leads Gorgias to agree, does only provide belief without knowledge because the rhetor, who claims to answer any question one may ask him, does not need to know what he is speaking about. Plato, in other words, lets Socrates explain why rhetoric cannot be considered as an art, but only as a practice (ἐμπειρία) aiming at persuading stirring pleasure in the hearers (*Gorg*. 462 B-C). Any art — Socrates says — is founded on knowledge. Rhetoric, on the contrary, is only founded on opinion. Far from knowledge and truth, therefore, the rhetor can persuade his listeners only because, though speaking about things which he does not know, he speaks to an audience that does not know what he is speaking about either (*Gorg*. 459 B-C). As producer of this kind of persuasion, says Socrates, rhetoric is actually only a flattery towards the souls of men, as well as cookery is a flattery towards their bodies (*Gorg*. 463 B). Both of them, namely, are irrational skills that produce gratification and pleasure without knowing what is good for men (*Gorg*. 462 C-D). Plato, to sum up, refuses, through Socrates' words, to give the name of art to what is irrational because — as he says — it is unable to tell the cause of anything (*Gorg*. 465 A).

This mention of the epistemic deficiency of rhetoric allows us, anyway, to understand what is missing in this persuasive process that Plato several times qualifies as "ridiculous". It is Aristotle who helps us. Even if, also according to him, rhetoric is not concerned with the truth, but only with what, happening for the most part, is similar to the truth in the opinion of men, Aristotle reverses the situation. Indeed, keeping the goal of rhetoric (the attainment of persuasion) apart from its task (discovering how to persuade), he lets the awareness of the cause of persuasion transform what Plato considered irrational into a rational process that deserves the name of art. The first consequence of this shift of the focus is a different definition of rhetoric itself: rhetoric is not "a producer of persuasion" anymore. It is the ability — says Aristotle — to investigate what can be persuasive in each particular case (*Rhet*. 1355 b 25 f.) and its function "is not to persuade but to see the available means of persuasion in each case, as it is true also in all the other arts"(*Rhet*. 1355 b 10 f.). Thanks to this distinction between aim and task any art can actually be considered as such even if it does not achieve its aim. The best example is medicine: its task — says Aristotle — is indeed not "to create health but to promote this as much as possible; for it is nevertheless possible to treat well those who cannot recover health" (*Rhet*. 1355 b 9 ff.). In this perspective orator will only be, we read in Aristotle's Topics, "he who can see what is a plausible argument on any occasion and omits nothing" (*Top*. 149 b 24 ff.). As any other art, moreover, rhetoric is concerned with universals, not with particulars because particulars are infinite and therefore not knowable (*Rhet*. 1356 b 32 f.). As the medicine — Aristotle tells us in the *Rhetoric* — "does not specify what is healthful for Socrates or Callias but for persons of a certain sort ... neither does rhetoric theorize about each opinion — what may seem so to Socrates or Hippias — but about what seems true to people of a certain sort" (*Rhet*. 1356 b 30 ff.). This is actually what distinguishes art from experience.

It is reading the beginning of the *Metaphysics* that we can understand the reason of this statement. There Aristotle calls attention to the successive steps that lead to knowledge (*Met*. 980 a 28 ff.). Any living being — he says — is born with the power of sensations, but only some acquire the faculty to remember them. Among those who remember, men are able to put these sensations down to experience: "It is from memory — he explains — that men acquire experience, because the numerous memories of the same thing eventually produce the effect of a single experience". At this point, however, Aristotle introduces an interesting warning: experience — he says — "seems very similar to science and art, but actually it is through experience that men acquire science and art; for as Polus rightly says 'experience produces art, but inexperience chance'"(*Met*. 981 a 4 ff.). What does this quotation from Plato's *Gorgias* mean? Does Aristotle really share Polus' understanding of the birth of the art? We must be careful not to misunderstand Aristotle's statement. He now does what Polus did not, namely he explains how experience can give birth to art. Experience becomes art — he says — when from several similar experiences, by means of an inductive process, we get a single universal judgment (*Met*. 981 a 6 ff.): it is therefore only keeping in mind this rational step that we can say that experience is the starting point of art. The difference between experience and art is indeed only a question of knowledge: experience is the knowledge of particulars, art of universals. Who relies on experience, consequently, only knows that single things happen, who relies on art knows why they happen (*Met*. 981 a 28 ff.). To explain his thought Aristotle, also here, uses as an example of the art of medicine: knowing that a certain treatment is useful to Socrates or Callias or anybody else suffering from a certain illness is indeed — he says — a matter of experience; knowing that a treatment is useful to all persons of a certain group, considered as a class, suffering from the same disease, is, on the contrary, a matter of art (*Met*. 981 a 8 ff.).

We don't need to wonder, therefore, if according to this interpretation of the concept of art Aristotle considers also rhetoric as an art. Rhetoric — he says at the beginning of his *Rhetoric* — is actually concerned with such things as are, to a certain extent, within the knowledge of all people. Because of that all people are able to defend themselves and attack, with the only difference that some do these things randomly while others do through an ability acquired by habit. If this happens in the nature of things — Aristotle continues — it is possible to observe the cause and to trace a path, i.e. it is possible to create a methodos that people can exploit to attain persuasion. Everybody would agree — he concludes — that is the task of any art (*Rhet.* 1354 a 1-11). It is this intellectual effort to discover why rhetoric can persuade, therefore, that according to Aristotle allows us to consider rhetoric as an art. At this point we can also understand why Aristotle distinguishes two kinds of proofs, the πίστεις ἄτεχνοι and the πίστεις ἔντεχνοι (*Rhet.* 1355 b 35). The first preexist to the art and are already available to the orator who only needs to exploit them, the second, on the contrary, are embedded in the art, i.e. they can be found only if the orator masters the art. Task of his art — says Aristotle — is indeed discovering how he can appear credible exploiting his own ethos, how he can arouse the emotions of his listeners and how he can find the suitable premises for his argumentation. Even the arousing of the feelings, toward which Aristotle is so critical, becomes in this way object of a rational process of investigation: the orator would indeed never be able to arouse a certain emotion without discovering "what each of the emotions is and what are its qualities and from what it comes to be and how" (*Rhet.* 1356 a 22 ff.).

This is the meaning of Aristotle's mention of an "artistic methodos" that can "trace a path" (*Rhet.* 1355 a 2 f.). One detail, however, is still missing in Aristotle's so clear understanding of the artistic nature of rhetoric: an explanation of how it is possible to transform the results of the intellectual discovering of the cause of persuasion into this "artistic methodos". The question has been discussed at length later by Cicero in his famous dialogue on the ideal orator. Giving voice to the interlocutors of the dialogue as Cicero, as well as Aristotle, focuses on the natural eloquence of men and on the possibility to transform into an art of the data of the experience. Requested by Sulpicius to express his opinion about the debated question whether rhetoric can or cannot be considered as an art, Crassus answers that the controversy only concerns the meaning of the word "art": "If art is defined ... as consisting of matters that are thoroughly scrutinized and clearly known ... an art of rhetoric does not exist ... If, however, the procedures that have been followed in the actual practice of speaking have been observed and recorded by skilled and experienced people, and described through definitions, and defined by division into classes and subclasses ... I don't see why this shouldn't be called an art" (*De orat.* 1.109). If in the first case it is evident that what is hinted at is the Platonic understanding of the concept of art, in the second case, on the contrary, the Aristotelian claim that observing why somebody speaks better that others allows to "trace a path" is integrated with a brief explanation of how this is possible.

As the question for the dialectic method of division, definition and composition that Plato in his *Phaidrus* (265 D – 266 B) said to be the foundation of knowledge. Crassus himself is well aware of the odopoietic function of this "artistic methodos": it is, he says, what reminds "the orator of the points of reference for each occasion, which he must keep in sight in order not to stray from whatever goal he has set for himself" (*De orat.* 1.145 f.). Cicero explicitly considers this dialectic process is essential for the birth of any art: "it is impossible — Crassus says — to reduce any subject to a systematic art, unless the same person who understands the material that he wants to establish as an art first possesses the knowledge of how to construct such an art out of things that are not yet systematized into an art" (*De orat.* 1.186). Not only rhetoric, therefore, but any other art is the result of the use of dialectic, the only art capable to join together rationally what before was in disorder and scattered far apart (*De orat.* 1.187 f.).

As Cicero, several other authors called attention to the essence and the property of rhetoric. Quintilian, as we know, discussed (*Inst.* 2.15) this question at length, pointing out what was wrong with several definitions of rhetoric. He said, for example, saying that rhetoric aims at persuasion was not correct because many other things can persuade, as money, authority, the wounds in the chest or the naked body of Phryne (*Inst.* 2.15.3-9). He also found fault with Aristotle's definition because focusing on the intellectual effort to find the suitable arguments includes only *inventio* and wrongly excludes *elocutio*, which is an indispensable aspect of rhetoric (*Inst.* 2.15.13); Quintilian also regards limiting the use of rhetoric to the "questions of the citizens" (*civiles quaestiones*), as had often been done, is an improper restriction which prevents rhetoric from being applied to other fields (*Inst.* 2.15.20).

The question was of some interest there after. At the beginning of Nicolaus' *Progymnasmata*, e.g., we read that a kind of natural rhetoric had always been available for men, but that only after having consciousness of its parts it has been possible to create a methodos (1,16-2,3 Felten). According to Troilos and Marcellinus what allowed this shift from natural eloquence to the art of rhetoric was the focus on the περιστάσεις, that is the determining elements of a case, as the place, the time, the manner, the reason or the person. Several of the *Prolegomena* collected in the past century by Rabe mention different definitions of rhetoric. Sometimes they are simply quoted but sometimes they provoke criticisms and disagreements. Only one definition, is referred to with admiration and praise. It was given by Dionysios of Halicarnassos — we read in an anonymous text — the result of good sense and attention, neither faulty because too narrow nor faulty because too broad, mentioning the genre and summing up all the necessary *differentiae*. Saying that rhetoric is "the ability given by art to compose a persuasive speech on a political issue, aiming at speaking well", Dionysios had fully expressed the essence and the property of rhetoric.

Today, far from being neglected, the artistic nature of rhetoric has called the attention of several modern scholars, such as Jonathan Barnes or David Roochnik who still used as titles for their articles for the old question "Is Rhetoric an Art?". Its definition, however, would be definitely broader today: not only would rhetoric be considered as "the ability given by art to compose a persuasive speech on a political issue, aiming at speaking well", but it would also be considered as the starting point for any advertisement or for the quick communication through the social networks. Why then so many people, when they want to persuade their audience of their sincerity, continue to say that they are speaking "without rhetoric"?

What Medieval Europeans Talked about When They Talked about Rhetoric

Martin Camargo
(University of Illinois, USA)

Abstract: This article cites evidence from Western European rhetoric textbooks written in Latin between the twelfth and the fourteenth centuries to dispel three myths about medieval rhetoric that often are repeated by historians of rhetoric whose focus is not the Middle Ages and sometimes by medievalists whose focus is not rhetoric. It shows that (1) medieval rhetoricians treated argumentation in some detail and so were not concerned exclusively or principally with stylistic ornamentation, (2) medieval rhetoricians paid close attention to oral delivery and so did not limit their instruction to the characteristics of written texts, and (3) medieval rhetoricians were alert to the need for creative adaptation to different rhetorical situations and so did not rely almost entirely on the mechanical application of inflexible rules.

Keywords: medieval; rhetoric history; argumentation

One of the benefits of accepting your generous invitation to address this conference is the opportunity it provides for me to learn more about Asian rhetoric, a subject that I know little about. If your lack of knowledge about medieval European rhetoric matches my lack of knowledge about Asian rhetoric — as I suspect it does — then you have a very good excuse. Even among historians of Western rhetoric, accurate and detailed understanding of medieval rhetoric is more the exception than the rule. For reasons that are easier to explain than to overcome, historians of Western rhetoric prefer to ignore the medieval period. They justify doing so by invoking some generalizations about medieval rhetoric that have been repeated for a long time and have only recently been challenged in a systematic way by medievalists.

In this paper I will try to dispel three myths about medieval rhetoric that one often encounters in published scholarship and in conversation with historians of rhetoric who are not medievalists:

1. medieval rhetoric is concerned only or principally with stylistic ornamentation

and never or only rarely with argumentation,
2. the object of medieval rhetoric is to produce written texts rather than spoken ones,
3. medieval rhetoric consists almost entirely of inflexible rules that reduce or eliminate the possibilities for creative adaptation to different rhetorical situations.

To make my case I will rely as much as possible on specific examples of medieval rhetoric rather than on generalizations about medieval rhetoric. I will conclude by indicating briefly some ways in which medieval rhetoric might be relevant not only to those who teach rhetoric in contemporary colleges and universities but also to those who study rhetoric with a view toward its practical usefulness in their professional careers.

Before I try to describe what medieval rhetoric was, I should pause to explain what I mean by "medieval" and by "rhetoric". The term "medieval" — from the Latin *medium aevum*, meaning "middle age" — refers to the period of time between classical antiquity and the "renaissance" or rebirth of classical scholarship that is associated with early modernity. In Western Europe the beginning of this period is marked by the fall of Rome to northern invaders in the fifth century of the Common Era. The end point of the Middle Ages is not so precisely marked, but most of the developments that are thought to characterize early modernity were well under way in most parts of Western Europe by the end of the fifteenth century.

This medieval period of about one-thousand years encompassed multiple cultures. While they were linked in some respects, most notably by a shared Latin Christianity, they differed in many other ways. In these brief remarks I will not attempt to represent the cultural diversity of the Latin Middle Ages but will take most of my examples of "medieval rhetoric" from the region and the time period that I know best, namely, England during the two centuries between about 1200 and about 1400.

From classical antiquity to the present day, the definition of "rhetoric" has been contested in the West. For example, is it a natural talent or a teachable art? Is it "an ability, in each particular case, to see the available means of persuasion," as Aristotle maintains, or is it the bombastic, deceptive, empty, or otherwise disreputable sort of discourse that the average person is prone to dismiss as "nothing but rhetoric"? Once again, I cannot hope to represent the full range of meanings that the term "rhetoric" had during the Middle Ages, and so I will focus on what rhetoric meant as a component of formal education in the schools and universities of late medieval England.

Even in this more limited context, the scope and meaning of rhetoric cannot be specified as simply as I would like. In theory, rhetoric was one of the three distinct verbal arts that made up the "trivium" (the "three ways"), a basic curriculum that traces its origins to classical antiquity. In practice, however, rhetoric tended to overlap with each of the other two trivial arts — grammar and logic — in ways that blurred the outlines of its disciplinary identity. In medieval English schools, for example, grammar and rhetoric usually were taught by the same teacher. A student of grammar learned how to use the Latin language "correctly" and rhetoric taught him how to use it "effectively", but a particular teacher's textbook might alternate between the two subjects without drawing a clear line between them. In England, the student's native language was not derived from Latin, as it was in the romance-language-speaking regions of Europe, and the extra challenge of mastering Latin as a "foreign" language would have contributed to the grammatical character of rhetorical instruction. Poetry tended to be more closely associated with training in grammar, and prose with training in rhetoric. Grammar tended to focus on the analysis and production of small units of discourse, like a single sentence or a line of verse, while rhetoric focused more on larger units of discourse, like a letter or a sermon. However, many of the same teaching methods were applied across this spectrum in the treatises on general composition from which I will take most of my examples of medieval rhetoric — treatises that have rightly been called "arts of poetry and prose".

The boundary between grammar and rhetoric was fluid even in classical antiquity. In the first century of the Common Era, for example, the Roman rhetorician Quintilian observed that grammar teachers were taking over more and more of the preliminary exercises (*progymnasmata*) that traditionally had been part of the instruction offered by rhetoric teachers. The same was true of rhetoric's relationship to dialectic, which Aristotle thought was particularly close since the central concern of both disciplines was argumentation. Theoretical treatments of rhetoric in the Middle Ages also tended to emphasize its close relationship to dialectic. One could claim that dialectic contains rhetoric because it is the general science of argumentation and rhetoric is a particular kind of argumentation; but one also could claim that rhetoric contains dialectic, since logical argument (*logos*) is the only one of the three means of persuasion that Aristotle identified as the subject of rhetoric, the others being the audience's emotions (*pathos*) and the speaker's character (*ethos*). At the University of Oxford around 1400, the only required textbook on rhetoric was Book 4 of Boethius's treatise on the topics, which identified and explained the differences between rhetoric and dialectic. According to Boethius, the most important distinction between the two arts is that the dialectician seeks to discover what is true in all situations while the rhetorician seeks to discover what is plausible in a specific situation.

The emphasis on argument in medieval scholastic treatments of rhetoric brings me to the first of the three myths about medieval rhetoric that I want to challenge. Of course, those who say that medieval rhetoric is all about stylistic ornamentation rather than argumentation are speaking as much about the practice of rhetoric as about the theory of rhetoric. However, John O. Ward has pointed out that until the twelfth-century medieval teachers devoted more intensive study to Cicero's textbook *On Invention* (*De inventione*) than to any other work on rhetoric and did so in ways that suggest they found it particularly relevant to practical contemporary needs. Since Cicero's treatise does not treat style but only argumentation, for those who made copies of it; wrote glosses, commentaries, and adaptations of it; and derived their understanding of rhetoric from it, the essence of rhetoric in practice as well as theory must have been orgued.

By the end of the twelfth-century medieval rhetoricians had shifted the focus of their attention to the *Rhetorica ad Herennium*, a work that they incorrectly thought was also written by Cicero. The *Rhetorica ad Herennium* had the advantage of treating aspects of rhetoric that are not treated in the *De inventione*. The definitions and illustrations of sixty-four figures of speech and thought in Book 4 of the *Rhetorica ad Herennium* were especially influential in the teaching of rhetoric during the later Middle Ages, and that influence contributes to the impression that medieval rhetoricians paid more attention to stylistic surface than to argumentative substance. However, the *Rhetorica ad Herennium* also devotes extensive space to invention and arrangement — the parts of rhetoric treated in similar fashion by the *De inventione* and the ones most directly associated with argumentation — and it provides briefer treatments of memory and delivery. Thus the shift of emphasis from the *De inventione* to the *Rhetorica ad Herennium* does not signal the abandonment of argumentation in favor of stylistic ornament so much as a greater desire to exploit the full range of rhetorical doctrine available in ancient sources.

Some twelve centuries separate the composition of the *Rhetorica ad Herennium* from its revived study in the Middle Ages, and society had changed a great deal in the meantime. The political and legal institutions of ancient Rome were not the same as those of medieval Europe, and those differences have obscured the practical relevance of ancient rhetoric to medieval realities. Scholars have been too quick to assume that the dominant varieties of ancient rhetoric — the deliberative rhetoric of political assemblies and the judicial rhetoric of the law courts — could have no valid application apart from the specific stages on which they were originally practiced. Therefore, they have been too quick to conclude that in the absence of such classical contexts, medieval rhetoricians simply ignored legal and political rhetoric and restricted their practice to the third variety of rhetoric that was recognized in the ancient treatises, namely, the demonstrative or epideictic rhetoric employed on ceremonial occasions. Such a view, which denies much of what medieval rhetoric teachers sought to inculcate in their students, feeds the myth that their overriding or even exclusive goal was to facilitate ostentatious displays of stylistic virtuosity.

Now let's turn to a specific example of a more broadly conceived and typically medieval rhetoric curriculum in which the teaching of argumentation is well represented. Before students at Oxford would have studied Boethius on the differences between dialectical and rhetorical argumentation they would have been trained in applied rhetoric, that is, in how to communicate effectively in Latin. In the year 1400, two textbooks were used more frequently than any others to provide such instruction at Oxford. One of them, the *Poetria nova* (the *New Poetics*), had been written around 1200 by the Englishman Geoffrey of Vinsauf. The other was an anonymous treatise that was called by its first two words "*Tria sunt*" and probably was no more than ten years old in 1400. Both textbooks were strongly indebted to the *Rhetorica ad Herennium*, and the *Tria sunt* was also indebted to the *Poetria nova*. In fact, it is very likely that the person who composed the *Tria sunt* deliberately set out to complement the earlier work by Geoffrey of Vinsauf, both by elaborating important points of doctrine that Geoffrey treated in a compressed fashion and by treating aspects of rhetoric that the *Poetria nova* does not include.

Like the *Rhetorica ad Herennium*, the *Poetria nova* covers all five of the traditional parts of rhetoric: invention, arrangement, style, memory, and delivery. It provides more detail on arrangement and style than on the other three parts, and for that reason a good deal of what the *Tria sunt* adds to the *Poetria nova* has to do with invention or the means by which one discovers persuasive arguments. The author of the *Tria sunt* was particularly interested in the attributes of persons and actions, an important source of persuasive argument that the *Poetria nova* mentions without developing in any detail. For those of you who are not familiar with the attributes as a component of rhetorical invention, these are "topics" or "places" of argument such as the physique, temperament, age, nationality, or gender of a person and the time or place of an action. The author of the *Tria sunt* devotes one of his longest chapters to the attributes, and he goes to uncommon lengths to gather information on the rhetorical theory of the attributes. His many sources include classical texts such as Cicero's *On Invention* and Horace's *Art of Poetry* (*Ars poetica*), twelfth-century texts such as Matthew of Vendôme's rhetorical treatise the *Art of Versifying* (*Ars versificatoria*) and Alan of Lille's learned poem the *Anticlaudianus*, as well as scholarly commentaries on several of these works. The amount of space he devoted to the attributes and the amount of labor it must have taken to research and compile this chapter are good evidence of the importance that this anonymous English rhetorician placed on argumentation as a component of his teaching.

He also was careful to show how the doctrine of the attributes could be applied in rhetorical practice. Since the *Poetria nova* is written entirely in verse, all of the examples it includes to illustrate rhetorical techniques are of necessity poems. Freed from this constraint, the author of the *Tria sunt* included specific instructions on how to compose letters, the most versatile and hence the most widely taught variety of prose in the Middle Ages. The attributes of persons are emphasized in his instructions, since a major function of letters was persuasion: "every sort of person," he says, "should be described in such a way that the description causes the maximum support of belief to be extended and so that what is true or plausible is said about this person." Besides being useful in formulating plausible arguments, study of the attributes gave the student practical opportunities to represent the hierarchical relationships between different categories of senders and recipients. Getting these relationships right was an essential precondition of successful persuasion in the highly stratified medieval society.

Making topical invention an essential part of the process of composing letters is only one way in which the author of the *Tria sunt* underscored the central role of argumentation in medieval epistolary rhetoric (in Latin, the *ars dictaminis*). He also draws attention to the argumentative structure of letters, a structure modeled on that of the ancient Roman speeches that were the subject of a work such as the *Rhetorica ad Herennium*. The first part of a medieval letter, the greeting (in Latin, the *salutatio*), serves a persuasive function by evoking the proper hierarchical relationship between sender and recipient and employing the formal language appropriate to the status of each party. The second part — the introduction (in Latin, the *exordium*) — provides the basis for the argument that is the main substance of the letter. This basis usually takes the form of a popular proverb, a quotation from a well-known and respected text, a historical example, or some other kind of "authority". In the statement of facts (in Latin, the *narratio*), the particular circumstances surrounding this letter are described in a way that shows them to be a specific example of the general rule articulated by the introduction. Then the request (in Latin, the *petitio*) makes explicit the desired action that follows logically from the premises and the evidence that were set forth in the previous two parts of the letter. The fifth and final part of a letter, the conclusion (in Latin, the *conclusio*), may wrap up the argument by returning to the premises of the introduction with a confirming citation of authority, or it may echo the greeting with a formal closing that reinforces the hierarchical relationship between sender and recipient and recalls the duties that are associated with each party in that relationship.

The core structure I have just described replicates a logical syllogism: the letter's introduction resembles the major premise, its statement of facts the minor premise, and its request the conclusion. This resemblance is not lost on the author of the *Tria sunt*, who shows how to use an opening proverb or exemplum to generate a tightly constructed letter whose syllogistic reasoning can be amplified and enhanced by means of the stylistic resources that are discussed at some length in his textbook.

He begins his discussion of letters by emphasizing the primacy of the inventional process: "First, let us pay close attention to three things: the nature of the subject matter, the nature of the persons involved, and the reason that moves one to write." The next step is to "find an appropriate proverb or exemplum" that is associated with the subject matter; then from this "proverb or exemplum one should discover the statement of facts, which is to be proved by means of reasons, probable arguments and effects of arguments, and certain conjectural proofs that work to the advantage of the case". These "conjectural proofs" will be taken from "the attributes of person and actions". He goes on to say that the "request and conclusion" also should be discovered from the initial proverb or exemplum. He concludes by reemphasizing that this method of composing a letter is one of rhetorical invention: "For invention is the devising of probable arguments for the advantage of our case, that is, for making persuasive that which we have in mind. And 'an argument is reasoning that provides proof, by which one thing is inferred through another,' as Quintilian says in *On the Education of an Orator* (*De institutione oratoria*)."

The author of the *Tria sunt* then puts these methods of persuasive argumentation into practice in two model letters, but I want to save those letters and use them to illustrate my points about oral delivery and creative adaptation to circumstances. Hence, I will turn now to an earlier, related treatise for a brief and relatively unadorned model letter that nicely illustrates the basic process of composing persuasive letters that is advocated in the *Tria sunt*. Just as explicitly as the anonymous fourteenth-century English author of the *Tria sunt*, the anonymous twelfth-century French author of the *Flowers of Rhetoric* (*Flores rhetorici*) underscores a letter's syllogistic structure by reducing its essential parts to three — the introduction (which he calls "the proverb"), the statement of facts, and the request. He does this by detaching the greeting from the body of the letter and by either eliminating the conclusion altogether or redefining it as a "final proverb" that is a mirror image of the introduction. He illustrates the structure so described with a brief letter in the plain style on a topic well calculated to arouse the interest of his intended audience of students: "The proverb should be adopted in this way: *A mother who does not relieve her son's poverty reeks of stepmother in her behavior*. The statement of facts: *It is a long time since I entered upon my studies at Paris, and I have already spent my money on necessities*. The petition: *Therefore you should provide me with what I need and so relieve my poverty with cash*. Final proverb: *For it is natural in a mother to relieve her needy son.*" Not content simply to label each part of the model letter, this considerate teacher goes on to provide a brief summary of the lesson he wants his students to learn and to apply in their own compositions: "Notice how you have an elegant proverb and how it is positioned in the text according to its close relationship with the request. Also notice how you have a brief and useful statement of facts and how the final proverb corresponds to the first and how it is properly joined to the request and how everything included in the text is assigned its proper place." The extreme brevity of this example — only one sentence per letter part — makes its structure crystal clear, and that is deliberate. Once students had mastered the basic principles for creating a persuasive argument, they could apply them in more expansive and complex ways, as we will see.

In teaching their students how to compose letters rather than judicial and political speeches, medieval rhetoricians clearly did not abandon argumentation in favor of style; but, in shifting their focus from one prose genre to the other, did they abandon live performances in favor of written texts, as the second myth about medieval rhetoric asserts? Once again, there is abundant evidence that medieval teachers trained their students to be effective public speakers, even if the venues in which those students went on to practice what they had learned were not identical to those in which classical orators held forth. Ambassadors and other diplomats, advisers to princes and bishops, civil and ecclesiastical administrators, members of parliament, participants in theological controversies, and legal advocates all had to present their arguments and rebut those of their opponents before an audience. Perhaps the largest group of public speakers were the priests who were required to preach sermons as part of their regular duties. In fact, a distinct variety of medieval rhetoric — the art of preaching (in Latin, *ars praedicandi*) — developed alongside the art of letter writing to provide preachers with guidance in composing and delivering their sermons. In some parts of Europe, especially in Italy, a rhetorical art of public speaking (in Latin, *ars arengandi*) was created by borrowing precepts from the art of letter writing and adapting them to specific forms of civic oratory.

More widely influential than such specialized training in particular types of public oratory, various exercises in oral performance were part of the basic rhetorical instruction provided by courses associated with general composition textbooks such as the *Poetria nova* and the *Tria sunt*. Usually one has to look carefully in the surviving textbooks to find the traces of such classroom practices, but occasionally they are closer to the surface. Geoffrey of Vinsauf provides an exceptionally clear example in the *Poetria nova*, when he illustrates his methods for teaching apostrophe, the rhetorical technique in which a speaker addresses an absent or eavesdropping audience. Geoffrey offers a comic speech about how to perform apostrophes, complete with descriptions of the tone of voice and the facial gestures that will make the performance all the more memorable for an audience of rhetoric students. As I try to perform the passage for you, notice especially the many asides or short apostrophes to the audience in the form of stage directions and sarcastic commentary (which I have underlined in the text):

> If you wish to rise up in full strength against the ridiculous, assail them in this form of speech: offer praise, but in a facetious manner; reprove, but with wit and grace; have recourse to gestures, but let these be consistently fitting. Give your speech teeth; attack with biting force — but let your manner rather than your lips devour the absurd. Lo, what was hidden in darkness will be revealed in full light. A lively theme is under discussion: "*Boys are raised up and made masters.*" Let their "masterly status" evoke laughter:
>
> *Now he sits, loftily graced with the title of master, who up to now was fit for the rod. For laymen, the cap on his head guarantees him authentic; as do the cut of his robes, the gold on his fingers, his seat at the head, and the crowd in his study.*
>
> You can laugh at the absurd situation; it is indeed a ridiculous thing:
>
> By his own and by popular verdict this is a learned man. But you perceive the same thing that I do: he is a very ape among scholars.
>
> I said that in a whisper, let no one hear it aloud.
>
> He boasts of himself, indeed, and rattling on, promises marvels. Hurry up, one and all; now the mountain's in labour, but its offspring will be only a mouse.
>
> Going before him, bid the master good day; but smile, too, at times, with a sidelong glance. Mock him with a kind of "beak" of your hands; or pull a wry mouth, or draw in your nostrils: for such expressions of ridicule it is fitting to use not the mouth but the nose. (*Poetria nova*, 431-54; trans. Nims 32, with my changes in formatting and some wording.)

Because apostrophes typically expressed strong emotions, such as outrage or grief, performing them encouraged students to practice the full repertoire of stylistic as well as non-verbal techniques for arousing an audience. Rhetoric teachers had their students compose and deliver such speeches, but they also had them practice rhetorical delivery by performing apostrophes and other emotionally charged passages from classical and medieval literature. Marjorie Curry Woods has identified late medieval manuscript copies of famous classical poems, such as the *Aeneid* of Virgil and the *Achilleid* of Statius, in which emotionally charged passages have been divided up and labeled as if they were rhetorical orations, and Jan Ziolkowski has shown how similar passages were marked with musical notation (neumes) in manuscript copies made earlier in the Middle Ages. Both types of gloss were intended to guide students as they performed such texts for their teachers and fellow students.

Even letter writers needed to practice such skills. While we moderns might think of letters in terms of writing and silent reading, such was not the case in the Middle Ages. The sound of a letter received at least as much attention as its structure in the rhetorical treatises on the *ars dictaminis*. Each sentence of a letter was divided into distinct parts, called *distinctiones* in Latin, and each of these "divisions" had to end with one of a limited set of cadences known as the *cursus*. Some teachers went so far as to distinguish particular intonations of voice appropriate for each of the three types of division: a rising tone for the *comma* that is incomplete in itself and for the *colon* that contains a complete thought but leaves something more to be said, and a falling tone for the *periodus* that allows no continuation. These and other points of doctrine clearly indicate that letters composed according to the rules of medieval rhetoric were meant to be heard as well as read.

We can only guess at the desired sound effects: there are no recordings of performances of medieval letters, and the cadences of the *cursus* are as difficult to translate into English as the metrical qualities of medieval Latin verse. Nevertheless, I will try to give you some sense of what such letters might have sounded like by reciting my translation of the second of the two model letters that are included in the *Tria sunt*. In this letter I have used English versions of the three types of cadence from the version of the *cursus* employed in the original Latin letter: the "plain" (Latin: *planus*), the "slow" (Latin: *tardus*), and the "rapid" (Latin: *velox*). Each of the letter's major divisions ends with one of those cadences. Even if you cannot hear the cadences, you will know when I reach the end of a division by a change in the pitch of my voice and a brief pause, both of which also are elements of epistolary performance that are discussed by medieval rhetoricians. In your printed copy I have inserted square brackets at each pause and indicated the type of division just concluded and the type of cadence I have employed in the translation to mark. The stressed syllables in each cadence have been underlined. Arrows pointing upward (ˆ) or downward (ˇ) indicate whether the pitch of my voice is meant to rise or fall at the end of a division.

The subject matter of the fictional letter that I will read aloud is based on historical events of 1203. The fatal conclusion of those events imparts a pathos that would have enhanced any emotional effects that a skilled performer might have been able to create with voice and gesture. The speaker is the sixteen-year-old Prince Arthur of Brittany, now a prisoner, who appeals in vain for mercy from his uncle King John of England:

(1) To John, (ˆ) his master most reverend, (ˆ) [*comma; tardus*] King by God's grace of England, (ˆ) [*comma; planus*] Arthur, albeit his captive, (ˆ) [*comma; planus*] asks that you take pity on your nephew's abundant misfortunes. (ˇ) [*periodus; planus*]

(2) Royal wrath should be tempered by clemency, (ˆ) [*colon; tardus*] and princely mercy punishes less precisely. (ˇ) [*periodus; velox*]

(3) I have earned, I confess, (ˆ) I have earned the penalty that I suffer. (ˇ) [*periodus; velox*]

(4) Indeed, after the days of my father, (ˆ) [*comma*] after the life of my grandfather, (ˆ) [*comma*] after the vicissitudes of my uncles, (ˆ) [*comma; velox*] in you only would I have had the assurance of kinship and friendship. (ˇ) [*periodus; planus*]

(5) But against so great a friend I shamelessly presumed to plot warlike follies and insidious altercations, (ˆ) [*colon; velox*] deceived to be sure by hostile suggestion. (ˇ) [*periodus; planus*]

(6) Not my uncle, (ˆ) [*comma*] not my father, (ˆ) [*comma*] not my own blood (ˆ) [*comma*] was I competent to remember. (ˇ) [*periodus; velox*]

(7) But now I give thanks to the mercy of Heaven, (ˆ) [*colon; planus*] which has granted me both to recognize what I am and to repent my deluded stupidity. (ˇ) [*periodus; tardus*]

(8) So may God restore me to your friendship (ˆ) [colon] or at least provide me milder imprisonment. (ˇ) [*periodus; tardus*]

(9) I would not wish that I, (ˆ) completely exempt, (ˆ) had not tasted this prison, (ˆ) [*colon; planus*] which has brought me back to my uncle (ˆ) [*colon; planus*] and freed me from the Gallic seducer. (ˇ) [*periodus; planus*]

(10) Your discretion knows what punishments I have suffered already: (ˆ) [*colon; planus*] I have deserved them, to be sure, (ˆ) [*colon*] but spare the penitent who confesses. (ˇ) [*periodus; velox*]

(11) If you think the penalty inflicted on me not yet equal to my guiltiness nor sufficient, (ˆ) [*comma; velox*] consider how you would have treated a nephew, (ˆ) [*colon; planus*] how you could handle a captive. (ˇ) [*periodus; planus*]

(12) Because if neither relation (ˆ) [*comma; planus*] nor even compassion, (ˆ) [comma; planus] at least let your graciousness hasten to pity. (ˇ) [*periodus; planus*]

(13) To a mind truly distinguished (ˆ) [*comma; planus*] the power of punishing suffices for mercy. (ˇ) [*periodus; planus*]

We know from the fourteenth-century Oxford university statutes that students would have had to perform their own epistolary compositions from memory and so probably employed a wider range of gestures in their performances than I did in my reading. Presumably their teachers and their fellow students would have provided them with criticism and advice on how to improve their delivery techniques, but this kind of instant feedback would have been given orally and so has not been preserved for us to share.

Like choosing the most persuasive arguments, speaking effectively before a live audience requires creative adaptation to particular circumstances. Medieval rhetoric teachers knew this as well as their classical predecessors and their modern successors, and they provided their students with opportunities to practice the intellectual agility and linguistic versatility that a professional rhetorician needs even more than formulas and rules. Rules and formulas abound in the textbooks those teachers composed, to be sure, and that fact has contributed to the last of the myths I want to question, namely, that their teaching consisted of little else. Some aspects of medieval rhetoric were bound by fixed rules: for example, a sermon always had to begin with a short quotation from the *Bible*. A preacher had to learn and obey such rules in order to fulfill the most basic expectations of his listeners. Likewise, some types of persuasion were accomplished most efficiently by means of formulaic language. Many treatises on letter writing contain long lists of model salutations because it was so important not to alienate those in positions of power by failing to greet them in language appropriate to their precise status and dignity. A breach of protocol at the very beginning of a letter would doom the most skillful arguments to failure, no matter how well they were presented.

In evaluating the evidence of the textbooks, we also need to bear in mind that they served in part as reference books and as schematic outlines for classroom practices that would have been much richer and more varied than they indicate by themselves. By comparing many different textbooks we can glimpse a certain number of those practices, as in the excerpts I have shared from the *Poetria nova* and the *Tria sunt*, but we cannot hope to reconstruct the teaching program in its entirety. It is less in the formal precepts and more in the illustrative examples of the medieval rhetoricians that we can see how they encouraged their students to be flexible and creative in applying the rules. An important means of accomplishing this crucial goal was "serious play," a technique I have illustrated already with Geoffrey of Vinsauf's lesson on how to deliver an apostrophe.

The author of the *Tria sunt* employs the same technique in the first of his two model letters, in which a student writes to a former classmate who had boasted about his accomplishments until he was exposed as a fake and had to leave the university out of embarrassment. In essence the letter is a kind of practical joke — its rhetorical purpose is supposedly to persuade its recipient that he is stupid; but the inventive playfulness of its stylistic excess is a calculated pedagogical strategy:

To A. of B. the greeting with which he deserved to be greeted. The hypocrisy of a gilded wall, as the pride of its gilding grows old, honest irony, the common exposer of lying pride, through the lie of its honesty exposes by lying honestly. By the same service of exposure, the feigned hyperbole of a tongue that takes pride in a pride of the superlative degree by covering over a poverty of the positive degree, by the true marvel of ironic exposure, as it becomes positive degenerates superlatively. Truly, how the wealthy abundance of your incomes had endowed you, how exceptional knowledge of the laws had instructed you, how subtle practice of legal cases had put you ahead of all others the common irony of a specific denunciation speaks by mocking in a genuine piece of writing. Don't you cast yourself down by raising yourself up in this way? Don't you make yourself foolish by being wise in this way? Don't you grow dumb by speaking in this way? Don't the people proclaim: "Let the deed overcome the word; boasting lessens renown"? Wherefore, once you have banned any hypocrisy of gilded pomposity whatsoever, you should hasten to assist the departure of an arrogant tongue, lest rumor lend the belief of the listening people to an ironic exposure.

The chief lesson this model letter teaches has to do with stylistic choice in relation to audience. Its style is deliberately obscure, especially at the beginning, for two reasons: (1) at the level of the epistolary fiction, its difficulty will defeat the pretentious former student's efforts to understand it and thus will provide him with an object lesson in his own ignorance; and (2) equally important but implied rather than stated, the student author's ability to produce and to understand such difficult language testifies to the skills he and his fellow students are acquiring from their rhetoric teacher. Thus, the letter simultaneously deprecates the outsider's ignorance, flatters the insider's sophistication, and advertises the rhetoric course and its teacher.

The letter also incorporates many auditory features that would be appreciated only in performance: not only the rhythmic cadences of the *cursus* and the tonally accented pauses of the *distinctiones* but also the densely clustered figures of speech that create the letter's deliberate obscurity while delighting the ear with their patterns of repetition and variation. Finally, as the author of the *Tria sunt* goes on to observe, the letter is an example of persuasive argument that builds upon the carefully chosen opening exemplum that compares the vainglorious poseur to a painted wall whose superficial gilding eventually peels off to reveal the base matter underneath. Properly appreciated, a model letter such as this one gives the lie to all three of the myths about medieval rhetoric teaching that I have been challenging. It demonstrates the function of structured argument in rhetorical persuasion, deploys the sound effects that heighten the impact of oral delivery, and illustrates the ingenuity and flexibility that enable an attentive rhetorician to adapt his treatment of any subject matter to any audience or even, as here, to more than one audience at the same time.

The author of the *Tria sunt* varies his rhetorical strategy in his own teaching, just as he expects his students to be able to do once they have left his classroom to pursue careers as professional communicators. After explicating the playfully excessive letter to a former student, he acknowledges that "in the foregoing letter the words seem too decorated" and for that reason he "will supply still another model letter, plainer in words but weightier in meaning," namely, the letter from Prince Arthur that I read to you earlier. However, even that stylistically simpler and more serious letter involves a certain amount of play. To compose such a letter a student must pretend to be another person and invent a rhetorical argument that one person could have used in a specific situation.

Like the many smaller-scale exercises that medieval students performed in order to develop verbal dexterity in Latin, such structured play more closely resembles what modern students are asked to do in a creative-writing class than in a typical rhetoric and composition class. However, the ultimate goal of this pedagogy was not to encourage self-expression but rather to develop the verbal craftsmanship needed to speak from authority. The compositions that medieval students performed for their rhetoric teachers were often quite different in content and even in style from what they would go on to compose in their professional careers, but the skills that they acquired in composing and performing such exercises served them very well in those careers.
Could similar methods work for modern students? Confronted with the complex syntax, arcane technical vocabulary, and seemingly arbitrary formulaic conventions of specialized disciplines, modern students often feel as if they, too, are being asked to read and reproduce a foreign language. Moreover, the single greatest communication challenge facing such students, no matter what discipline they are learning, is the same one faced by their medieval counterparts, namely, how to master the language and the logic that will give their own words authority. In Western Europe, from classical antiquity through at least the seventeenth century, rhetoric teachers met this challenge by assigning their students brief compositions, often treating highly dramatic subjects, with explicit formal constraints, including the structure of a specific genre (such as a letter) and the requirement that the argument be elaborated from a concise citation of some recognized authority, and by requiring those students to take ownership of their words by performing them to an audience of their peers. These methods worked well for thousands of years, proving highly adaptable even in the face of profound cultural changes. It might be worth trying to revive and adapt them once again.

References:

[1] Camargo, Martin. The Pedagogy of the *Dictatores*[J]. *Papers* on *Rhetoric*, 2002, 5: 10-11.

[2] Vinsauf, Geoffrey. Poetria Nova[J]. *Pontifical Institute of Medieval Studies*, 2010, 6: 97-114.

The Reappearance of an Ancient Rhetorical Dilemma in Modern Western Democracies

Helena Moelgaard Hansen
(University of Copenhagen, Denmark and New York University, USA)

Abstract: In this academic essay I will discuss the prevailing, yet ancient, rhetorical dilemma: Whether rhetoric is a matter of persuasion rather than a question of ethics in modern Western democracies. Despite the fact that this rhetorical debate dates back to the time of Isocrates in Ancient Greece, my recent experience as a speechwriter at the national parliament of Denmark has demonstrated that rhetoric is perceived very differently in politics compared to academia. This prompted me to readdress rhetoric's perpetual dilemma to discuss rhetoric's role and value as an academic discipline in modern Western democracies. My experience led me to the preliminary conclusion that academic rhetorical studies perhaps insist too much on rhetoric's inherent ethics, yet I will argue that rhetoric's normative function is essential to the concept of democracy, at all times.

Keywords: rhetoric; perpetual dilemma; democracy; political communication.

Most rhetoricians agree that the ancient Greek orators from the Classical period (5. – 4. BCE) designate the beginning of the Western rhetorical tradition. However, here the agreement ends: Some scholars regard ancient Greece as the golden age of rhetoric, whereas others warn not to write an idealistic history of rhetoric concealing the merits of other periods and cultures.

Isocrates was possibly the first scholar to shed light on the different views on rhetoric's purpose as he dissociated himself from the sophists who used rhetoric as an instrument of persuasion regardless of truth or falseness. Isocrates, conversely, argued in favor of the "vir bonus" — the idea of the natural union of communication and ethics — which likely is the very first conception of how rhetoric requires and fosters ethics. Aristotle later developed this conception further, sparking the debate of the role of *form and content.*

Even though this rhetorical debate is more than 2,500 years old, it is still highly ongoing. While working as a speechwriter for the government party at the national parliament of Denmark, Folketinget, in the period August 2011 to January 2012, I got exposed to the political machinery and the modern sophists, also known as political speechwriters and advisors. The game of politics made me readdress the ancient rhetorical dilemma and wonder who is right and who is wrong in this debate: Is rhetoric rather a matter of persuasion than a question of ethics in modern Western democracies?

Through a critical examination of the rhetorical history consisting of analyses of rhetorical texts from different historical periods I will claim that a somewhat idealized notion of rhetoric is prevailing among rhetoricians. Even in periods where rhetoric was reduced to merely elocutio, widespread idealism among rhetoricians whom believed in rhetoric's social and ethical value has been observed. Conversely, non-rhetoricians have criticized rhetoric for being a potential means of manipulation and demagogy. My personal experience from working at the parliament indeed planted a seed of doubt in my otherwise firm believe in rhetoric's educative force.

In this article I will reassess and discuss rhetoric's ongoing dilemma: Whether the art of rhetoric has inherent norms of communications that works as power-regulating forces in modern, democratic societies. Before describing my work at the parliament, I will, firstly, introduce the dilemma that the Greek sophists and Isocrates outlined almost 2,500 years ago which has haunted the field of rhetoric ever since. As my next point, I will briefly describe the parliamentary processes at the Danish parliament, leading me to introduce some newer social scientific theories, from which I will pinpoint current tendencies and changes in the political system that have changed the power mechanisms between Danish politicians and the media. I will argue that these changes have affected the relationship between rhetoric and its audience fundamentally, so that it is crucial to acknowledge and fully understand rhetoric's perpetual dilemma in order to maintain rhetoric's relevance as a normative science.

Although the ethics of communication has been central to modern rhetoric since Chaim Perelman and Kenneth Burke, I still find that empirical research and practical fieldwork could greatly advance our understanding of the actual norms of communication today. The conditions for political communication has changed a lot since the days of these two founding fathers' contributions to modern rhetorical theory and it is constantly changing due to information technology and globalization. Hence, I find it necessary to confront the often abstract and idealized notions of much modern rhetoric with actual political communication in different media.

Clash of Notions

Isocrates wrote the simulated speech "Against the Sophists" back in 400 BCE with which he wished to distance himself from the contemporary sophists. According to Isocrates, the sophists made rhetoric into smart, fast courses in speechwriting, and Isocrates was concerned about the possibilities for exploiting the practical part of rhetoric as he saw the sophists did it. For Isocrates himself, the finest assignment of rhetoric was to establish consensus through debate and eloquence in the ancient Greek democracy. The sophists, on the other hand, had — according to the American scholar Thomas Conley — a behavioristic approach to rhetoric, in which rhetoric was used to achieve power through stimuli and responses regardless of truth or falseness. Thus, the different and clashing notions of rhetoric were established as early as 500 BCE with the isocratic, ethical notion on one hand, and the sophistic, instrumental notion on the other.

Modern studies of rhetoric are to a great extent founded on the basis of Isocrates and Aristotle who believed in rhetoric's educative, normative, and ethical force. However, through my fieldwork I found that this notion of rhetoric did not have much in common with the political realitises at the Danish parlament.

Most of these challenges originated from the Department of Research and Information in the party that I worked for. This particular department is the architect behind the party's image and can, more or less, be regarded as a modern sophistic machine. Every single press release, speech for the parliament, and political initiative is controlled and streamlined by this department. Among others, the department has its own research unit that provides favorable statistics, which are useful in debates, articles and the like. This may seem very indecorous but all the big parties have their own research unit who, likewise, produce similar logos appeals for their politicians and support bases.

However, a problem occurs when the different parties' research units have reached different conclusions. Conflicting reports are actually sent to the media quite often. They are a definite proof of the lack of empirical evidence and reveal, furthermore, how twisted the conclusions must be. From this, it is evident that traditional, democratic values were devalued and general voter optimizing outweighed political ideals. This prioritization develops a democratic problem, since the consideration for audiences no longer forms the center of the democracy. Additionally, the impartiality of the reports illustrates how the truth-value was disregarded, which according to Conley characterizes a sophistic approach to rhetoric. The practical application of rhetoric and its systematic approach to audience, persuasion, and framing, were very useful to the department. However, the extremely controlled and targeted communication challenged the ideals of rhetoric.

The Development of Political Communication

The focus on targeted communication — also known as political communication — is a tendency that generally has emerged in Denmark and similar Western democracies during the last couple of centuries. Not only is the strong control of political communication a big democratic problem, but there are other problems as well. Power struggles between politicians and the media made the communication even more blurred. Offhand, one may think that the professionalized communication makes the politicians the dominant operator in a democracy such as Denmark. However, the constant focus on press cutting and media coverage reveals that the politicians themselves ascribe significant dominance to the media. Hence, it is my experience that the politicians adopt a comparatively reactive role in relation to the media.

The Danish professor of media studies, Stig Hjarvad, identifies the relationship between politicians and the media as a "reciprocal dependence relationship". Here, the "newsworthiness" is negotiable as long as both parts meet the unwritten requirements. Those are deadlines, relevance, entertainment, and editorial meetings on the one side, and internal competition among the news agencies and statements and stories from the politicians on the other. Hence, some sort of competition of capturing the audiences' attention takes place. The question of why this tendency of political communication emerged remains. Several scholars explain the development by two general social changes:

Firstly, the Danish media and journalism scientist, Finn Rasmussen, suggests that the public domain has turned into a communicative battlefield, in which the public authorities, the media, lobbyists, and companies fight for the audiences' attention. The fight for attention affects the political system for which reason the politicians and the parties have to devise professional targeted communication, if they want to stay in contact with the audience.

Secondly, the media's role in the society has changed. Traditionally, the politicians have been in contact with the audiences at local halls, workplaces, and political societies. However, the attendances at these communication platforms have dramatically decreased in favor of media coverage during the last couple of decades. Rasmussen emphasizes how this change, generally speaking, has given the media monopoly as political communicator.

Hjarvad concurs with Rasmussen's view and further argues that the media have developed from being an instrument for conveying the political reality into an instrument that to great extent produces the political reality. These two social changes have resulted in a systematic and intense use of spin-doctors, communication advisors, and press officers as communication tools in the political system. The Danish social scientific scholar Sigge Nielsen argues that the professionalized communication has made the audience into consumers and votes into something one can negotiate with. This point, moreover, substantiates the democratic problem that is under way.

The Devaluation of Democratic Core Values

Traditionally, the public conceived as audiences who are capable of being mediators of changing forms of the pivot of a democracy. But does the public still have this central role? Nothing is arbitrary in the professionalized communication. And therefore one may ask whether the professional and strongly controlled political communication favors or harms the enactment of democracy. On the positive side one may argue that appropriate and lucid information that is directed to a certain target audience may get one's political point across and creates better understanding of a given political issue. On the negative side, this may just as well function as a negative factor as a positive, under circumstances where the control with the information slides into being downright manipulation. Isocrates would certainly have been outraged at my sophistic role at the parliament! However, I also experienced that Isocrates and my fellow rhetorical colleagues seem to take a rather isolated stand. In the social democratic support base, my linguistic skills were highly appreciated and the argumentation that I made was — regardless of its uprightness — "business as usual".

Based on my field experience, I will argue that rhetoric can be divided into at least two overall notions. The first notion is the academic, ideal notion of rhetoric in which norms of ethical communication are fundamental. This particularly applies to the Danish as well as the American academic tradition being taught at the University of Copenhagen, for instance. The second notion is the general notion of rhetoric as a more instrumental, practical tool, which primarily exists outside the academic institutions.

It is not the first time in the rhetorical tradition that rhetoric's role in society has changed. In addition to the time of Isocrates and the sophists, rhetoric was primarily a study of elocutio during the medieval times in Italy. Thus, the function of rhetoric has changed throughout the rhetorical tradition. What is important is for rhetoricians to observe and accept that rhetoric to some is regarded as a mere communicative tool, at present — just like rhetoric being regarded as mere ornament during many periods of history. This, of course, challenges our academic notions of rhetoric and questions its normative and ethical functions.

I do not want to argue in favor of an instrumental, strategic defintition of rhetoric. I, nevertheless, believe that my observations are similar to what many other candidates of rhetoric experience in their jobs. We should use these observations constructively in order to maintain our ideals about rhetoric as being both a normative and descriptive science. If academic rhetoric is not confronted with the actual conditions for, political communication as an example, there is a danger of getting stuck in antiquated notions about rhetoric. It may also lead to a misconception of the role of academic rhetoricians in the public debate. This appears partly from an idealistic writing of the rhetorical tradition, and partly from an ethical notion of rhetoric in which its immanence is somewhat taken for granted.

A Critical Examination of the Histories of Rhetoric

Most rhetoricians agree that the ancient Greek orators from the Classical period designated the beginning of the Western rhetorical tradition. However, here the agreement ends. Some scholars regard ancient Greece as the golden age of rhetoric, whereas others warn not to write an idealistic history of rhetoric concealing the merits of other periods and cultures. The American professor of communication, Carole Blair, for instance, warns that the histories of rhetoric themselves are rhetorical, but that rhetoricians, ironically, are "blind to their own rhetoric". Blair, furthermore, argues that critiques of historiographical assumptions and procedures have multiplied, and that the problems that the critics identify in traditional histories of rhetoric are legion. Especially, the histories of rhetoric have been criticized for containing embedded and unacknowledged presuppositions about either history or rhetoric. Moreover, the assumptions of these stances have culminated in partial historical accounts that mask their own partiality.

If one defines rhetoric as an embodied relationship between form and content, rhetoric has surely had its ups and downs. This appears from a comparison between the rhetorical history and analyses of original, rhetorical texts from the different historical periods. Thus, on the basis of Blair's article I will, argue that to the extent that we take the history of rhetoric seriously, we must take the historians' choices as seriously. Rhetoric's inherent ethics is not per se. The critical examine of the histories of rhetoric proves that. This leads me on to a discussion of rhetoric's normativity.

Rhetorical Evangelism

According to Danish rhetorician Lisa Villadsen, rhetoric is generally defined as a descriptive and normative science with a practical aim. According to Villadsen, it is rhetoric's self-assured and insisting focus on norms of communication that distinguishes rhetoric from other subjects that also deals with communication, but which do so at a more descriptive level. In her article "Who Do the Rhetoricians

Think They Are?", Villadsen enhances the American scholars Lundberg and Gunn who question rhetoric's tendency to so-called "rhetorical evangelism". By "rhetorical evangelism", the two controversial scholars refer to an ethical and self-righteous notion of rhetoric, in which rhetoricians without self-evaluation preaches norms for civil culture. Their point is, among others, that it would suit rhetoricians if they generally respond less opinionated to the notion that rhetoric in itself is a matter of ethics. According to Lundberg and Gunn, it is a fundamental self-understanding among rhetoricians that needs to be challenged.

Applied to my field experience at the parliament, one may argue that Lundberg and Gunn have a point. If the majority is to decide the norm, the ideal form and content notion of rhetoric should be deselected in favor of the Danish media and politicians' general notion of rhetoric as a practice tool. Does it mean, then, that the modern Danish sophists at the parliament are not at all wide of the mark, but that the rhetoricians themselves are?

In order to answer this question, I will return to the democratic problem that has developed as a result of the emergence of the political communication. As mentioned earlier, it is problematic if the audience cannot see through the game of politics as it may lead to the manipulation of the audiences. In that connection, I believe it is the rhetoric's responsibility to maintain a sort of ethical barrier of what is acceptable within the frames of rhetoric. That is due to rhetoric's both analytical and practical aims. As Villadsen articulates: If one does not have a notion of what good rhetoric is, one cannot counsel other of how to get better in expressing oneself. Rhetoricians can simply not go without a normative point of orientation and, therefore, rhetoric must relate to what good and ethical communication is, at all times.

This discussion has clarified a democratic problem in the political system, which rhetoric — because of its normative function — can and should take part in restraining. Lundberg and Gunn's point is nevertheless more relevant. These scholars keep rhetoricians reassessing the ideals of good rhetoric and how these are developed. Likewise, the discussion illustrates rhetoric's essential role for democratic purposes and how crucial it is to a rhetorician to maintain one's ethical values in a society, where the foundation of rhetoric and democracy is disputed and tested.

My field experience has given rise to an important discussion of rhetoric's role in modern Western democracies in which rhetoric's perpetual dilemma has turned out to be just as prevailing as was the case 2,500 years ago. By continuously discussing the goal and role of rhetoric, rhetoric will continue to be as relevant and useful as an academic discipline as it has proved to be in this particular case. With a final quotation from Blair I shall conclude this article: "Rhetoric as a universal human activity has naturally left its records in a wide variety of cultures and languages over thousands of years of civilization. Consequently our efforts to understand its complexity need to be as sophisticated as the subject itself."

References

[1] Conley Thomas. *Rhetoric in the European Tradition*[M]. Chicago IL: University of Chicago Press, 1994.

[2] Easton David. *A Systems Analysis of Political Life*[M]. New York: John Wiley, 1957.

[3] Hjarvad Stig. *Det selskabelige samfund*[M]. Samfundslitteratur, 2003.

[4] Hoff Jens, Storgaard Kresten. *Informationsteknologi og demokratisk innovation – borgerdeltagelse, politisk kommunikation og offentlig styring*[M]. Samfundslitteratur, 2005.

[5] Isokrates. *Fire taler, herunder "Mod sofisterne"*[M]. Copenhagen: Museum Tusculanums Forlag, Københavns Universitet, 1986.

[6] Nielsen Sigge Winther. *Sæg politik som du sæger bananer*[M]. Publiceret i, 2011.

[7] Rasmussen Finn. *Massemedier og politisk kommunikation*[M]. Columbus, 2007.

[8] Roer Hanne. Helenas pris[J]. *Publiceret i Rhetorica Scandinavica*, 2007, 41: 6-8.

[9] Villadsen Lisa Storm. Hvem tror retorikerne egentlig de er[J]. *Publiceret i Retorik Magasinet*, 2011, 82: 12-15.

第二部分

传播修辞研究

Imagination in Rhetorical Communication and Persuasion[1]

WooSoo Park

(Hankuk University of Foreign Studies, Repulic of Korea)

Abstract: Imagination means a faculty or power of making images in mind. Imago is a form, a simulacrum, an edidolon, an idol, an icon(eikos) that gives a form and appearance to something perceived. An image brings a noumenon of abstract quality into light of illustration, illumination, and phenomenon. An idea is brought into our perception in and through images. Imagination is the mediator participating in both perception and conception. In order to understand some conceit or idea we need perceive it in concrete images. Even medieval theologians admitted the role of fancy in our access to invisible God. The power of imagination determines the depth and intensity of engraved impressions. Only when imagination works on reason with its touch of images and revealing light does reason affect on our will, which induces us to an action. Therefore imagination is a potential action working on both reason and will: it instigates a desire for an action, basically derived from emotions of pleasure and pain. Imagination as a mediating power and energy activates a movement of soul in desire and appetency. When the energy of imagination is great, the movement becomes vital and speedy to that extent: that is why vivid expressions both in poetry and oratory transport us in ecstasy. As a moving energy imagination is a necessity for sympathy and social commerce. Rhetorical communication and persuasion is founded on imaginative sympathy. But for the imaginary change of situation is not possible a true commerce and communication, let alone persuasion and identification. Imagination and imaginative sympathy come before rhetorical persuasion and identification. Imagination is a light energy that breaks darkness and comes into appearances. Before the god of creation was the god of imagination, and the latter created the world out of dark chaos by means of the light of imagination (phantasy).

1 This paper was prepared by the HUFS 2013 research grant.

Hence imagination is Jacob's ladder on whose rung we can step along to reach the invisible god. Therein we have the moral theology of imagination for human society and communication. Imaginative sympathy is a kind of electric affinity circulating in discourses, and rhetorical communication and identification is possible only when it works as *qi* (in Chinese, meaning energy or vitality).
Key words: imagination; rhetorical communication; medialogy

Imagination means a faculty or power of making images in mind. Imago is a form, a simulacrum, an edidolon, an idol, an icon (eikos) that gives a form and appearance to something perceived. An image brings a noumenon of abstract quality into the light of illustration, illumination, and phenomenon. An idea is brought into our perception in and through images. The more vivid and vital the image is, the stronger and more energetic the impression is engraved on the tracks of memory. Plato is not immune from the fatal attraction of eidos when he denigrates the phenomenal, "Insubstantial" world of images: his transcendental world of ideas (eidos) is still haunted by images, even though they are arguably archetypes or images beyond images. An obscure and abstract idea is embodied by imagination as a concrete entity in the fluxes of the sense, and is surfaced in understanding by way of perception. If the myth of the Edenic Fall is significant in the history of Christianity, it is mainly because it implies an irrecoverable gap between things and words, actuality and potentiality, signified and signifier, image and idea. It further implicates a human fall from the happy state of unification of idea with image, perception with understanding until the advent of the Redeemer as perfected Logos. If the art of lying and truth-like lies is the byproduct of the Fall, we are condemned in Biblical narratives to live the irredeemable world of phenomenon and noumenon and to understand the transcendental signified through worship of idols and images. We are similar in nature to Moses' Israelites in the wilderness of their mental hunger for the visible and the graspable, who forged a golden calf in place of a hidden and cloudy deity. When we characterize the postmodern age as blurring and re-drawing the line of the real and the simulacra, we are at the last skeptical stage of heathenism which takes images (icons) for the real. Though we cannot accept as a "real" reality the virtual reality as it is, this kind of blurring and deterritolialization is remarkable, for it is symbolic of the sublime power of images affecting intelligence and reason. We are living the last phase of the Romantic Age because we are ironically experiencing its ideal aspiration of uniting the word and the thing, emotion and reason, the multeity in one and one in multiety. Hence chiasmus as a via media is the typical idiom and rhetorical device of our age of commerce and communication. We are on the crossway hesitating and indeterminate like free floating signifiers hovering for a location to settle in.

Imagination as a Medialogy

If imagination is the via media between perception and understanding, we have to go through the gate of imagination in order to reach understanding. As a mediator between perception and understanding, imagination is placed in a crucial and dangerous position that can color, twist, and help perception and understanding. It is assumed to play a two-edged role, both positive and negative, in intelligence and understanding. As Aristotle says in his vein of empirical psychology against Plato's metaphysics of transcendental presence and logos, imagination is inevitable in thinking. Though "phantasia differs from both perception and thought even though it cannot exist without perception and serves as a precondition of belief" (*De Anima* 427b), "every time one thinks one must at the same time contemplates some image" (432a). Though Aristotle makes it clear that imagination (phantasia) is a kind of motion causing a desire resulting from sensation, he avows positively the perception-dependent role of imagination in thinking and belief:

> The thinking soul apprehends the forms in images, and since it is by means of these images that it determines what is to be sought and what avoided... Moreover, it is by means of the images or thoughts in the soul, which enable us to see (the future), that we calculate and deliberate about the relationship of things future to things present. (*De Anima* 431b).

If it is possible for us to see through time or things not present at the moment of deliberation, it mainly because of the power of memory relevant to imaginary sensations. Deliberation in images is a species of conceptual memory, whereas perceptive is the mental operations of memory when the memory image is a copy of external reality. Memory is similar to phantasy in that it is both perceptive and conceptive at once. For Aristotle "deliberation involves the consideration of possible future outcomes and it also involves imagination" (Kearney 419 n. 43). Deliberation, memory, and imagination are siblings in the family of mental operations and they grow together. What is remarkable in the Aristotelian psychology is that every faculty of mind is irretrievably interwoven in unity of being with each other. This interwoven configuration of the faculties of mind is analogous to the ontological and hierarchal chain of beings in the universe. Deliberation is ethical when it tries to avoid pain and/or pleasure, and ethical deliberation in the regulation of our conducts is actively imaginative when it is permeated by imaginative sensations, both perceptive and conceptive. Ethical deliberations may bring a substantial change in the deliberator, and the latter may enhance ethical deliberations in return, so they are mutually in the dynamic movement. Imagination is a vital energy (*energeia*) and potential act of movement when it leads to a desire of knowledge and avoidance. Imagination, as its Greek equivalent *phantasy* includes the etymological word, *phao* (light), is in itself a strong energy of light that breaks the barrier of obscurity into open appearances. As in Dante, "the towering fantasy" beholds the eternal light as reflected splendor, when the vigor of speech fails to give conception birth. Imagination is moving in both senses that it causes a movement of desire and at the same time re-moves perceptions to conceptions of reason.

Since the material things of the phenomenal world are real, Aristotle assumes, the motion of phantasia serves to the king of reason to make it possible for it have a contact with the sensible world of reality. As Richard Kearney argues, "the image serves as the internal representation of sensation to reason," and imagination differs from sensation "in its capacity to relay our impressions of reality to the inner activities of reason" (108). Phantasia as a kind of light and motion participates actively in both perception and understanding. And in perceiving some material thing, it causes an action of appetency. In moving an appetite for a thing, phantasia may go against the dictate of reason. However, even in this case, phantasia is not wrong, but the object of desire may be. Since phantasia as a kind of movement includes a movement of appetency, learning and belief in the soul is impossible without a phantasm. Phantasms work as sensational presence in providing absent things before the eyes of mind. Even the mathematical abstraction of the mind, like the general idea of a triangle is possible in Aristotle based on the concrete and particular image(s) of a triangle, unlike the other way round as in Plato. As Murray Bundy rightly puts it, "Aristotle was apparently trying to avoid the pitfalls of Platonic dualism, when, building upon Plato's conceptions, he defines a power concerned both with perception and conception, sensation and thought, body and soul. Phantasy for Aristotle bridges the gap" (73). Here we can safely assume that in Aristotle imagination as an image-making faculty is not a stone in the stream to hinder the current of epistemological recognition, but a helping genius to the way. Imagination is actively working in perception and conception, and conception is not possible without the mediation of imagination delivering the sense impressions to the mental operations of mind. Aristotle's vision of imagination foreruns the Romantic vision of it as the highest mode of intelligence and as a unified being associating sensibility with thinking, body with soul, and the phenomenal with the noumenal. Cicero is wrong when he points out the Socratic moment as the fragmentation of prudence as a comprehensive science of rhetoric. Aristotle is shown to try to combine every faculty of mind and consequently to overpass the Platonic dualism.

The English Romantics inherit the legacy of David Hume's identification of imagination and understanding. Hume says of understanding as "but the general and more established properties of the imagination(*Human Nature*, I. IV, in Anderson 266). For Hume imagination is the unifying power of all the endeavors of the mind and upon it depends the unity of reality and consciousness(Anderson 267). This synthesizing power of imagination in its various conjunctions with senses, memory, understanding, and reason is crystallized in S.T. Coleridge's idea of imagination. Though Coleridge started as a Hartleian psychologist of association, he developed his idea of imagination from a reproductive or representative power to a more creative and productive co-adunating power, the "power by which one image or feeling is made to modify many others and by a sort of fusion to force many into one" (Raysor, I, 212). Imagination as an esemplastic power is like a metoptric chamber of mirrors reflecting and transforming one into many and many into one. For Coleridge imagination is like a triune God manifesting itself in the trinity of the Father, the Son and the Holy Ghost: it is a multeity in one, and one in multeity. The man of genius reconciles in imagination the objective and the subjective, the represented and the representative, the unconscious and the conscious, thing and thought (*Biographia Literaria*, II, 258). In its balance of reconciliation, creative imagination is related to the primal creative forces of the universe. In its highest sense imagination repeats in the finite mind the eternal act of creation. Though Coleridge sometimes hesitates to fully identify imagination with reason, he tries to fuse them in the ideality of imagination.

Though Thomas Hobbes and his followers confined in their own versions of empiricism imagination to materialism of sensation, and memory to "decayed sense," imagination as creative power and embodiment of reason and insight keeps up its vitality and energy in the English Romantic poets, going back to the tradition of the Cambridge Platonists. However, the Platonist is a misnomer as far as the holistic function of imagination is concerned. Rather English Romantics return to Aristotle who tries to bridge the gap in Plato's dualism. Now we can derive from Aristotle the medialogy of imagination mediating perception and conception. We cannot perceive what we cannot imagine, and we cannot understand what we cannot perceive. And what we conceive, we conceive in and through images and memory of them. When we begin to identify imagination with invention and judgment, rhetorical communication and persuasion is brought under the sphere of imagination. If imagination is conducive to thinking and belief, persuasion is not possible without the mediating power of imagination as a vital energy. The brighter and stronger the illuminating power of imagination is in speech and communication, to such an extent the more easily we are likely to be transported out of our own identity into a sublime loss of the self. Imagination is the very energy needed for soul's movement. We will illustrate the rhetorical power of imagination in eloquence.

Imagination as *Evidentia* or *Claritas*: The Power of Language

Imagination as a powerful energy of movement manifests itself in vivid and sublime expressions (energeia). The history of rhetoric has appropriated imagination as devices that enhance the power of transportation and movement of audiences. In order to achieve persuasion and identification the audience must be first of all moved out of their own proper selves (ex-tasia), and for this purpose verbal pictures that portray concrete and particular events and situations are claimed to appeal directly to the eyesight, provoking emotions. As Shakespeare's Volumnia says in *Coriolanus*, "action is eloquence, and the eyes of th' ignorant / More learned than the ears" (3.2.76-77). Similarity of poetry and painting as sister arts is expressed in the idea of paragone between poetry as speaking picture and picture as silent poetry. As Longinus says, "genius does not merely persuade an audience but lifts it to ecstasy. The astonishing is always of greater force than the persuasive or the pleasing" (in Gilbert 147). Judicious use of metaphors is one of the best ways to achieve this admiring effect on the audience/readers. A metaphor, as its Latin translation, *translatio*, clearly indicates, involves a movement of place. Metaphors when well-used, as products of an imaginative genius, are moving in the soul because they give us great pleasure and wonder of discovering apparently veiled resemblance among disparate things. A sudden joy of intellectual recognition is revealed in novel metaphors which uncover unexpected patterns of analogy between seemingly different things. And intellectual joy of a new finding is stronger and more long-lasting than physical distractions because it is harder to get. What is harder to get needs more energy since it wants much longer movement of your desire, and when you get your long desired object after much toil and task, you get greater satisfaction than an easy procurement. According to Aristotle, "the pleasures of thought are superior to the pleasures of the senses" (*Nichomachean Ethics*, 285). As imagination as a species of moving energy involves a movement of appetency, so metaphor as a subspecies of imagination activates a soul movement in terms of wonder and admiration. In this sense Longinus compares violence of metaphors to the sweeping torrent, "The right time for their (metaphors') use is when the feelings roll on like a spring torrent and sweep along the whole mass of them as though they were inevitable" (182). The use of a highly figurative language requires as a necessity thereof the enthusiasm of both the speaker and the audience. The bursting violence of a metaphor in imagination flashes like a thunderbolt and lightning and blinds, though temporarily, the discerning eyes of the audience. That powerful energy of light in metaphor works an ecstatic transportation, and an enthusiastic madness is more violent and powerful than persuasion in oratory.

Energetic is the power of imaginative presence when it puts something, physically absent, just before your eyes. Almost synonymous in rhetorical communication are the two words: energeia as an energy of enactment and moving appetency and enargeia as vividness (evidential, visibility). Here is Longinus again on the energy of imagination:

"Imaginative pictures (the name by which some people call poetic images) are highly effective in producing massiveness, grandeur, and energy. The name imagination is commonly applied to any idea that enters the mind and produces speech, but the meaning that prevails is the one I employ, namely, that in your enthusiasm and strong feeling you seem to see what you speak of and put it before the eyes of your audience. It will not escape you that imagination is defined in one way by the orator and in another by the poet, nor that in poetry it strives to strike the hearer with a sudden shock, but in oratory it seek vividness. Both, however, aim at the latter and at excitement. (165)"

Imagination brings us a sudden shock of recognition and a passion of excitement working in energy. Enthusiasm as a kind of rhapsodic madness is a heightened desire and that sublime desire is in itself as an accumulated mass of energy: that is why we are moved and removed in and out of ourselves when we are in a state of enthusiasm and passions. Mark Antony wins over Brutus in the logomachy in the Roman forum over the body of Julius Caesar because he is good at moving his audience by taking advantage of the energy of concrete and vivid presence while Brutus is devoted to abstract virtues. As Chaim Perelman argues, "presence, at first a psychological phenomenon, becomes an essential element in argumentation" (*The New Rhetoric*, 117). Presence works in images and in imagination of both the speaker and the audience as a kind of logos. As passions can provide a support for a positive argument, imagination in the form of Baconian idols is not separable from reasoning in argumentation. Here we find an unexpected similarity between Perelman and Coleridge in terms of imagination as a unified vision. Our reason works on our will only when it touches our affections by means of imagination as a power of movement and energy. Vividness in an elevated language and emotion realizes imagination as a medialogy as it affects both perception and conception in its moving energy of tension and vibration. As Longinus links literary excellences with social freedom of democracy, imagination of violent transportation is oriented toward communion and community because a true fellowship and society is possible when we escape from the prison-house of self. Imagination is a prerequisite for sympathy.

Imagination as Sympathy

Pity or compassion depends on imagination. Only imagination can deliver us out of self-love into sharing of pleasures and pains of other people. According to Adam Smith,

> As we have no immediate experience of what other men feel, we can form no idea of the manner in which they are affected, but by conceiving what we ourselves should fell in the like situation... By the imagination we place ourselves in his (our brother's) situation, we conceive ourselves enduring all the same torments, we enter as it were into his body, and become in some measure the same person with him, and thence form some idea of his sensations, and even feel something, which though weaker in degree, is not altogether unlike them. (*The Theory of Moral Sentiment*, 9)

It is by changing place in imagination with the sufferer that we can come to have sympathies or fellow feelings with him. For Smith sympathy is founded on imaginary change of situation. This sympathetic imagination is related with our desire of praise-worthiness and our aversion to blame-worthiness. Hence moral judgment leading to an action is derived from sympathy or antipathy. The man of self-command watches in the mirror of his mind pains of his fellow sufferers, unaffected and seldom perverted by his self-interest and self-love, though it must be admitted that "even the judge within is often in danger of being corrupted by the violence and injustice of our selfish passions" (141). Adam Smith calls this man an impartial spectator, whose moral judgment is the jurisdiction of the man within. This impartial spectator or the man within the breast transports himself in imagination to a vantage point from where he can survey all the situations his fellows are placed in. In Aristotelian words, "sympathetic understanding is a correct critical sense or judgment of what is fair; and a correct judgment is a true one" (*Nichomachean Ethics*, 165). This man of imaginative sympathy and of divine extraction makes him "a citizen of the world, a member of the vast commonwealth of nature" (140). Imagination can conjure up an impartial spectator within, free from the limitations imposed by the real spectator without, so as to make him reach objective judgments of perception and moral actions. Smith's impartial spectator is the ideal moralist gazing at the looking-glass of conscience because he can exercise self-command and self-control in the stoic tranquility of mind regardless of turbulent events and situations of reality which can affect his passions. However, in actuality he is more likely to remain a passive spectator with indifference to fellow feelings. At most, if he is motivated to sympathy or antipathy by his innate desire of praise-worthiness and aversion to blame-worthiness, still haunted is he by his inescapable sense of egotism. Nevertheless, what matters with Adam Smith is that his crucial idea of an impartial spectator is aimed at universal morality which makes possible the construction of the universal commonwealth of human nature and citizenship of the world. This ideal moralism, working only in and by imagination, reflects Smith's astute awareness of the economic man governed by his self-interest. Despite real conflict between theory and praxis in Smith, remarkably it is imagination that makes an ego-bound man transcend his own atomic being and converge himself on a conglomeration of society. Imagination, by its medialogy of moving power which realizes and reveals itself in and by the media of language, signs and symbols, is the proper energy needed for unifying and synthesizing atomic sense data for a unity of being and fellow-feelings. On imagination is founded a societal man of sympathy.

Imagination is the mediator participating in both perception and conception. In order to understand some conceit or idea we need perceive it in concrete images. Even medieval theologians admitted the role of fancy in our access to invisible God. The power of imagination determines the depth and intensity of engraved impressions. Only when imagination works on reason with its touch of images and revealing light does reason affect on our will, which induces us to an action. Therefore imagination is a potential action working on both reason and will: it instigates a desire for an action, basically derived from emotions of pleasure and pain. Imagination as a mediating power and energy activates a movement of soul in desire and appetency. When the energy of imagination is great, the movement becomes vital and speedy to that extent: that is why vivid expressions both in poetry and oratory transport us in ecstasy. As a moving energy imagination is a necessity for sympathy and social commerce. Rhetorical communication and persuasion are founded on imaginative sympathy. But for the imaginary change of situation is not possible for a true commerce and communication, let alone persuasion and identification. Imagination and imaginative sympathy come before rhetorical persuasion and identification. Imagination is a light energy that breaks darkness and comes into appearances. Before the god of creation was the god of imagination, and the latter created the world out of dark chaos by means of the light of imagination (phantasy). Hence imagination is Jacob's ladder on whose rung we can step along to reach the invisible god. Therein we have the moral theology of imagination. The whole man is made possible by the functional synthesis of will, reason, and imagination, characterized by emotional intensity and sincerity. Imagination is "the reconciling and mediatory power, which incorporates the reason in images of the sense, and organizes, as it was, the fluxes of the sense by the permanent and self-circling energies of the reason" (Anderson 531).

References

[1] Anderson. *Theory of Fancy and Imagination in English Thought from Hobbes to Coleridge*[D]. Vanderbilt University, 1953.

[2] Aristotle. *De Anima*[M]. Trans. R. D. Hicks. Cambridge: Cambridge University Press, 1907.

[3] Aristotle. *Nicomachean Ethics*[M]. Trans. Martin Ostwald. Prentice-Hall, N.J.: The Library of Liberal Arts, 1999.

[4] Bundy, Murray. *The Theory of Imagination in Classical and Medieval Thought*[J]. University of Illinois Studies in Language and Literature, Vol. XII 1927: 1-289.

[5] Coleridge, Samuel Taylor. *Shakespearean Criticism*[M]. London: Dent, 1960.

[6] Coleridge, Samuel Taylor. *Biographia Literaria*[M]. Oxford: Clarendon, 1907.

[7] Fogle, Richard. *The Idea of Coleridge's Criticism*[M]. Berkeley: University of California Press. 1962.

[8] Kearney, Richard. *The Wake of Imagination*[M]. London: Routledge, 1988.

[9] Longinus. "On Literary Excellence" *Literary Criticism from Plato to Dryden*[M]. Detroit: Wayne State University Press, 1962.

[10] Perelman, Chaim, Olbrechts-Tyteca. *The New Rhetoric*[M]. Trans. John Wilkinson & Purcell Weaver. Notre Dame: University of Notre Dame Press, 1969.

[11] Read, Herbert. *The True Voice of Feeling*[M]. London: Faber & Faber, 1968.

[12] Smith, Adam. *The Theory of Moral Sentiment*[M]. Oxford: Clarendon, 1976.

[13] Thorp, Clarence. *The Aesthetic Theory of Thomas Hobbes*[M]. Ann Arbor: University of Michigan Press, 1940.

[14] Tuveson, Ernest Lee. *The Imagination as a Means of Grace*[M]. Berkeley: University of California Press, 1960.

[15] Warnock, Mary. *Imagination*[M]. Berkeley: University of California Press, 1978.

修辞传播：传播效果研究的重要课题[1]

惠东坡

（［中国］北京联合大学）

摘　要： 传播效果研究作为传播学的核心课题，在研究思路、研究意识、研究内容和方法上和修辞学有着密切的历史渊源。纵观传播效果研究的历史和修辞传播的历史演进，我们可以看出两者发展的关联逻辑：（1）修辞意识：传播效果研究的一条暗线；（2）修辞技巧：传播效果研究的微观考察；（3）修辞语境：传播效果研究的宏观关照；（4）修辞话语分析：传播效果研究的重要方法；（5）修辞批评：传播效果研究的另一种视野。因此，修辞传播作为一种以谋求预期效果为目的的积极主动的传播活动，应成为传播效果研究明确而重要的课题。

关键词： 修辞学；修辞传播；传播效果研究。

修辞学是以传播效果的产生、机制、要素、目的、结果为研究对象的。古典修辞学时期，亚里士多德在《修辞学》这本专著中就论述了在各种公共语境中进行有效说服的问题，并研究了话语的各种结构和机制的不同效用。当代修辞学认为传播活动几乎都是修辞活动，修辞是运用话语和象征来达到某种目的的传播活动。传播效果研究作为传播学的核心课题，在研究思路、研究意识、研究内容和方法上与修辞学有着密切的历史渊源。纵观传播效果研究的历史和修辞传播的历史，我们可以看出两者发展的关联逻辑。因此，修辞传播作为一种以谋求预期效果为目的的积极主动的传播活动，应成为传播效果研究明确而重要的课题。

一、修辞意识：传播效果研究的一条暗线

不管传播技术如何进步、传播形态怎样演进，传播效果研究一直是人类传播活动最重要、最核心的研究课题。在文字发明之前的口语传播时期和文字发明之后的手抄传播阶段，人际传播、群体传播、组织传播成为重要的传播渠道。在这一传播阶段，传播效果主要从微观层面考察，是指带有说服动机的传播行为在受传者身上引起的心理、态度和行为的变化。1456年，古登堡的机械印刷术把人类的传播活动带进了印刷传播的新阶段，由此开始了大众传播的新时代。此后，人类社会又从电子传播阶段进入新媒体传播时代。在这一传播阶段，传播效果研究主要从综合和宏观的层面来考察负载着不同功能的大众传播活动对受传者和社会所产生的一切影响

1 本文系北京市教育委员会2013年社科计划面上项目阶段成果（项目编号：SM201311417004）。

和结果。可见，传播效果研究的是带有目的和倾向性的传播活动的影响和结果。在这一点上，我们认为，传播效果研究和修辞有着极为密切的关系，因为，修辞是有目的、积极谋取效果的传播艺术。综合考察传播效果和修辞的研究核心，我们不难发现，两者都把有目的、谋取效果的传播活动及其各种影响因素作为研究对象。

当代新修辞学又一次扩展了修辞的内涵：运用话语和象征来达到某种目的的传播行为。认为修辞蕴藏于人类的一切传播活动中，而且它组织和规范人类思想和行为的各个方面。新修辞几乎把修辞活动等同于传播活动。随着新修辞学把研究的视角从传统的政治活动投向以言语为主的象征交流活动，修辞学逐渐向传播学演变。因此，“我们可以说，从20年代开始以演讲和话语为研究主体的现代修辞学的复兴为现代传播学播下了种子，作了理论准备”。[2]“大众传播研究一直被一种‘效果导向’（Effect-Orientation）主导”[3]以追求话语效果为核心的修辞精神和思想渗透于传播研究的各种模式和理论中。也就是说，修辞意识一直是传播效果研究的一条暗线。

古典修辞的话语过程、机制、策略等理论在众多解释媒介效果的理论框架中若隐若现。不论是拉斯韦尔的5W模式还是申农–韦弗模式都和亚里士多德的话语模式十分相似。这与其说是科学研究中的机缘巧合，不如说是对传统的扬弃或互相启发。而且，以拉斯韦尔为首的一些学者进行的宣传术研究重点探讨的也是修辞技巧。但由于其缺乏量化程序，所以有人称之为“旧式修辞研究”。由于历史条件的限制，古典话语修辞所使用的研究方法是思辨、批评和缺乏数理论据支持的推论等阐释性的定性研究，虽然这种研究方法在解释话语传播的微妙特征、功能和结果等方面比定量研究方法更有效。但是，由于越来越多的研究采用基于社会科学的观点和方法为指导的定量调查方法这种主流的求知方式。因此，带有浓厚人文思辨色彩的旧式修辞研究的日趋式微也就顺理成章了。[4]

1929年至1932年佩恩基金研究表明，电影对儿童的影响成为使媒介调查领域科学化的先驱。从此，实验和定量分析才开始在媒介调查中占主导地位。重要的是，这项调查对旧式修辞的研究模式进行了改进。这直接影响了后来的研究，“它预言了到现在才提出的意义理论、模型理论，并且还关注了一些新兴的研究领域中的课题，如态度转变、休眠效应、使用与满足、内容分析、模仿的影响和现实的社会性建构（Social Construction of Reality）。”[5]

如今，传播学理论和方法蔚为大观，其实，只要我们追根溯源，进行知识考古式地探究，我们仍然可以看到古典修辞的光辉。他们以新的视角、新的方法、新的

2 大卫·宁：《当代西方修辞学：批评模式与方法》，常昌富、顾宝桐译，中国社会科学出版社，1998年12月第1版。

3 洛厄里、德弗勒：《大众传播效果研究的里程碑（第三版）》，刘海龙等译，人民大学出版社，2009年6月第1版。

4 惠东坡：《我国重大突发事件新闻话语修辞研究》，人民日报出版社，2013年。

5 洛厄里、德弗勒：《大众传播效果研究的里程碑（第三版）》，刘海龙等译，人民大学出版社，2009年6月第1版。

理论改进、发展、丰富了修辞话语的各种要素、机制、规律。其实，不只是大众传播，其他一切或具体或抽象的文化形式都成为修辞学研究的对象。现在，谈到修辞学的定义，西方修辞学界比较认同的观点是“现代修辞学研究的是人类使用符号相互交流的能力，这种能力是人类所特有的，人类使用符号来构建自己的世界，来认识自我，来和其他人一起互动，使生活更有意义”。[6]

20世纪六七十年代在西方国家开始广泛出现的具有重大影响的社会文化思潮——后现代思潮将一切符号化、话语化，也就是将一切建构化，这实际上是将一切修辞化，这直接影响了大众传播的效果研究。从目前的发展趋势来看，短期的、预期的效果研究将更多地让位于长期的、非预期的效果研究。也就是说，从魔弹论开始，线性的单向影响模式逐渐向更为宏观的以文化、受众为中心的模式发展。

这恰恰反映了修辞研究和传播效果研究从微观研究逐步拓展到宏观研究，这是因为传播过程的各种要素和环节都会对传播效果产生重要影响，而且这种影响是各种因素相互作用的结果。以效果作为关注点的修辞意识贯穿了整个传播过程。修辞意识是制约传播活动的首要因素，是事先对传播活动进行的策划、组织和安排，也是传播活动实施、监控、检查的必不可少的环节。也就是说，在修辞活动实施之前，传播者就对自己的修辞目的、修辞表现方式有着清醒的认识。具有修辞意识意味着对传播过程各环节及其各影响因素的规律和特点的敏感。传播活动中的许多问题都与修辞有关，传播者、传播内容、信息载体、媒介渠道、传播技巧、传播对象等要素和环节都可提出种种修辞要求。修辞意识可帮助我们根据传播活动的要求、目的，迅速准确地进行传播活动的定位、策划、实施、监控或修改。修辞意识是指在传播活动中的修辞主体意识、修辞策略和修辞技巧意识、语体意识、语境适应意识、受众分析意识。

二、修辞技巧：传播效果研究的微观考察

东西方修辞学都有着悠久的历史传统并产生了深远的影响。东西方修辞学产生于言语传播的社会实践，都研究修辞的手段和方法，都重视修辞技巧的研究，关注人类的言语传播规律。这种研究的目的是追求最佳的传播效果，从言语和语言的本体层面探讨言语传播的效果是微观的考察，也是最直接的研究。

关注言语运用的技巧和规律一直是修辞学研究的核心内容之一，也是狭义修辞学的主要特征之一。20世纪的中国修辞学，从辞格研究起步，直到同义结构的讨论，其中自有种种变化，但总体上还是遵循同一个研究范式，这就是语言的艺术化的技巧及其选择。把修辞看作是“语言技巧”的选择，是从语音、词汇、句式的变异运用出发，具体有“修辞方式”研究、“同义结构”研究、“语言风格”研究、“语体特征”研究等。虽然，当代语用学逐步把修辞技巧拓展到“言语行为”规律的探讨，但我国的修辞技巧研究已经取得了辉煌的成就。

6 胡曙中：《现代英语修辞学》，上海外语教育出版社，2004年7月第1版，导论，第2页。

修辞方法是指人们使用语言时用来提高言语效果的各种方法的统称。修辞技巧通常和修辞方法、修辞手法、修辞手段、修辞方式、修辞格等术语混用，有时又指包括辞格在内的所有修辞技法。修辞方法是指表达者为了适应表情达意的特殊需要、为了提高语言表现力和增强表达效果，实现预定的交际目标，在说写活动中所运用的言语方式和技巧。修辞方法主要是对语言材料进行选择、加工和配置的方法。从选词择句到谋篇布局以及适应不同的语体风格都要讲究修辞方法。也就是说, 人们为了适应社会交际的需要, 根据民族语言内部发展规律所创造的具体修辞方法, 如拟人、比喻、夸张、标点、句式、音律、感情、风格, 等等。[7]陈望道先生把所有修辞方法区分为消极修辞和积极修辞，前者“力求意义明白”“尽传达事理的责任”，后者“却要使人‘感受’”“要它有力，要它动人”。[8]

大众传播时代，随着社会科学研究的“语言学转向”，很多社会科学领域的研究课题都试图从以语言为基本传播手段的话语中寻求问题的答案。在传播学中，对信息内容的研究形成了独特的内容分析方法。内容分析从本质上说就是微观的言语技巧和规律研究，也可以说是修辞技巧研究。即使是宏观的传播效果研究也往往是从最基础和微观的层面展开的。从总体来看，修辞技巧就修辞本身所具有的传播本质属性而言，不应局限于辞格、语音、词汇、句式等语言本体研究，而应该综合考察言语行为、传播过程及其他影响因素。

三、修辞语境：传播效果研究的宏观关照

早在古希腊时期，亚里士多德在其名著《修辞学》中就论述了在演讲中影响演讲效果和听众理解的诸多因素，例如不同社会环境、历史背景、身份地位对听众的心理、道德观的影响等。这些当时并未完全被认定是“修辞情景”的因素就是后来修辞学家们研究的“语境”。1923年，波兰语言学家马林诺夫斯基（B. Malinnowski）在《意义的意义》一书中提出了“语境”的概念。他把言语行为发生时的具体情境称为“Context of Situation（情景语境）”，把说话者所处的社会文化的语境称为“Context of Culture（文化语境）”。功能语言学“伦敦学派”代表人物弗斯（J. R. Firth）继承、发展了马林诺夫斯基的观点，弗斯认为文化、信仰、整个社会环境、参加者的关系、参加者的身份和历史等都属于语境的组成部分。

1964年，英国语言学家韩礼德（M. A. K. Halliday）在弗斯语境理论基础上提出了“语域”这一概念，语言情境由“场景（Field）”“方式（Mode）”“交际者（Tenor）”三部分组成，三个部分都可以产生新的语域。此后，美国社会语言学家菲什曼（Fishman）又提出了“语义场”（Domain）的概念，认为语义场就是受共同行为规则制约的社会情境，包括时间、地点、对象和主题。另一位美国社会语言学家海姆斯（Hymes）认为语境还包括话语本身的形式和内容（Form and Content of Text），这进一步扩展了语境的内涵。

---

7 王德春：《修辞学词典》，浙江教育出版社，1987年。

8 陈望道：《修辞学发凡》，上海教育出版社，1997年。

劳埃德·比彻（Lloyd F. Bitzer）以政治家的演讲为基础论述了修辞具有情景性。他认为情景是修辞活动的基础。修辞情景可定义为“人物、事件、物体和关系的组合造成一种实际的或潜在的事变状态，而这一状态可以被全部或部分消除，如果言语在运用到这一情景中以后可以制约人的决定或行为以使这一状态发生重大变化的话。”[9] 美国当代著名修辞学者肯尼斯·博克(Kenneth Burke)把修辞环境“上升到哲学的高度”，归纳出普遍的“人的环境”，他认为“修辞环境永恒地存在着”，“人一旦运用语言，就不可避免地进入修辞环境”。[10] 随着认知语言学和语用学的兴起、发展，语境的内涵得到了进一步的拓展。1986年，斯波伯和威尔逊提出了认知语境（Mutual Cognitive Environment）的概念，交际双方共享的具体时空知识、上下文知识、各种知识图式被视作语言交际的基础。动态语境概念的提出把传统的对语境静态的历时研究引向了动态共时的分析。

在我国春秋战国时期，作为儒家学派经典著作之一的《论语》就有关于要根据交际的社会背景、时机、交际对象等环境因素调整言语活动，以取得预期交际效果的论说。如“邦有道，危言危行；邦无道，危行言孙。（《论语·宪问·四》）”。后世的《韩非子》、《荀子》、《墨子》、《春秋繁露》、《论衡》、《文赋》、《文心雕龙》等著作中，虽没有明确提出“语境”这一概念，但都有从不同的角度对影响言语活动的环境因素的论说。

1932年，陈望道在《修辞学发凡》中提出“修辞以适应题旨情境为第一要义”的观点，并认为“情景上的分题”包括何故、何事、何人、何地、何时、何如等“六何”。1963年，张弓教授在《现代汉语修辞学》中提出语境包括社会环境、自然环境及上下文，并认为“结合现实语境”是“修辞的原则”。1982年，王德春提出“语境学是修辞学的基础”。他把“语境”定义为“时间、地点、场合、对象等客观因素和使用语言的人的身份、思想、性格、职业、修养、处境、心情等主观因素所构成的使用语言的环境”。[11] 张志公认为“语言环境，从比较小的范围来说，对语义影响最直接的，是现实的语言环境，也就是说话和听话时的场合以及话的前言后语。此外，大至一个时代、社会的性质和特点，小至交际双方的情况，如文化教养、知识水平、生活经验、语言风格和方言基础等，也是一种语言环境”。[12] 王希杰强调语境是修辞的生命。在《修辞学通论》中他把语境分为语言内的语境即上下文语境和非语言语境，包括物理世界语境、文化世界语境和心理世界语境等不同层次的类别，还提出零度语境、语境偏离、语境差等概念。陈汝东教授认为语境因素可以划分为三个层次：话语层次、修辞主体层次、社会文化层次。这三个层次的

9 劳埃德·比彻尔：《修辞情景》，《当代西方修辞学：演讲与话语批评》，常昌富、顾宝桐译，中国社会科学出版社，1998年12月，第124页。

10 常昌富：《20世纪修辞学概述》，中国社会科学出版社，1998年12月，第16页。

11 王德春、陈晨：《语境学》，《语境研究论文集》（西槙光正编），北京语言大学出版社，1992年，第132页。

12 张志公：《现代汉语》，人民教育出版社，1982年，第214页。

因素在人们的修辞交际行为中起着不同的作用。[13] 他在《当代汉语修辞学》中进行了详细的探讨。张宗正在《理论修辞学：宏观视野下的大修辞学》的第三章专门论述了修辞语境的性质和系统。

总之，语境是中西方修辞学的重要研究对象，语境的构成、性质、功能、分类是共同的研究内容。虽然目前还没有确切统一的语境理论，但是不可否认的是语境是在语言使用过程中生成的，语境与修辞有着天然的密切关系。“语境是由某种动态过程创造出来的——是由受话人和释话人之间、与‘客观外在’的现实相联系的互动过程创造出来的。”[14]“切实的自然的修辞多半是对应情境的，或者对应写说者和读听者的自然环境、社会环境。”[15]

我们认为，修辞语境是新闻传播效果研究的宏观关照，这是因为新闻话语的建构、传播、解构大都是依据实际发生的具体事件情景和宏观的社会政治、经济、文化、心理、历史、技术背景进行的。因此，所谓新闻语境，是指在新闻话语建构、传播、解构过程中动态存在的社会环境、自然环境和具体的新闻情景。其对新闻话语的建构、传播、解构起到制约、影响、解释、控制、协调、补充的作用。根据新闻语境的层级构成和形成规律，我们可以把新闻语境分为话语语境、情景语境和自然、社会语境。话语语境包括语体语境和上下文语境；情景语境就是新闻事实实际发生的环境，具体包括事件语境、人物语境、时间语境、地点语境等；自然、社会语境包括主观语境、客观语境，主观语境包括人文背景、社会角色、社会关系、个性心理等，客观语境包括自然环境、社会文化、社会政治、社会心理等。每类新闻语境还可以再向下细分，例如事件语境还可以细分为事件性质、事件场所、事件进程等；人物语境可以向下细分传者语境、受者语境、受访者语境等。（见表1）

表1 新闻语境的分类

自然、社会语境		情景语境	话语语境	
主观语境	客观语境	事件语境	语体语境	上下文语境
人文背景	自然环境	人物语境	报纸语体	句子
社会角色	社会文化	时间语境	广播语体	句群
社会关系	社会政治	地点语境	电视语体	段落
个性心理	社会心理		网络语体	篇章
	民族心理		手机语体	
	种族心理			
	宗教心理			

在这三类新闻语境中，话语语境是“小语境”，它的形成和变化受“情景

13 陈汝东：《当代汉语修辞学》，北京大学出版社，2004年，第334页。

14 耶夫维索尔伦，钱冠连、霍永寿译：《语用学诠释》，清华大学出版社，2003年，第127页。

15 陈望道：《修辞学发凡》，复旦大学出版社，2008年，第8页。

语境”和“自然、社会语境”的影响和制约；“情景语境”是基础，属于“中语境”，作为新闻事件实际发生的环境，它直接影响了“话语语境”的生成，同时，情景语境的相关因素又可以在自然、社会语境中得到解释；自然、社会语境是“大语境”，它直接或间接、显性或隐性地影响着“情景语境”和“话语语境”。

新闻语境，尤其是宏观的社会语境影响和制约着新闻选择、新闻价值的大小、新闻的时效和时机、新闻的传播效果和影响。客观发生的事实能否成为新闻，有很多的选择标准，但这都受到当时社会语境的制约和影响。社会语境不仅决定着新闻的选择，在一定意义上影响着所选择的事实的新闻价值的大小。很小的事件，只要它吻合了时代或社会的语境，就可能成为大新闻，发挥大影响。在奉行节约的大环境下，“一厘钱精神”就会得到提倡，相关的单位和个人就会被树立为社会典型。因此，新闻语境是新闻事实选择的重要依据，它常常成为衡量新闻工作者业务水平的重要标准和尺度。[16]

四、修辞话语分析：传播效果研究的重要方法

修辞的研究范围随着人类认知和社会的发展不断地深化。以20世纪中国的修辞学研究为例，“修辞观”经历了从传统的“修饰观”“技巧观”“努力观”“美辞观”逐步发展到“过程观”“组合观”“言语交际行为观”“认知行为观”的过程。[17]

修辞学除研究语言体系中的修辞手段外，还研究言语规律，其研究对象已从词句修辞跨入话语修辞，从话语层次研究修辞效果，从而形成话语修辞学。从话语修辞学的角度来看，不分析整个话语而孤立地讲究修辞是不可想象的。超句结构的交际作用和修辞价值是一般修辞手段和方法所不能代替的，话语信息量远不是词句相加的意义，话语风格的研究必须依赖于对整个话语的分析。所以，话语修辞学成为现代修辞学的重要领域，引起语言学界的广泛重视。[18]

话语修辞分析的依据是古典修辞学的五大要素：构思、组织、风格、记忆和实际演说。当代西方修辞学主要有四种比较有影响力的修辞批评模式与方法（实际就是话语修辞分析模式），分别是新亚里士多德主义修辞批评模式、戏剧主义修辞批评模式、社会学修辞批评模式、后现代主义修辞批评模式。

在当代，话语修辞研究也得到了我国修辞学界的关注。王德春在《现代修辞学》中专设一章论述了话语修辞学的研究内容，包括句子功能分析、话语衔接手段、句际关系类型、对话和语篇分析。陈汝东教授在其专著《当代汉语修辞学》中对话语建构、话语理解进行了专门论述，揭示了话语建构、话语理解的规则、内容和价值。李军在《话语修辞理论与实践》中把修辞研究拓展到了整个言语交际领域，重新阐释了话语修辞的本质。“话语修辞的实质应该是言语交际中的话语效果调控行为，即发话人有效调控言语交际过程和交际的各种参与因素，运用最具针对

16 惠东坡：《我国重大突发事件新闻话语修辞研究》，人民日报出版社，2013年。
17 陈汝东：《当代汉语修辞学》，北京大学出版社，2004年8月，第511-512页。
18 王德春、陈晨：《现代修辞学》，上海外语教育出版社，2001年9月，第389-390页。

性的话语策略，最大限度地促使发话人所期望的话语效果的成功实现。修辞学是一门具有鲜明目的趋向性的话语效果调控科学。”[19]

从历史上说，话语分析可以追溯到古典修辞学。[20] 古希腊伟大的修辞学家亚里士多德已经详细论述了话语的各种结构和在公共话语中的说服功能。20世纪中叶以后，随着语言学研究由语言研究转向言语研究，同时发轫于语言学、文学理论、符号学、社会学等学科的现代话语分析在60至70年代得到了迅速发展。与此同时，修辞的本质、属性被重新审视，修辞被界定为运用话语和象征来达到某种效果的传播行为，研究对象几乎涵盖了我们社会生活的一切传播行为。修辞开始在各个领域、各种话语系统的话语分析中扮演重要角色。它的定义已经从传统的遣词造句、美化语言、说服策略、结构调控等演变成建构话语、生产知识、象征力量等更宏观、更广义的一种理论和方法。

在这个意义上，我们认为修辞是知识、信息、思想、意识的生产、组织、传播、接受、认知所遵循的那个原理、原则或者说是规律。[21] 话语就是人类知识、信息、思想、意识的外在表现形式，或者说话语是知识、信息、思想、意识进入交际和传播的言语形式。根据杨信彰的归纳和分析，话语分析的方法有五种：结构分析法、社会文化分析法、认知分析法、批评话语分析法、综合分析法。如前论述，这五种话语分析方法都隐含着修辞学的思想和理念。修辞概念内涵和外延的演变反映了人们对话语的建构、传播、解读规律和特点的认识和把握。因此，从历史渊源、关注内容等方面来看，话语分析实质上是一种修辞分析。

综上所述，我们认为，话语修辞分析就是对话语生产、传播、认知、接受、效果等机制的考察和分析。话语修辞分析就是对话语内容，话语的言说方式、原则，话语效果，话语交流、传播的制约因素等所进行的研究。话语修辞分析不仅考察话语与社会、话语与思维的关系，还关注话语的构成，更重视研究话语如何被建构，如何被赋予价值、意义和意识形态并在特定的社会语境中承担了功能。[22]

从话语的角度来理解新闻传播，可以更好地把握新闻传播的本质。新闻话语是随着大众传播事业的飞速发展，在实践中长期运用而逐渐形成的最有影响力的一种公共话语类型。在阶级社会中，它经过了个体、团体、集体的过滤，必然也就具有倾向性、党性、阶级性。新闻话语修辞现象和规律是客观存在且时刻被运用却未被系统研究的领域。

五、修辞批评：传播效果研究的另一种视野

修辞意识在人文科学领域的迅速蔓延使得西方思想界将这一变化看成是继“语

19 李军：《话语修辞理论与实践》，上海外语教育出版社，2008年1月，第60-61页。

20 梵·迪克，曾庆香译：《作为话语的新闻》，华夏出版社，2003年，第18页。

21 惠东坡：《我国重大突发事件新闻话语修辞研究》，人民日报出版社，2013年。

22 惠东坡：《我国重大突发事件新闻话语修辞研究》，人民日报出版社，2013年。

言转折”“解读转折”之后出现的又一重大智力思潮，并被称为“修辞转折”。伴随着这一转折，修辞学本身也转向了“批判性”。

1925年，维切恩斯（Herbert A.Wichelns）发表《演讲的文学批评》，从此，修辞批评在当代西方修辞学界产生了广泛的社会影响。维切恩斯的“修辞批评”是指批评家根据作者的意图及所处情景对拥有特定听众的作品所进行的效果分析。可见，修辞批评是一种效果研究。后来，修辞批评远远超过了传统的修辞学范围，可以运用到包括新闻传播活动在内的任何人类的行为、过程、产品和人工制品上。

美国修辞批评的历史大致分为传统范式阶段和多元范式阶段。传统范式阶段的修辞批评主要是新亚里士多德模式。多元范式阶段的修辞批评包括众多模式，如心理批评模式、戏剧主义批评模式、幻想主题批评模式、社会运动批评模式、体裁批评模式、女权主义批评模式、意识形态批评模式等。

批判性修辞更加注重修辞的过程，力图通过演绎的方式批判性地还原和解析修辞过程，以帮助修辞学成为“向其他学科提供用以解读和分析修辞现象的权威理论资源”，“也唯有具备批判性，修辞学才可能破解社会文本，揭示文本的社会特征、文本所蕴涵的社会认知和文本自身各种复杂社会权力关系对说服性话语的操控等”。[23] 如前所述，修辞天然具有传播的属性。因此，我们认为修辞批评是传播效果研究的另一种深层拓展，它揭示了制约和影响传播活动的更复杂、更深层、更隐蔽的多种因素。

参考文献：

[1] 陈力丹. 解析中国新闻传播学[M]. 北京：人民日报出版社，2010.

[2] 李军. 话语修辞理论与实践[M]. 上海: 上海外语教育出版社，2008.

[3] 刘亚猛. 追求象征的力量：关于西方修辞思想的思考[M]. 上海：三联书店，2004.

[4] 刘亚猛. 西方修辞学史[M]. 北京：外语教学与研究出版社，2008.

[5] 娄开阳. 现代汉语新闻语篇的结构研究[M]. 北京：世界图书出版公司，2008.

[6] 谢立中. 走向多元话语分析：后现代思潮的社会学意涵[M]. 北京：人民大学出版社，2009.

[7] 梵·迪克. 作为话语的新闻[M]. 曾庆香译. 北京：华夏出版社，2003.

[8] 费尔克拉夫. 话语与社会变迁[M]. 殷晓蓉译. 北京：华夏出版社，2003.

[9] 詹姆斯·费伦. 作为修辞的叙事：技巧、读者、伦理、意识形态[M]. 陈永国译. 北京：北京大学出版社，2002.

[10] 洛厄里·德弗勒. 大众传播效果研究的里程碑（第三版）[M]. 刘海龙等译. 北京：人民大学出版社，2009.

23 曲卫国：人文学科的修辞转向和修辞学的批判性转向，《浙江大学学报》(人文社会科学版)，2008 年第1期，第113-122页。

[11] Biagi, Shirley. *Media Impact: An Introduction to Mass Media*[M]. Belmont, CA: Wadsworth Publishing Company, 1990.

[12] Bittner, J. R. *Mass Communication, An Introduction* (4th Edition)[M]. Englewood Cliffs, NJ: Prentice-Hall, 1986.

[13] Hansen, Anders, Simon Cottle, Ralph Negrine, Chris Newbold. *Mass Communication Research Methods*[M]. Basingstoke, Hampshire: Macmillan, 1998.

[14] McCroskey. *An Introduction to Rhetorical Communication*[M]. Englewood Cliffs, NJ: Prentice-Hall, 2005.

[15] McQuail, Denis. *Mass Communication Theory: An Introduction* (2nd Edition) [M]. London, Newbury Park: Sage Publications, 1987.

[16] Richardson, J. E. *Analysing Newspapers: An Approach from Critical Discourse Analysis*[M], Princeton, NJ: Macmillan, 2007.

[17] Tan A. S. *Mass Communication Theories and Research* (2nd Edition)[M]. New York: Wiley, 1985.

Rhetoric Communication: An Important Topic of Communication Effects Research

Hui Dongpo
(Beijing Union University, China)

Abstract: As a core topic in communication studies, communication effects research has close historical ties with rhetoric in research ideas, research awareness, research contents and methods. Throughout the history of communication effects research and the evolution of rhetoric communication, we can see the logic connection between the two. (1) Rhetorical awareness: a dark line of communication effects research; (2) Rhetorical skills: micro-inspection of communication effects research; (3) Rhetorical situation: macro-study of communication effects research; (4) Rhetorical discourse analysis: an important method of communication effects research; (5) Rhetorical criticism. another view of communication effects research; Therefore, as pro-active communication activities to seek the desired effect, the rhetorical communication should be a clear and important research topic of communication effects studies.

Keywords: rhetoric; rhetorical communication; communication effects studies

电视谈话节目话语控制的修辞策略

杜敏　李晓寒

（[中国] 陕西师范大学）

摘　要：话语控制的修辞策略在电视谈话节目中有充分表现，体现了交际双方为实现电视传播的目的在语言上采取了有效的修辞手段。在控制话轮时，谈话节目主持人因其机构性地位，出于对时间、会话进程及方向、会话目标的考虑，会采用控制力较强、礼貌性较低的打断方式来取得话轮。但另一方面，出于对嘉宾的尊重及对嘉宾信息提供者身份的认同，主持人会较少地采用插入方式，给予嘉宾充分的话语权。在放弃话轮时，主持人更多地采用了指定下一说话人的方式，而嘉宾采用让听话人自我选择以放弃话轮的比率极低，体现了嘉宾对节目的高度参与与配合。另外，嘉宾较少采用让听话人自我选择的方式，也体现出其在对会话方向的控制方面处于弱势地位。在持有话轮时，主持人因其引导者身份，会主动将提供信息的任务交由嘉宾，而嘉宾能充分认识到自己信息提供者的身份，较多地持有话轮。

关键词：谈话节目；话语控制；话轮；修辞策略

中国电视谈话节目始于20世纪90年代的《东方直播室》，经过近20年的发展，不仅节目数量多，类型也日趋丰富多彩。从选题内容看，既有涉及经济、文化、政治、社会等公共性话题的栏目，如《实话实说》、《大家》；也有以个人生活、经历、情感为话题的个人性栏目，如《鲁豫有约》、《杨澜访谈录》。从节目风格看，既有就大众话题进行讨论的纪实类节目，如《面对面》，又有以放松身心为目的的娱乐类节目，如《艺术人生》。电视谈话节目之所以在中国快速发展，取决于它的低成本制作，又与它可视性强、讲究修辞策略具有重要关系。本文从话语分析的角度，以10期《杨澜访谈录》为语料，探究电视谈话节目话语控制的基本策略。

一、电视谈话节目话语控制的修辞性

修辞实际上就是一种言语行为，是修辞者在特定的语境中，针对不同的交际对象，为了特定的交际需求，对语言所做的一种加工、选择和控制，是一种复杂而高级的语言行为。这其中有多种要素参与、多个环节起作用，具有鲜明的目的性和系统性，使用多种不同的修辞手段和策略。电视谈话节目正是借助大众传媒呈现的、具有鲜明言语修辞特征的一档“脱口秀”，其话语的修辞性体现在这样几个方面：

首先，借助双方或多方的言语交际来修辞。电视谈话节目是指由主持人引导，相关嘉宾（有时有群众）参与，在演播室或特定环境中，在一种轻松愉悦的氛围里，就公众普遍关心的问题即兴发表意见，表达心声，实现信息共享、观点共识、情感共鸣的一类电视节目。依据话语交际参与方的多少，谈话节目分为双方交流、三方交流和多方交流。双方交流是主持人与嘉宾的交流，录制现场的观众只是“看客”，在很少的情况下才得以参与到会话中，如《杨澜访谈录》之中，杨澜说：

“尊敬的王后殿下，非常感谢您百忙之中接受我们的采访。这是您第二次访问中国了，您刚刚同北京大学的年轻人进行了一场非常有趣的对话……”

在此例中，杨澜采访了约旦王后拉尼娅·阿卜杜拉。在会话一开始，她首先问候了嘉宾，随即与其展开话题，观众较少进入节目的谈话之中。有的节目，根本没有观众在场，如《今日说法》；三方参与指的是主持人、嘉宾、观众共同交流，如《对话》等，观众很好地参与到谈话中，是谈话的重要组成部分。

其次，控制话语以实现吸引大众的修辞目的。受大众传播特质的要求，吸引观众、提升收视率，是贯穿谈话节目始终的根本目的。围绕这一终极目的，谈话节目既要营造某种修辞语境，又要给出谈话内容的线索，还要不断引导嘉宾在规定的节目时段说出能吸引观众的话题内容，最终与观众进行某种形态的交流，使之成为会话节目现场的交际对象或者节目播出时的间接交际对象，最终实现其传播目的。这使得谈话节目的话语控制性特别鲜明。无论是在话题的背景介绍、话题的开始部分，还是在谈话的展开部分，以及节目的结束部分，其控制性体现在话语节目整体结构的方方面面。如在《杨澜访谈录》节目的不同阶段，均可能设置各种背景内容，一方面为观众预告每期节目的内容，介绍嘉宾的经历与有关资料，为话语交际营造某种语境；同时，这种背景材料，又可作为节目的话题，成为展开话题的引子，起到承接上一轮谈话，开启下一轮谈话的目的。例如：

“他出身草根，尝尽冷暖，数十年埋头奋斗成就一代天王巨星，而今人到中年，魅力不减却烦恼不断，事业、婚姻、未来，46岁的男人有了哪些新感悟，《杨澜访谈录》带您走近刘德华。”（背景介绍）

此段背景介绍在旁白讲述时，伴有刘德华荧屏前后的画面，而背景介绍为观众点明了此次访谈节目的主题内容是刘德华不惑之年对生活的感悟和困惑，嘉宾与观众需要按照设定好的主题来配合访谈节目，访谈节目的背景介绍起到了方便观众理解和控制访谈内容的双重作用。

又如在会话的主体部分，主持人围绕话语修辞的目的有意识地提问，嘉宾对此提问进行回答，在谈话的过程中，主持人通过各种手段与方式引导及掌控话语，使话题既展现嘉宾的独特魅力、丰富的经历、有趣的个性等，又力求被广大的观众所喜爱和接受，同时，昭示主持人机构性媒介人的地位与权力。如：

杨澜：大家非常好奇对于发生在您这样一位魅力十足的王后身上的神话，在您遇到您的丈夫前，您那时的生活是什么样的？职业规划和生活规划呢？

拉尼娅：谢谢你的赞美。我从小是个普通的女孩，我父亲是个儿科医生……

杨澜：您还记得你们第一次见面时，在晚宴上都聊了些什么吗？

拉尼娅：我们第一次见面是在大家共同的一个朋友家，我们当时的确都对对方有意……

杨澜：那时您的丈夫还不是王储，所以结婚时您也没有期望做王后，谁告诉您您成了王后？

拉尼娅：你说得对，我们结婚时我的丈夫还不是王储，所以我们结婚时我的头衔是王妃……

此例中，杨澜根据节目修辞的需要对拉尼娅王后进行提问，拉尼娅王后根据问题来回答，话题与拉尼娅的生活息息相关，满足了大众对王后生活的好奇心，吸引了大众的眼球，同时显示出主持人对于话语权的掌控与把握。

第三，以丰富的策略性作为修辞的手段。言语修辞行为是一种系统性行为，关系到多方交际者、交际语境、交际的话题内容、交际的手段、交际的效果等多个环节。而大众传媒上的谈话节目，尤其要考虑言语修辞的策略和手段，因为这种修辞，一方面考虑节目在时长上的限制，一方面要保障谈话的顺畅进行，另外要考虑节目播出后的广泛可视性。

修辞策略是话语人为实现某种交际目的而采用的交际修辞的方式、手段与途径。修辞策略的优劣直接影响着交际活动的过程及效果，因为谈话节目的修辞，是不断反馈的双方修辞过程。在《杨澜访谈录》中，杨澜就根据节目话题内容、嘉宾的谈话状态，采用多种修辞策略，不仅掌控访谈的进程，而且对话题的深入程度把握得恰到好处、收放自如。面对嘉宾愿意畅谈的话题，她乐于倾听却又控制得当，面对嘉宾刻意回避或羞于谈论的敏感话题，她循循善诱，机智、巧妙地打开话题，却又深浅适中，不事苛求。她以其“绵里藏针”的独特主持风格，既对嘉宾的经历、观点给予了足够的理解与尊重，又坚守自我，与嘉宾的观点碰出了思想的火花，同时恰到好处地满足了观众的猎奇心理。许多观众在《杨澜访谈录》中得以了解嘉宾真实的一面。下面着重分析电视谈话节目修辞中的话语控制策略。

二、电视谈话节目话语控制的修辞策略

电视谈话节目控制话语的修辞策略集中地体现于访谈节目用时最长、展开话题、实现目标的主体部分。主持人凭借节目赋予自己的机构性身份，在与嘉宾对话轮的合作与竞争战中，采取各种策略赢得了绝对的话语权，主导了整个谈话节目。这体现在争取话轮、放弃话轮、持有话轮等几个方面。

（一）争取话轮

争取话轮就是在会话进行过程中，听话者进行的自我选择。在会话的展开阶段，听话者出于某种目的，往往会有发言的需要，此时他会争夺话语权，争取话轮。其方法可分为两种，即插入和打断。

1. 插入。发生在话轮转换关联位置处，现在的说话者并未选择下一个说话者，而听话者主动自选获得话轮。听话者往往可以预测出说话者话语语义语法的结尾处，即转化关联位置，在转换关联位置处趁机插入句子以取得话语权。插入的动机可能是评价说话人的观点，或是表达自身的看法。“插入”方式遵循了话轮分配的“一次只有一个人能说话”的机制，在获得话语权的同时，充分考虑到了礼貌原则。如：

黄奇帆：农民工的问题其实本质上不是一个户口转换的一个问题，中国的户口制度体现了国家对老百姓的各种利益，比如我们一个城市户口，就绑架着城市居民的养老保险、医疗保险、住房制度、小孩读书的制度，以及就业的制度。

杨澜：还有医疗……

此例，重庆市长在谈中国户籍制度，杨澜在其话轮转化的关联位置，即一个语义语法单位完成后运用了插入的方法，发表了自己的意见，补充了黄奇帆的信息，帮助其完成了话轮。再如：

杨澜：《弟子规》里所讲述的人生的一些基本规范、规矩和教养是很多父母都没有做到的，所以你光给孩子教，让孩子去背去实践，但是他看到的父母，可能是粗俗的、无理的，这里面说怎么样，不要谄富，不要骄贫，他的父亲就是谄富和骄贫的，所以这个时候，实际上是教育大人的问题，而不是教育孩子的问题。

钱文忠：所以，我不赞成把《弟子规》叫作儿童读物，我认为它是启蒙读物。

在这里，嘉宾使用了插入手段来争夺话轮。当杨澜谈到家长在规矩教养方面匮乏，不能为孩子做好榜样时，钱文忠在杨澜话轮中转换关联位置处插入了话轮，因为教育问题是钱文忠感兴趣的话题，《弟子规》是他研究领域内的问题，所以钱文忠在谈话中具有强烈地表达自己看法和观点的意愿。钱文忠通过插入争取话轮的行为也显示出了他参与节目的积极态度。

通过分析《杨澜访谈录》10期节目，主持人与嘉宾在争取话轮时，各自采取的插入手段的次数统计如表1所示：

表1 主持人与嘉宾争取话轮策略统计表

控制方式	插入		打断	
主 持 人	536	39.41%	95	87.96%
嘉宾	824	60.59%	13	12.04%

主持人在争取话轮时，采取插入手段536次，而嘉宾在争取话轮时，采取插入手段824次，主持人采取插入手段的次数占插入手段总次数的39.41%，而嘉宾采取插入手段的次数占总次数的60.59%。很明显，嘉宾在争取话轮时，采用的插入手段较主持人更多。究其原因，从嘉宾方面来看，嘉宾采取更多的插入手段，是其积极参与会话

的需要。电视谈话节目的目的是从嘉宾身上获取更多的信息，作为信息来源，嘉宾需要通过插入这种手段来拓宽发散信息的渠道。从主持人方面来看，主持人较少使用插入手段，显示其对嘉宾的尊重及友好的态度；另外，主持人也期待嘉宾使用更多的插入手段，以提供更多的话题点，为其开拓更多的话题提供足够的资源。所以，嘉宾更多地采用插入手段，并不代表着主持人失去了对节目的主导和控制权。

2. 打断。发生在话轮构建成分内部，现在的说话者并未选择下一个说话者，而听话者在说话者语义与语法单位表达未完整时就介入的行为，这种争取话轮的方式就是“打断”。“打断”是对话轮转换机制的有意违反，更是一种否认当前说话者话语权的行为，违反了礼貌原则。主持人借助“打断”这种方式以控制话题的发展、表达自己的意见，或者出于时间的考虑，或在嘉宾表达不清时，帮助观众理解，还可能是在嘉宾语塞时，帮助嘉宾进行表达。如：

冯小刚：这个电影放完了，可能很多人只要到机场……
杨澜：到机场就说：“葛成生 please。”
冯小刚：葛成生 please，他就会了。可是你拿到那么一个《夜宴》的电影……
杨澜：我怎么觉得你一下就好像进入一个特别难受的状态里面……
冯小刚：就是说你的脑子是“卡拉就给关上了”。

在此处，面对侃侃而谈的嘉宾冯小刚，杨澜使用了打断的策略来控制话题的方向。冯小刚是一位性格较为开朗、非常健谈的嘉宾，在谈论机场发生的趣事带给他的灵感时，谈兴颇浓，对此话题费时过多，这时就需要主持人有意识地对其进行必要的控制，打断其正在进行的话语，为其他话题的进行赢得时间。再如：

钱文忠：他（季羡林）说我最近这两天，他那时候正在开人大会，耽误了几天，所以你可能收信会晚几天，非常抱歉。……这个把我给惊呆了，这我一辈子都不会忘了，这就是一位大学者，所以这种对我是……
杨澜：你更加敬仰他了，就是说必须要去学巴利文。

钱文忠在表达他对季羡林的敬仰之情时，不知如何形容自己的心情，产生语塞，杨澜通过打断的方式帮助其表达，使得会话顺利进行。

表1显示，主持人在争取话轮时，采取打断手段95次，而嘉宾在争取话轮时，采取打断手段13次，主持人采取打断手段的次数占采取打断手段总次数的87.96%，而嘉宾采取打断手段的次数占总次数的12.04%。这样明显的差距，表明在电视谈话节目这样的半机构性谈话中，主持人享有机构性权力，他们可以利用打断这种方式争取话轮，从而控制话语按照预期规定的时间和话题进行。

从以上数据可以看出，主持人争取话轮时，较多地采用了插入手段，而很少打断嘉宾的谈话。因此，插入在主持人争取话轮策略使用中占明显优势。这是因为插入是争取话轮最礼貌的策略，主持人在使用插入来争取话轮时，运用的机构性权力最小，最为礼貌，对维护主持人与嘉宾的友好关系最为有益。另外，我们也看到了主持人争取话轮方面的修辞策略，一方面，主持人考虑到电视谈话节目的流畅进行，以及与嘉宾的友好互动关系，不会轻易打断嘉宾的话语。另一方面，当嘉宾持有话轮时，是主持人决定嘉宾在哪里停止，决定了话题的展开程度，控制了会话的进行。

（二）放弃话轮

放弃话轮指的是当前说话者出于某种原因，不想或不能继续说话，而将话语权移交给听话者的言语修辞行为。根据当前说话人是否主动从听话人中选择下一说话人，放弃话轮可以分为两种：第一，当前说话人指明下一说话人。第二，当前说话人未指定下一说话人，听话人自我选择成为下一说话人。

1. 当前说话人选择下一说话人。当前说话人选择下一说话人最直接、最常见的方式就是点名，通过直呼其名、提请注意的方式让指定听话人做好接过话轮的准备，使得话轮正常自然地转接下去。很多情况下，指定听话人的名字可能依语境而省略。如：

杨澜：但是，最近其实两位也有一个很好的合作……那王菲你觉得这首歌吸引你的地方是什么？其实要你接一首歌是很难的，对不对？并不是只是因为亚鹏在里面出演，你就接了这首歌吧？

王菲：有好几个因素吧……

在此例中，嘉宾王菲是一个寡言少语的人，很少会主动争取话轮，所以杨澜需要指定其回答问题，通过点名的方式施压，让其参与到会话中，以此移交话语权。杨澜通过指定下一说话人的方式很好地控制了话轮的转换，让被动的嘉宾获得了合理的说话时间，让每一位嘉宾都有机会说话，突出了电视谈话节目互动交流的特点。

杨澜：先说说为什么，我是觉得有点紧张，然后我一看王菲的微博，说她好紧张啊，好紧张啊，你先说说为什么你紧张啊？

王菲：我紧张，因为我本身就不是做很多采访的……

在此例中杨澜从两位嘉宾中选择了王菲作为下一说话人。杨澜通过提问的形式抛出了话语权，而移交对象则是王菲，杨澜并未直接指出王菲的名字，而是通过“你”替代了王菲的名字。

嘉宾同样也可以通过指明下一说话人的方式来转让话轮。如：

贾达·萍克·史密斯：在家里，我们明白我们是一个团体，我们同心协力去做事情，所以贾登的成功也是维罗的成功。我们分享成功。

维罗·史密斯：但是我不理解，我不理解他的成功也是我的成功。我只想是我自己。

贾达·萍克·史密斯：你现在明白了？

维罗·史密斯：是的。

此例中，贾达·萍克·史密斯在谈及个人成功属于集体成功时，女儿维罗·史密斯提出了异议，贾达·萍克·史密斯在获得话轮的同时，通过提问“你现在明白了”将话轮让给女儿维罗·史密斯，实现了嘉宾间的相互交流。再如：

杨澜：那么，凯蒂，在丈夫遇到困难的那些时刻，对他微笑是一件难事吗？
凯蒂：其实一点也不难。事实上，当我被4.4环震惊以后，我倒是笑了出来。

杨澜在采访埃蒙斯夫妇时，埃蒙斯是访谈节目的主角，而凯蒂则扮演的是他身后女人的角色。在问及埃蒙斯赛场失手的情形之后，为了让作为配角的凯蒂也有机会说话，杨澜采用了点名的方式将话轮移交给凯蒂，并以此切入了本次访谈节目的核心部分：夫妻间的相互理解、支持、宽容、不离不弃才是成功的前提。

主持人与嘉宾在放弃话轮时，各自指定下一说话人的次数统计如表2：

表2 主持人与嘉宾放弃话轮次数统计表

	主持人	嘉宾	合计
指定下一说话人	165	8	173
让听话人自我选择	63	5	68
合计	228	13	241

主持人在放弃话轮时，指定下一说话人的次数为165次，而嘉宾指定下一说话人的次数为8次。主持人指定下一说话人的次数占指定下一说话人总次数的95.38%，而嘉宾指定下一说话人的次数占指定下一说话人总次数的4.62%，主持人指定下一说话人的比例远远高于嘉宾指定下一说话人的比例，这样的差异显示了主持人对会话享有更多的控制权。而这种控制权一部分是由指定下一说话人这种方式实现的。指定下一说话人是一种强有力的、机构性的放弃话轮的方式。主持人处于机构性权力阶层的顶端，通过指定下一说话人，可以合理地分配话语权，使得嘉宾充分参与到会话当中，实现主持人引导、嘉宾讲述的合理局面，从而控制会话方向，避免个人过长时间持有话轮。而嘉宾很少使用指定下一说话人的方式来放弃话轮，是由于其处于权力阶层的底端，很少有机会控制话轮的走向。

2. 当前说话人已表达自己的观点并准备放弃话轮时，除指定下一说话人之外，也会采取另一种方式放弃话轮，就是让嘉宾通过自我选择的方式来接过话轮。就电视谈话节目而言，主持人一般会以提出问题的形式来放弃话轮，问题不设特定对象，这时在嘉宾中，自我选择将会发生，首先自我选择的人有权成为下一说话人。

主持人采用的自我选择方式如：

杨澜：所以说雅典是你的第一届奥运会？
埃蒙斯：是的。
杨澜：你也是吗，凯蒂？
凯蒂：是的，那也是我的第一届奥运会。
杨澜：在那之前你们互相认识吗？
凯蒂：在雅典之前，我们只是像其他人一样在赛场上见过……

在此例中，杨澜采用了自我选择方式来放弃话轮。杨澜通过对在座的两位嘉宾提出问题的方式，让嘉宾通过自我选择接过话轮，凯蒂在杨澜采用自我选择策略后，首先接过了话轮，获得了话语权。

嘉宾采用自我选择方式放弃话轮的次数很少。如下：

杨澜：是否有时候你们会对某些事情或某种行为比较苛刻？

贾达·萍克·史密斯（妻子）：当然了。

威尔·史密斯：我们是否偶尔对你们有一些苛刻？

贾登·史密斯（儿子）：哎，岂止一点点。

此期，杨澜对好莱坞巨星威尔·史密斯一家进行了采访。在谈及史密斯夫妇对孩子的行为及思想是否会不理解时，威尔·史密斯的妻子首先接过了话轮，后来威尔·史密斯随即接过了话轮，但接过话轮的同时，又放弃了话轮，威尔·史密斯未指名下一说话人，儿子贾登·史密斯和女儿维罗·史密斯均有机会获得话语权，此时，贾登·史密斯首先接过了话轮。换句话说，威尔·史密斯采用让听话人自我选择以获得话轮的方式放弃话轮，贾登·史密斯通过自我选择获得了话轮。

根据表2显示，主持人在放弃话轮时，让嘉宾通过自我选择获取话轮的次数为63次，而嘉宾放弃话轮时，让听话人自我选择获取话轮的次数为5次。主持人让听话人自我选择的次数占自我选择总次数的92.65%，嘉宾让听话人自我选择的次数占自我选择总次数的7.35%。可以看出，采用让听话人自我选择以放弃话轮这种形式的主要是主持人，嘉宾很少以此方式来放弃话轮。一方面，当主持人想从嘉宾那里获得大量信息时，他会通过让嘉宾自我选择的方式放弃话轮；另一方面，嘉宾采用让听话人自我选择放弃话轮的比率极低，这表明了嘉宾对节目的高度参与和配合，为主持人与观众提供大量的信息，而不是选择时机放弃话轮。

综上所述，放弃话轮策略的结合使用，既保证了主持人实施机构性权力，对电视谈话节目进行严格把握，又实现了嘉宾与主持人轻松的互动氛围，使得会话顺利进行。

（三）持有话轮

持有话轮指的是说话人在讲话过程中，为完成自己的讲话内容，而避免听话人介入话轮。换句话说，就是说话人尽量避免在话轮未完成时出现放弃话轮的特征。如果放弃话轮的特征出现，那么会引起听话人对转化关联位置判断的失误，从而引发争取话轮的行为。持有话轮的方式可分为语言和非语言两种。此处，我们仅探讨持有话轮的语言策略。说话人可以通过发出这些言语特征来持有话轮。

1. 独白。根据Sacks的毗邻对理论得知，会话中前一说话人的话语会限制后一说话人的话语形式及内容。而独白则是指当前说话人无视前一说话人的谈话内容，而兀自谈论自己话语内容的行为。如：

杨澜：所以你妈妈过去有两个孩子了？

成龙：有两个女的，我爸爸有两个男的，现在我拍完这个纪录片，本来不是给人家看的，我是写我自己，我为什么姓房，我叫房仕龙，我爸爸是逃难要饭，不想给人家知道他姓房，所以改姓成了，所以一直改下来，就改到我今天这个样子，哦，原来我族谱，现在写的是叫房仕龙。

在此例中，杨澜向嘉宾成龙提出问题，询问成龙的妈妈过去是否有两个孩子。成龙仅需遵循合作原则回答“对，有两个女的”就足够了，但是成龙乐于向主持人和观众转达更多关于自己名字由来的信息，这些故事都与杨澜提出的问题并无直接关联，但他的独白使得人们对成龙的身世更加了解，达到了电视谈话节目交流信息与情感的目的。再如：

杨澜：你说过在和雅虎的并购案之后，这十亿美元一到账你就开始做梦。梦见自己爬梯子，然后抓到那个石头都抓不住，要掉下来，这是不是某种心理压力的一种暗示？

马云：我想是，其实最近半年这种梦特别多，就像以前我觉得，以前我做梦特别多是考数学，三天两头考数学。其实我上个月还做过考数学的梦。然后醒过来一看，还好还好，现在已经上班了……

杨澜：当然这十亿美元进来是给公司的，不是给你个人的……

当杨澜问及雅虎并购案期间，马云是不是常常做梦时，她的意图在于知晓马云在雅虎并购案期间有何种压力。但是马云却兀自展开了关于压力做梦的讲述，即独白已经偏离了此时的话题。因此，杨澜及时争取话轮，将话题又引回雅虎并购案上。

2. 限制话轮长度

限制话轮长度指的是使用像“我要说N点，第一……第二……”或者“首先……其次……”这样的言语形式，以此来构拟出一个相当大的语言单位，提醒听话人此话轮的长度，使其了解到转换关联位置后说话人仍有话未尽，以防听话人的介入。如：

杨澜：从实施到现在，从农民工的角度，他们的反响热烈吗？我听说有的区只有十几个人去申请，为什么会这样？

黄奇帆：……所以我们是三个平台在推进这工作，首先是千家万户相关联的户籍警平台、派出所平台；第二是所有农民工工作的、有联系的单位平台；第三个才是农民工的家庭平台……

在此例中，当重庆市市长黄奇帆面对杨澜对重庆户籍改革制度的质疑时，他指出了工作进展慢的三个要素“我们是三个平台在推进这工作”，明确地告诉杨澜自己要探讨三个问题，防止中间被打断，在完整地传达自己的阐释后，主持人方可介入话轮。

3. 前置语列

前置语列指的是在说话人的话轮中，一些位置靠前的句子是后面句子或句子序列的先驱，预示着其后有话要说，话轮仍未终结。如：

杨澜：当您把雅虎的员工请到杭州来联欢的时候，大概有七百多人从北京过来，说那天晚上你还跳舞了，领舞了。你跳的什么舞啊？
马云：这个是这样，因为我们公司有一个叫FUN文化，英文的F、U、N，所以每年我们都会有一些"春节联欢晚会"，搞得很疯狂……

此例中，当杨澜问及马云的领舞经验时，马云使用了前置语列"这个是这样"来展开叙述，前置语列提醒主持人说话人仍有话要说。再如：

杨澜：你有什么可郁闷的呢？
钱文忠：比如我想，第一，咱们对知识分子怎么看，我们凭什么认为知识分子就应该过非常清贫的生活，什么时候中国的读书人是社会上贫穷的人？物质上是贫乏的，什么时候？大概只有很短的一到二十年。为什么呢？五六十年代知识分子都是高收入阶层……一个人物质生活的状态和精神生活的状态没有必然的联系。

在此例中，面对杨澜提出的大众对知识分子穷酸形象有着刻板印象的问题，钱文忠提出了质疑，在钱文忠的话轮中，他使用了自问自答的设问句来持有话轮。尽管钱文忠在此连续提出了几个问题，但是其意图并不是寻求答案，因为只有身为知识分子的他最清楚问题的答案，自问自答在此仅仅是持有话轮的一种修辞手段而已。

4. 话语标记语

话语标记语指的是在说话人的话轮中，一个句子完成后，紧接着使用表示句子尚未完成的连接词，如"还有、然后、但是、而且、如果、因为、所以"等。话语标记语可以把一个潜在的完成句变成一个非完成句，使得当前说话人持有话轮。如：

杨澜：虽然你出名很早，但是做摇滚乐本身有给你带来很大的经济上的收益吗？
崔健：可以说很大，但是不是说就是像西方的那种摇滚乐很成功，很早成功的摇滚乐一个歌手应该得到的一些，跟他们比的话，我是觉得我太少了，但是我非常的就是不在意这件事，因为我觉得我始终在干自己喜欢干的事，而且我的收益也比其他的中国的做摇滚乐的人要高得多，所以我在这方面说，我已经很知足了。所以说，我想对我说的这个，我对商业的看法应该负点责任，我希望能做出一个致富的好的榜样……

在此例中，崔健通过多次使用"但是""所以""而且""因为"等话语标记语，表达了自己对金钱与理想关系的复杂态度，这种复杂的态度并非几句简单的话语就能表达的，所以崔健利用话语标记语来继续保持话轮，从而全面地传达出自己的复杂情感。

主持人在有些情况下，也会使用话语标记语来持有话轮，如：

杨澜：我一直有一件事情，我觉得看了以后，我对你蛮有看法的，就是你说是在那个小龙女的事情之后，你和林凤娇通了很长的电话，然后她不仅还是支持你，而且还让你去照顾别人，所以你很感动，然后你说你消除了对她的戒心，你怎么可以20年对自己的太太有戒心呢？

成龙：因为我看到我几个朋友，你可以想象那老公一回来，整个家没有了吗？沙发都没有，空空的。

在此例中，杨澜为了让成龙理解问题的由来，使提问不显得突兀冒昧，也便于观众的理解，采用了陈述事由的修辞方式。在陈述时，杨澜通过“就是说、然后、不仅、而且、所以”等话语标记语来持有话轮，以此陈述了事情的经过，并在此基础上发问。

5. 重复

当说话人在话轮开始时未就言语内容和表达形式事先做好充分准备，却又想继续说话时，多采取重复词句的方式来维护会话的连贯，赢得时间，以继续持有话轮。当然，在很多情况下，重复不是由于时间不充分，而仅仅是说话人持有话轮的一种表达形式。如：

杨澜：你最紧张的一次演唱会是什么时候？

刘德华：最紧张，最紧张应该是第一次在香港，因为真的没底。

在此例中，刘德华通过重复“最紧张”赢得了时间来思考杨澜提出的问题，而且给杨澜以暗示，将继续持有话轮。

上文列举了持有话轮的5种语言策略，它们分别是独白、限制话轮长度、前置语列、话语标记语和重复。在电视谈话节目中，主持人和嘉宾均可采用这5种语言策略来继续持有话轮。本文分别对主持人与嘉宾采用的持有话轮的次数进行了统计，结果如表3：

表3 主持人与嘉宾持有话轮策略统计表

	主持人	嘉宾	总数
持有话轮	55	355	410
占有比例	13.41%	86.59%	100%

如表3所示，主持人采用语言策略来持有话轮的次数为55次，嘉宾采用语言策略来持有话轮的次数为355次。主持人采用语言策略以持有话轮的次数占持有话轮语言策略总次数的13.41%，而嘉宾采用语言策略以持有话轮的次数占持有话轮语言策略总次数的86.59%。在持有话轮方面，嘉宾采用语言策略的次数远远大于主持人采用语言策略的次数。究其原因，从主持人方面看，主持人很少持有话轮，这是由电视机构赋予其的机构性地位决定的。主持人是节目的引导者和控制者，而不是信息的主要提供者，不是节目的焦点人物，所以主持人很少持有话轮。而且其持有话轮的形式多是提出问题，在发出提问后，他们便会迅速地将话轮抛给嘉宾。从嘉宾方面看，嘉宾持有话轮的比例很高，这同样是由电视机构赋予其的机构性地位决定的。

嘉宾是节目的主角，是节目的采访对象，是节目中会话资源的宝库。嘉宾提供的信息具有新闻价值，嘉宾的高度参与和积极互动是电视谈话节目实现信息共享的关键。因此，持有话轮是嘉宾对其机构性地位的遵从与适应。

三、总结

根据对10期《杨澜访谈录》视频资料的转写和分析，我们发现谈话节目的主持人和嘉宾在言语修辞上常常采用不同的话轮转换策略以适应在谈话节目中的身份。

在访谈节目的背景介绍、开始和结尾部分，主持人的修辞往往通过使用特定的策略，如独白性话语、欢迎、感谢嘉宾、概括提炼观点等来施行其权力。

在访谈节目的主体部分，嘉宾在言语修辞时，在争取话轮、放弃话轮和持有话轮方面所使用的策略都体现出他们对自己机构性身份的顺应。

从会话的局部结构看，在争取话轮时，相较于嘉宾，主持人在言语修辞时，采用了更多的打断方式，而较少地采用了插入方式。其中，主持人因其机构性的地位，出于对时间、会话进程及方向、会话目标的考虑，会采用控制力较强、礼貌性较低的打断方式来取得话轮，但另一方面，出于对嘉宾的尊重及对嘉宾信息提供者身份的认同，主持人会较少地采用插入方式，给予嘉宾充分的话语权。

在放弃话轮时，相较于嘉宾，主持人修辞时，更多地采用了指定下一说话人的方式，主持人的机构性身份赋予其控制话轮走向的权力，这种权力可以通过指定下一说话人的方式来实现。同样，采用让听话人自我选择以放弃话轮这种形式的主要是主持人。双方放弃话轮策略的差异表明了：一方面，主持人因其机构性身份，可以成功指定下一说话人；另一方面，嘉宾采用让听话人自我选择以放弃话轮的比率极低，体现了嘉宾对节目的高度参与与配合；另外，嘉宾较少采用让听话人自我选择的方式，也体现出其在对会话方向的控制方面处于弱势地位。

在持有话轮时，主持人因其是引导者身份，通常会主动将提供信息的任务交由嘉宾，而嘉宾能充分认识到自己信息提供者的身份，较多地持有话轮。

综上所述，由于主持人与嘉宾机构性权力的不对等，导致其为了适应各自的机构性身份，而作出不同言语形式和策略的选择，形成了言语修辞的不同特点。

参考文献

[1] 高有祥. 电视新闻的理论与实践 [M]. 北京：中国社会科学出版社, 2002.
[2] 何兆雄. 新编语用学纲要 [M]. 上海：上海外语教育出版社, 2000.
[3] 于国栋. 会话分析 [M]. 上海：上海外语教育出版社, 2008.
[4] 张廷国. 话轮及话轮转换的技巧 [J]. 外语教学, 2003(4).

Hostess Rhetorical Strategies on TV Talk Show Programe

—— Taking "Interview with Yang Lan" as an example

Du Min Li Xiaohan
(Shanxi Normal University, China)

Abstract: Discourse control rhetorical strategies can be found in full performance on TV talk shows, in which both sides have taken effective rhetorical measures in language for the purpose of communication on television. Considering her institutional status, the time and target of program, the process and direction of the conversation, the talk show hostess will adopt a less polite way to interrupt and get the control of the conversation. On the other hand, the hostess will also give guests full time to express themselves, showing enough respect for them. While giving up the talking turns, the hostess tends to designate the next speaker, but guests seldom leave the right to audience, because they want to show their attitude of cooperation and participation. Moreover, it also shows the guests are in a weak position in the control of the whole program. During the talking part, the hostess usually asks the guests to provide information, and guests will take the initiative to be good information providers.

Keywords: talk show; control of discourse; turn-taking; rhetorical strategies

新闻记者职业角色认同的自我呈现
——基于厦门地区社会新闻报道的个案研究

熊慧
（[中国] 厦门大学）

摘　要： 剖析媒体从业者的角色认同与媒体内容之间的关系，是连结宏观与微观层面的媒体研究，理解大众媒体的生产过程、机制及其影响因素的关键。本文以厦门地区的报媒为例，通过深度访谈和叙事分析的方法，探索该地区从事社会新闻报道的报媒记者的职业角色认同与他们的新闻叙事策略之间的关系。研究发现，具有显要性的职业角色认同将呈现于新闻作品中，与特定叙事视角联系在一起。

关键词： 社会新闻；职业角色认同显要性；叙事视角

引言

“新闻自律”和“新闻专业主义”议题在20世纪90年代进入国内学界的视野。此时正值传媒改革的集团化阶段，有偿报道等新闻业乱象初现端倪。之后近20年间，国内学界持续目睹了新闻娱乐化倾向的加剧和“软新闻”“软广告”及虚假新闻的泛滥。在感慨新闻自律的不易、指出国内新闻记者角色的错位与越位、倡导新闻专业主义理念的同时，研究者开始尝试挖掘新闻业乱象背后的根源。社会转型、媒体改革以及技术创新等常被用于解释新闻业的种种乱象。这些论述在帮助我们理解新闻实践的社会历史语境方面颇具价值，但是在说明社会结构究竟在多大程度上、以何种方式透过新闻机构内外的人际关系网络，作用于记者个人，影响后者的价值和行为方面缺乏效力。

在这方面，陆晔和潘忠党关于新闻专业主义的研究为我们提供了一个良好范例：研究者从新闻从业者如何期待及建构专业名望入手，通过实地观察、深入访谈和阅读新闻工作者的自述发现，国内记者在新闻专业理念、政治宣传体制和商业传媒体制构成的话语体系中选择、评估自身实践活动并赋予其合法性；他们面临身份认同混乱的困境，但并未放弃启蒙理想和追求社会公平与正义的责任感。这一微观社会学分析路径在之后少数研究中得到强化。这一路径下的研究表明，现在断言国内新闻业职业道德沦丧还为时过早，以此解释新闻业乱象更有失之过简的嫌疑；唯有沉潜到新闻生产的微观层面，通过与一线新闻工作者的直接接触，了解后者的价值取向和行为模式，探寻二者之间的关联，才可能获得对新闻业运作机制的深入、客观的理解，进而对造成新闻乱象的可能因素展开合理推断。

受到新闻生产的微观社会学研究的启发，本文着眼职业角色与职业行为之间的关联，立意考量新闻记者职业角色认同的自我呈现机制，探索新闻记者的职业目标对于其新闻实践的影响。关注的议题有：作为一线的媒体从业者，国内新闻记者究竟如何看待他们的职业角色？他们倾向于赋予哪些职业角色以认同显要性？他们如何理解和评价具有显要性的职业角色认同的内涵？对职业角色认同的理解和评价将如何透过记者的新闻实践得以呈现？新闻记者职业角色认同的类型和内涵与新闻叙事策略之间的关联性究竟体现在哪里？什么因素可能影响着二者之间的关联？具体说来，本文将焦点对准了转型期社会历史语境的落脚点，对结构性张力体验异常深刻的群体——报社新闻记者，采用深度访谈和叙事批评的方法，对厦门地方报社新闻记者职业角色认同的自我呈现机制展开分析，以期见微知著，从个案研究中管窥新闻记者的价值取向与行为模式之间的关系。

一、研究背景

作为人类历史上第一种真正意义上的大众媒体，报纸尤其是廉价报纸促成了“阅读公众”向“阅读大众”的转变。在广播、电视出现以前，报纸一度是具有读写能力的人群了解外部世界的首要渠道。20世纪60至70年代电视的普及，曾催生“报纸消亡论”，20年后，电脑的发明、互联网技术的推广，再度引发类似论调的流行。历史已经向我们证明，新旧媒体之间绝非简单的替代关系，报媒的未来前景仍不明朗。然而，有一点毋庸置疑，那就是，在第二次传播革命势如破竹，传播新技术高歌猛进的今天，较之市场边界基本清晰的广播媒体和市场回报依旧可观的电视媒体，报媒实际承受的或者说自身感觉到的生存压力最大。国内报媒属于后一种情况——既有体制以及整个传媒体系的后发优势，使得国内报媒尚不必直面新媒体的冲击，但国际报媒走势和国内报业市场份额自2005年以来的低谷巡游状态，足以激发国内报媒的自危感。

令报媒对社会转型期外部语境格外敏感的另一原因，在于其新闻从业者的身份定位与认同。现代意义上的中国报业产生于近代。20世纪中前期，国内报人大多抱持儒家知识分子“以天下为己任”的责任感和启蒙理想，主张以言论报国，鼓吹改革与现代化，寻求救亡图存之道。新中国成立以后的40年间，虽几经政治革命和风波的洗礼，报社记者以知识分子自居的身份认同并未发生根本改变，只是在言论的表达上更加理性。20世纪最后10年至今，媒体改革进入白热化阶段。作为这场改革的排头兵，国内报媒最先感受到了来自于市场的巨大压力。报业结构深层调整的结果之一，是市民报的滥觞。这类报纸以市场需求为导向，强调新闻的服务意识。这一转向意味着记者与读者关系位阶的改变，使得昔日以开启民智为目标的知识分子认同显得有些不合时宜。较之报媒，广播和电视媒体的技术属性及其发展历程，让他们的新闻记者与儒家文化认同传统之间的纽带相对不那么紧密，在媒体改革浪潮中，后者完成角色转换的过程因此更快更容易一些。

对于社会转型期外部语境，如技术革新、媒体改革等的高度敏感，使得报社记者成为了本文的研究对象。在报纸新闻的诸多类型中，社会新闻与媒体改革的关系尤为紧密。何谓“社会新闻”，国内学界尚无定论，但就几方面达成共识：首先，社会新闻被国外学界和业界视为“软新闻”的典型代表，区别于政治、经济、科技报道等“硬新闻”； 其次，在我国，社会新闻古已有之，建国后曾一度被归入“资产阶级黄色新闻”范畴而受到压制，改革开放以后尤其是晚报兴起后，社会新闻开始复兴；第三，社会新闻的报道范围非常广泛，涵盖了社会风貌、社会动态、社会现象、社会生活、社会事件、社会问题等。最后一点共识为我们理解社会新闻这一如此难以界定的事物为何能在20世纪80年代以来的国内报媒改革中扮演独特、不可替代的角色提供了线索：正是其对社会状态的广泛关注，使社会新闻获得了国内报媒的青睐，党报引入社会新闻来改变其在读者心目中的刻板印象，市民报则通过大量的社会新闻报道来增加其内容的贴近性和可读性，提升发行量。回顾国内报媒的改革之路，我们不难发现，社会新闻复兴的过程，同时也是报媒改革逐步推进，市场化、商业化程度不断增强的过程。在社会问题丛生、个体利益和价值日益多元化的今日中国，较之其他记者，社会新闻记者需要更多地面对来自体制和市场的反弹，承受自我认同与社会期望的差距造成的巨大压力。选择这一群体作为研究对象，研究者有望直接触及转型期新闻生产过程的内在张力，使有关新闻记者职业角色认同的探讨建立在对新闻生产环境的深刻理解之上。

社会新闻记者在当今的新闻业中扮演着某种尴尬的角色：一方面，他们是保障报纸发行量的中流砥柱，另一方面，他们常常招致批评，与哗众取宠、低俗、浅薄、造假等负面声誉联系在一起。这一群体往往在追求社会新闻的教化功能，即弘扬真善美、揭露假恶丑，与娱乐功能，如提供心灵休憩的空间，帮助个人排解压力之间摇摆，时而强调社会新闻的多元价值，即在满足显著性、重要性、接近性、趣味性和一定时效性的要求的同时，还要兼具可读性和思想性，时而又抱着接近性、趣味性和可读性至上的态度，将思想性置于次要地位。这种自我矛盾、分裂的症候并非社会新闻记者所独有，但在这一群体中表现得更加明显。

本文尝试通过社会新闻记者的自我阐释，来理解这一症候背后的根源和机制。不过，受到时间和精力的限制，笔者仅选取了厦门地区的社会新闻记者作为具体的研究对象，力图通过对这一个案的细致分析来获得对社会新闻记者生存群像的了解。较之北上广等地区的报业，厦门报业的发展相对滞后，但它的成长历程却颇具特色：在过去短短十余年内，厦门报业经历了一轮井喷式发展，从“一家独大”迅速转变为多家报纸激烈竞争的格局。超常规的改革速度，使得厦门报业成为了观察市场化、商业化对于国内新闻实践的影响的良好窗口。

目前，厦门市共有四家综合性日报，分别是厦门日报报业旗下的《厦门日报》、《厦门晚报》、《海西晨报》和福建日报报业集团旗下的《海峡导报》，以及若干周报、专业报和在厦设有记者站的省内外报业的报纸，如《东南早报》、《海峡都市报》、《人民日报》等。就市场份额和自费订阅量等指标而言，四家综合性日报占据明显的优势地位：《厦门日报》是中共厦门市委机关报，1949年创立，以“传媒力量源于读者”为办报理念；《厦门晚报》创办于1994年元旦，以“走进市民中，办给市民看”为办报理念，目前是厦门地区发行量最大、综合影响力最大的报纸；《海西晨报》原名《厦门商报》，创办于1995年，原为厦门市市委宣传部机关报，1999年划归厦门日报社主管主办，2005年改版，以“追求最有用最好看的新闻”为办报理念，2012年9月5日起更名为《海西晨报》，定位从财经都市报向综合都市报转型；《海峡导报》创办于1999年，办报理念是“用服务的理念经营民生新闻”。以上四家报纸在定位和内容方面并无根本区别，作为市民报或具有市民报特色的党报的读者本位意识和服务意识非常明显，社会新闻是这些报纸争夺有限市场份额的重要砝码，社会新闻记者则是实现这一目标的行动者，他们的职业角色认同及其自我呈现方式，部分决定了报纸的办报理念转化为实际的新闻产品的程度。社会新闻记者在上述四家报纸日常新闻生产中的重要角色，使其成为了本文最终的分析对象。

二、理论架构

角色认同与角色行为，更确切地说，角色认同显著性与角色选择行为，是本文的两个核心概念。有关这两个概念的研究，大多受到了社会学领域的认同理论的启发。所谓“认同”，指的是自我的组成部分，它为人们在不同社会群落中扮演的角色提供意义来源。这一定义将认同与角色、自我联系在一起，为本文提供了最核心的概念和出发点。1934年，美国社会学家米德首次对“自我”进行探讨，将“自我”视为一种从社会经验中产生出来的社会结构，认为自我一旦形成，就可以为个体行动提供社会经验。在米德看来，社会形塑自我，而自我形塑个体的社会行为。以这一观点为基础，麦克和西蒙引入“角色认同”的概念，进一步揭示“自我”的生成机制。所谓“角色”，即人们对社会关系网络中处于不同地位者的行为的期望。将角色期望内在化，产生所谓的“角色认同”，即个体对自我的想象，想象自己处于何种地位，扮演何种角色，该如何行动。史塞克等人延伸上述观点，发展出“认同理论”，强调角色承诺、认同显要性和角色选择行为之间的关系。该理论认为，角色认同是多层次的，在不同的社会关系网络中，人们会占据不同地位，扮演不同角色；角色认同具有不同的显要性，后者表现为在不同情境中被激活，进而转变为个体行为的可能性；个体越觉得其他重要的人希望自己扮演某个角色，自己在不同情境中将该角色认同激活、据此行事的可能性就越高。

认同理论被证明在解释某些偏差行为以及角色期望的生成机制方面缺乏效力，但它依然是迄今为止解释社会与人类行为之关联的最有力的理论之一，其基本观点在社会科学的诸多领域得到认同，其中包括新闻传播学领域。受到该理论的启发，新闻传播学研究倾向于从“角色认知”（Role Perception）和“角色行为”(Role Behavior)两个维度来探讨记者的职业角色认同问题。多数研究都在前一维度下展开。

所谓“角色认知”，指的是个体在社会情境中对自我角色、他人角色以及角色期望的了解，是角色认同的基础。根据道斯巴赫的定义，记者的角色认知表现为“记者们相信社会或利益相关者对他们抱有某些期望”，这些期望被记者们视为可接受的规范，可能影响后者的工作表现。聚焦这一议题的研究为我们贡献了早期的记者角色类型学。科恩最早将记者角色分为“中立报导者”和“参与倡议者”，前者致力于事实的客观呈现和传递，后者致力于行使“第四权力”、代表公众监督和批评政府决策。韦弗和维尔霍特进一步提出“信息传递者”“诠释调查者”和“对立者”的角色划分。其他一些调查研究发现，中立、客观被视为新闻职业理念的核心，得到较多记者的认同。

国内有关记者角色认知的研究，大致延续了国外研究的发现，但更偏重角色认知的历史变迁。例如，陈阳认为，我国记者中存在“宣传者”“参与者”“营利者”和“观察者”四种职业角色，后两种角色的出现与传媒改革密切相关。陈力丹和江陵指出，国内记者的角色认知经历了从“党的宣传工作者”到“信息传播者”“社会守护神”，再到“记录者”的转变。周裕琼的调查发现，国内新闻记者的媒介角色认知正经历由传统（以宣传教化为主导）到现代（以信息监督为主导）的转变，互联网使用在一定程度上诱发了上述转变。多数研究者相信，信息发布、信息解释、舆论监督、社会批评、公共空间、娱乐、喉舌、教育、教化是国内记者承担的常规角色，后者的角色认知总体呈现出向中立记录者偏移的态势。

“角色行为”指的是个体扮演特定角色时的行为表现，是角色认同的呈现方式。记者的角色行为主要体现为与新闻制作相关的一系列实践活动，如新闻制作、新闻加工。相关研究呈现出两种取向：一是新闻生产的民族志研究，即通过对记者每日新闻制作的流程和策略的实地观察，深入挖掘新闻意识形态的来源。其中，塔奇曼和费什曼关于新闻选择机制的研究堪称典范。前文提及的陆晔等人的研究，亦属此类范畴。这一路径下的研究长于揭示意识形态在新闻生产尤其是选择过程的作用机制，但它对于新闻意识形态的影响问题，即记者的角色认同如何投射到新闻作品中并通过后者与受众互动的问题缺乏解释力，而这正是另一研究路径——新闻生产的符号学和语言学研究的优势所在。

后者主要采用叙事分析、内容分析或文本分析的方法，通过对新闻生产的产品——新闻文本中记者的“自我呈现”机制的考察，揭示记者角色认同的符号形态。在新闻报道日益故事化的当前语境下，叙事分析受到了较多研究者的青睐。例如，泽丽泽对肯尼迪遇刺案的叙事分析发现，电视记者在报道中将自己呈现为目击者、代言人、调查者和诠释者四种角色，以此确立其作为权威发言人的地位。巴伊姆比对了“尼克松水门案”和“克林顿绯闻案”的电视新闻，发现记者在报道中分别以“信息提供者”和“视觉叙事者”的姿态出现。类似的研究主题和架构被广泛采用。反观国内研究，虽不乏对新闻内容和业务的探讨，但大多关注媒体自身的价值倾向和新闻业务中的错误和偏见，鲜少聚焦角色问题。

总体而言，角色认知研究解答了“记者的价值取向是什么”的问题，但对于价值取向背后的意涵语焉不详；角色行为研究可以回答“价值取向是否以及如何转化为特定行为模式”的问题，遗憾的是，国外研究过度，系统研究不足，国内研究则基本处于起步阶段。正是在这样的背景下，本文选择探讨社会新闻记者职业角色认同的自我呈现机制，既沿袭先前的理论和研究架构，以自我—认同—角色为构件，采用实证方法考量社会新闻记者的角色认知，又对这些架构进行了拓展和创新，以角色认同为切入点，兼顾角色认知与行为，通过多元研究方法的使用，深入揭示社会新闻记者的角色认同显著性与角色选择行为之间的关联。

综合以上论述，本文将就角色认同显著性和角色选择行为的关系进行分析，致力于回答以下几方面问题：

第一，新闻记者的职业角色认同存在哪些类型？

第二，哪些职业角色被新闻记者认为是更受他人期许，从而被赋予更高的认同显要性？

第三，新闻记者如何理解那些较显要的角色认同的内涵？

第四，较显要的角色认同是否在记者的新闻作品之中得到反映？

第五，对于较显要的角色认同的内涵的理解，将如何影响该角色认同在新闻作品中的呈现状态和方式？

三、研究方法

本文拟采用深度访谈与叙事分析相结合的方法，对厦门地区社会新闻记者职业角色认同的自我呈现机制进行深入、系统的考察。作为质化实证研究方法的一种，深度访谈强调在宽松舒适的谈话环境中与能提供有用信息的谈话伙伴开展一对一的对话，灵活地讨论范围较窄的话题，以便获取话题的细节，了解行为背后的规则、意义和价值。该方法尤其适用于处理那些较敏感的话题或错综复杂甚至相互矛盾的主题。本文的研究目标之一是了解新闻记者职业角色认同的显要性以及他们对具有显要性的职业角色认同的理解，其间涉及体验、意义和价值等问题。深度访谈的方法，能帮助研究者从少量样本中通过多次交谈获取关于研究对象的价值观念、经验感受等的详尽、细致的一手资料，形成对上述议题的“深描”。

本文采用滚雪球抽样的方式，邀请四位厦门地区的社会新闻记者，采用面对面交谈的方式进行至少一轮访谈，了解他们对上述议题的看法。谈话伙伴的基本情况如下：

表1 谈话伙伴的基本情况

编号	性别	职业	从业年限
谈话伙伴No.1	男	编辑，记者	13
谈话伙伴No.2	女	记者	5
谈话伙伴No.3	女	记者	5
谈话伙伴No.4	男	记者	5

深度访谈采用结构性访谈与开放性访谈相结合的方式，先邀请谈话伙伴填写一份简单的问卷，主要测量其认同显要性，初步了解谈话伙伴在角色认同方面的观念；然后，据此进行开放性访谈，进一步了解谈话伙伴对具有显要性的职业角色认

同的内涵的理解；访谈结束后，研究者将要求谈话伙伴提供约10~20篇对他们来说具有特别价值或意义的新闻作品，以供之后的叙事分析。

作为叙事学的重要贡献之一，叙事分析在20世纪80年代进入新闻传播学领域，形成了分别着眼于新闻叙事的形式——话语结构和内容—故事结构的两类分析路径。这两条路径被广泛用于揭示新闻记者的个体经验尤其是有关自我和认同的观念如何透过新闻作品这一中介获得象征性的表达。过去数十年的市场化运作，使国内新闻日益成为一种叙事，社会新闻报道尤其如此，这构成了本文诉诸叙事分析方法的根本前提。更重要的是，市场化运作还使新闻具有了浓厚的非个人化表达的色彩，个人新闻作品的叙事结构往往反映了新闻机构制度化的运作规程，叙事分析因此可以与深度访谈相互补充，共同勾勒新闻生产语境与记者的新闻实践之间的关系。

从经典叙事学到新叙事学，叙事分析汲取了诸多领域的理论资源，形成了多元化的分析层次。结合特定的研究对象和目标，本文的叙事分析将主要从三个层次展开，分别是叙述者与聚焦者的关系，聚焦的视角，叙事的人称。具体操作如下：

1. 数据汇总。从四位谈话伙伴那里收集到约80篇新闻，形成叙事分析的语料库；
2. 开展叙事分析。具体过程如下：首先，分析叙述者、人物与聚焦者之间的关系，即新闻叙事采用叙述者作为聚焦者的视角或人物作为聚焦者的视角，分别产生何种效果；然后，分析聚焦的视角，即新闻聚焦是以全知、限知还是纯客观视角为主，分别产生何种效果；最后，分析叙事人称，即新闻叙事采用第一或第三人称，分别产生何种效果；
3. 探寻叙事视角及其效果与显要角色认同的类型及其内涵之间的联系。

四、研究发现

深度访谈表明，四位社会新闻记者的职业角色认同呈现出某种建制内的多元性。换言之，谈话伙伴在认同新闻专业主义的核心理念的基础上，赋予社会新闻记者的职业角色以不同的认同显著性和意涵。从谈话伙伴对于自身新闻工作状态和过程的描绘中，研究者发现了信息发布、信息阐释、社会批评、公共空间、教化、娱乐六种角色的存在。四位谈话伙伴偏向于对其中一种或几种角色的认同，如强调舆论监督、社会批评，或偏重娱乐等，对同一职业角色认同的阐释存在差异。

整体上，谈话伙伴都表达了对于中立、客观的专业主义理念的认同，或强调“局外人”立场的价值，如“在采访的时候……先要有局内人的参与融合，共同感受，但是写报道的时候，还是要有战略性思维，要有理性，要用局外人的眼光，视野来看”，或强调职业理念的约束效用，如“新闻确实要冷静，要中立，要客观……但是还是要有人情味。很多时候，你可能有一个范畴……我们做新闻不能超过这个范畴……包括一些道德的底线啊，人性的底线啊，职业的操守啊，职业的修养啊，在这个范畴之内，其实可以操纵的东西很多，可以自己把握的东西很多”。

尽管如此，受到报社导向、个体差异等的影响，谈话伙伴在自身新闻工作中会赋予职业角色以不同的认同显要性，有的遵循儒家知识分子“以天下为己任”的责任感和使命感，如“我对……体制更深层次的公平正义以及人性的这种复杂性，还有就是一个人之所以会成为今天这样的人，一件事之所以会发展到今天这样，会更感兴趣一点”，有的倾向于娱乐大众的职能，如“我个人还是喜欢关注这种趣闻”，有的则强调再现社会事件的功用，如“（记者在形成好稿的过程中）只是作为记录者”。

值得注意的是，即使是同一职业角色认同，也会被谈话伙伴赋予不同的意涵。这在对舆论监督者这一职业角色的认同方面表现得尤为明显。两位谈话伙伴表达了对这一角色的认同并赋予其较高的显著性。然而，在阐释该角色认同的过程中，二者呈现出一定的差异：一位谈话伙伴将舆论监督者角色理解为“我们希望通过报道，更好地让市民知道怎么保护自己的利益，也让政府知道他们应该尽起什么样的责任”，另一位谈话伙伴则认为舆论监督的意义在于“我们进行一些报道，能对其他人有一些帮助”“（政府的负面新闻）报不报道不重要，我其实给你们（事件中的受害者——作者注）讨个说法，我们把这个事情解决了最好”。二者都希望能通过自身的新闻工作监督舆论，但前者认为舆论监督的途径在于将事件转化为报道，监督的最终目的在于提升民众和政府的意识，后者则强调报道行为本身具有的监督效力，认为监督的最终目的在于促成问题的实际解决，是否能将事件最终转化为报道并不那么重要。相对于后一立场，前者的精英主义色彩更浓一些。

访谈结束后，四位谈话伙伴分别向研究者提供了35、14、10、17篇（含部分系列报道），共计76篇独立的新闻作品，构成本文叙事分析的语料库。经过对这76篇新闻作品的叙事视角的分析，研究者发现，所有的新闻作品都采用了第三人称叙事，绝大多数新闻作品都将人物作为聚焦，采用“限知”视角，部分作品采用叙述者聚集的“全知”视角，少数作品采用叙述者聚焦的“纯客观”视角。具体说来，谈话伙伴1的35篇新闻作品主要涉及两类视角——10篇新闻作品采用叙述者聚焦的“全知”视角，25篇新闻作品采用人物聚焦的“限知”视角；谈话伙伴2的14篇新闻作品涵盖前述三类视角——2篇采用叙述者聚焦的“全知”视角，2篇采用叙述者聚焦的“纯客观”视角，10篇采用人物聚焦的“限知”视角；谈话伙伴3的10篇新闻作品主要涉及两类视角——2篇采用叙述者聚焦的“纯客观”视角，8篇采用人物聚焦的“限知”视角；谈话伙伴4的17篇新闻作品同样涉及两类视角——3篇叙述者聚焦的“全知”视角和14篇人物聚焦的“限知”视角（见表2）。

表2 新闻作品的叙事视角

编号	“全知”视角	“限知”视角	“纯客观”视角
谈话伙伴No.1	10篇（40%）	25篇（60%）	0
谈话伙伴No.2	2篇（≈14%）	10篇（≈72%）	2篇（≈14%）
谈话伙伴No.3	0	8篇（80%）	2篇（20%）
谈话伙伴No.4	3篇（≈18%）	14篇（≈82%）	0

从上述表格看来，谈话伙伴1和4具有某种相似性，采用较多全知视角且都没使用“纯客观”视角。聚焦叙事者的“全知”视角常表现为新闻文本对背景、环境、气氛的细致描述，对人物心理和情绪的传达，对事件的评论等，可以表明叙事者对于事实信息的占有，是形成新闻叙事权威性的话语策略。从“全知”视角中呈现出来的一种占据道德高地的冷静与全面，与舆论监督、社会批评所追求的权威、高度和深度是一致的，因而被以上两位谈话伙伴使用。值得注意的是，谈话伙伴1尤为注重社会新闻报道对人性的发掘，这一追求与“全知”视角之间更为符合，后者因此在该谈话伙伴的新闻作品中被更频繁地使用。

谈话伙伴2和3均采用了“纯客观”视角。这是一种叙述者将自己严格限定在“记录者”的角色中，完全隐匿在文本背后的叙事方式，只描述人物言行而不进入其内心世界，也不提供相关背景、场景、气氛等。“纯客观”视角的客观是一种超然事外、甚至有些冷感的客观，它常被用于短新闻中，营造和强化记者作为纯粹记录者的氛围。在访谈中，谈话伙伴2和3均主动地与舆论监督、社会批评等角色拉开距离，前者倾心于趣闻的单纯和生活化，而趣闻通常篇幅短小，无关乎人物心理或背景，适合采用“纯客观”的视角；后者则直接强调记者作为纯粹记录者的角色，其内在的价值取向与“纯客观”视角的叙事效果完全一致。这正是“纯客观”视角在两位谈话伙伴尤其是谈话伙伴3的新闻作品中得到频繁使用的原因。

值得注意的是，聚焦人物的“限知”视角是所有谈话伙伴最多采用的视角。笔者以为，这一现象与市民报“读者本位”的宗旨和办报理念有着密切关系。“限知”视角以特定人物来感知和呈现对象，可以在细致再现场景和环境，深入发掘人物心理和情绪的同时，传递出一种客观真实的感觉。换言之，“限知”视角兼具“全知”和“纯客观”的优点，且能有效避免二者的不足，取信于读者的同时，还能更好地打动读者，激发读者的情感共鸣，不难理解这一视角为何能在市民报的社会新闻报道中得到最频繁的使用。在访谈中，研究者发现，报社的新闻生产惯例和管理评价制度，如采编分离、重点题材上层决策、多元评报体系等，对于记者的新闻实践有着最直接、深入的影响，得到报社认可的价值取向和报道策略自然也会更多地反映到记者的日常新闻实践中去，这正是“限知”视角在所有谈话伙伴的新闻作品中得到最频繁使用的重要原因。

五、结论与讨论

基于深度访谈和叙事分析的结果可知，显要的职业角色认同及其内涵在社会新闻记者的作品中有所呈现，与特定的叙事策略，如叙事视角等联系在一起。遗憾的是，叙事视角仅是叙事策略之一，由于时间的关系，本文未能使对新闻记者职业角色认同的探讨建基于完整翔实的访谈资料之上，也未能就新闻记者的职业角色认同的其他自我呈现机制展开探讨，这都有待于后续研究的跟进。

参考文献

[1] 陈力丹, 江陵. 改革开放30 年来记者角色认知的变迁[J]. 当代传播. 2008年第6期.

[2] 陈力丹 等. 艰难的新闻自律——我国新闻职业规范的田野观察/深度访谈/理论分析[M]. 北京：人民日报出版社，2010年.

[3] 陈阳. 当下中国记者职业角色的变迁轨迹——宣传者、参与者、营利者和观察者[J]. 国际新闻界. 2006年第12期.

[4] 李良荣. 公共利益是中国传媒业立足之本[J]. 新闻记者. 2007年第8期.

[5] 李金铨. 超越西方霸权：传媒与“文化中国”的现代性[M]. 香港：牛津大学出版社，2004年.

[6] 陆晔, 潘忠党. 成名的想象：社会转型过程中新闻从业者的专业主义话语建构[J]. 新闻学研究. 2002年第4期.

[7] 罗以澄, 侯迎忠. 新闻记者的角色冲突与道德失范：兼论记者的职业责任与社会责任[J]. 武汉大学学报(人文科学版). 2006年第2期.

[8] 孙光海 等. 2003中国内地报刊杂志影响力公信力调查报告（简体版）[EB/OL]. [2012-09-15]. http://www.1a3.cn/cnnews/yjzl/sun/200909/7003_6.html.

[9] 赵智敏. 社会转向器——记者的角色冲突与调适[J]. 新闻爱好者. 2007年第8期.

[10] 张志安, 阴良. 新闻生产：职业意识与社会环境的影响——以1987“深度报道年”为个案[J]. 新闻大学. 2009年第1期.

[11] 周裕琼. 互联网使用对中国记者媒介角色认知的影响[J]. 新闻大学. 2008年第1期.

[12] 米德. 心灵、自我和社会[M]. 霍佳桓 译. 南京：译林出版社，2012年.

[13] 戈夫曼. 日常生活中的自我呈现[M]. 冯钢 译. 北京：北京大学出版社，2008年.

[14] McCall, G. & Simmons, J. *Identities and Interactions: An Examination of Human Association in Everyday Life* [M]. New York: Free Press, 1966.

[15] Stryker, S. & Burke, P. J. The Past, Present, and Future of an Identity Theory [J]. *Social Psychology Quarterly*, 63(4): 284-297.

The Self-Presentation of Journalists' Occupational Identities: A Case Study of Societal News in Xiamen

Xiong Hui
(Xiamen University, China)

Abstract: A key to connect media research at the macro level with that at the micro level to understand the process, mechanism and influence factors of mass media is to dig out the relationship between media practitioner role identities and media contents. This paper employs the methods of in-depth interview and narrative analysis to explore the relationship between societal news reporters role identities and the narrative strategies they used for their reporting. It turns out that salient occupational role identity will be presented through specific narrative perspectives of societal news.

Keywords: societal news; salience of occupational role identities; narrative perspectives

第四部分

文化修辞研究

翻译与文化传播的修辞学
——亚瑟·韦利翻译修辞手法初探

张伟雄
（[日本] 札幌大学）

摘　要： 翻译是两种语言转移交换的行为。翻译活动，是对原文进行一种新的解释，实施新的语言表现。这种“解释与表现”可以称之为“翻译语言的修辞实践”活动。修辞是运用语言的艺术，就是对语言的“调整与选择”。因而考察翻译行为，也就是对译者的修辞行为进行研究的过程。很多翻译家都对翻译的过程中对语言的“调整与选择”有明确的观点并将其应用到实践活动中。我们进行翻译的研究，可以从修辞研究的角度切入，探讨其翻译的遣词造句是否适合语境，是否达到交际目的。研究译者通过翻译，如何运用具有不同表达形式的语音、词语、句子等来有效地表达原著的文采以及思想感情等。本文拟以英国的翻译家亚瑟·韦利为例，探讨其翻译行为中的修辞手法，及其翻译修辞手法所起到的文化传播效果。

关键词： 翻译与文化传播；语言的调整与选择；文化的变异；《谷行》

一、翻译语言的调整与选择

翻译是两种语言转移交换的行为。翻译活动，是对原文进行一种新的解释，实施新的语言表现。同时翻译也是两种不同文化碰撞的过程，以及通过碰撞而追求文化越境的过程。文化在以翻译的形式试图越境的过程中，将会遇到很多障碍，这些障碍一般认为来源于以下几个方面：一，原文与译文语言结构的不同；二，原文存在而译文不存在的固有词汇；三，原文与译文各背负着不同的文化；四，原作者与译者各有不同的人生经历等。翻译修辞研究往往从这四个角度去审视译文，探讨译者是如何通过翻译语言的调整与选择、用其有效的修辞技法来超越以上障碍的。同时，人们进行翻译的目的意义是非常明确的，就是试图将一种文化传播到另一种文化中去。因而我们探讨翻译问题时，这种文化传播的问题也势必映入视野里。

本文将结合着比较文学的研究方法之一“翻译研究”，从“翻译与修辞”的角度，对日语作品《谷行》的亚瑟·韦利英译本进行分析，探讨其翻译通过对语言的“调整与选择”，如何试图超越翻译中的障碍的。本文主要从以下两个角度来考察：一，原文存在而译文不存在的固有词汇是如何翻译的；二，原文与译文各背负着不同的文化，在文化移植的过程中，译者的修辞手法使其发生了何种变异。

亚瑟·韦利于1889年出生在伦敦南部的Tunbridge Wells。大学时代，在剑桥大学攻读希腊、拉丁古典文学。大学毕业之后，韦利于1913年到大英博物馆工作。在那儿他有机会接触到了敦煌的出土文物。从此他对东方学产生了莫大的兴趣。他开始学习汉语和日语，同时积极地把中国和日本的优秀作品翻译成英文，并写下了不少有独到见解的中日文化论的专著。他的译作可以说囊括了中国和日本的主要名著。[1]

在翻译方面，亚瑟·韦利有他独到的理论，关于翻译他曾有过以下的论述：

> Different kinds of translation are needed for different purpose. If one is translating a legal document all one needs to do is to convey the meaning; but if one is translating literature one has to convey feeling as well as grammatical sense. The author puts his feelings — exasperation, pity, delight — into the original. They are there in his rhythm, his emphasis, his exact choice of words, and if the translator does not feel while he reads, and simply gives a series of rhythmless dictionary meanings, he may think he is being "faithful", but in fact he is totally misrepresenting the original.[2]

韦利把翻译的对象文本分为两种，一种为法律性的文件（Legal Document），一种为文学作品（Literature）。他主张翻译法律性的文件时，翻译的重点放在意思（Meaning）上，而翻译文学作品的时候，则要把翻译的重点放到情感（Feeling）上去。他特别强调翻译文学作品时，要把全身心都投入到作品中去，充分地为原作者代言。韦利的这种积极态度是值得肯定的。这个为原作者代言的阶段，重要的工作就是"翻译语言的调整与选择"。原作者所投入的激情，翻译者如何去体验，然后再如何通过他的遣词造句，使用"his exact choice of words"来履行他的翻译行为，这是一个极其微妙的过程。这里也充满了危险性，不小心的话，译者会驾驭不了他自己的情感，会远离原作者，将自己个人的情感极度迸发出来，感性超越理性，令译文出现强烈的变异。以下就从"翻译语言的调整与选择"的角度，探讨亚瑟·韦利在文学作品翻译的过程中，导致了何种文化变异，以及这种变异与其修辞手法的关系。

1 亚瑟·韦利的代表性译著有：*The Tale of Genji*；*Japanese Poetry, The 'Uta'*；*The No Plays of Japan*；*The Pillow Book of Sei Shonagon*；*The Way and Its Power*；*The Book of Songs*；*The Analects of Confucius*；*Monkey*；*The Poetry and Career of Li Po*；*The Life and Time of Po Chu-I*；等等。

2 *Madly Singing in the Mountains — An Appreciation and Anthology of Arthur Waley*. London, G.A & Unwin, 1970. p.152.

二、词语的转换

亚瑟·韦利在翻译的时候，首先碰到的障碍就是原文存在而译文不存在的固有词汇的问题。1921年，亚瑟·韦利翻译了日本的“谣曲集”，题名为 The No Plays of Japan。谣曲集中有一篇作品名为《谷行》，作品讲述了孝子、师们和宗教等方面的故事。

古时候在日本，佛教修验道的行者入山修行的时候有一个规定，如果遇上同行者生病，就必须将其抛下山谷。谣曲《谷行》所描写的就是关于这样的修验者入山修行的故事。故事讲述了：住在京都今熊野的一位高僧决定入山修行，年幼的弟子松若在其母亲的恳求下，得到了许可一同入山修行。在入山的途中，松若得了病，按照修验道的规矩，人们把他推下了山谷。后来在高僧的祈愿下，伎乐鬼神显灵使得松若起死还生。在作品的开端，有高僧登场自我介绍的场面：

これは今熊野椰の木の坊に、帥の阿闍梨と申す山伏にて候。さても某弟子を一人持ちて候が、かの者の父空しくなり、母ばかりに添ひて候。又某は近き間に峯入を仕り候程に、暇乞の為に唯今京仕り候。[3]

（本人住今熊野木坊，身为阿阇梨高僧，是入山修行的导师。为师的有一个弟子，弟子的父亲已过世，他与母亲相依为命。本人近日要入山修行，特前往告辞。）

这里的阿阇梨高僧“山伏”在修验道中特指修行者的导师。在入山修行的时候，山伏又是修行者的向导，隐居深山的僧人。此山伏与一般的老师不同，具有很重的宗教色彩。但是韦利在他的译文中，没能恰当地表达出这种气氛。他的译文如下：

I am a teacher. I keep a school at one of the temples in City. I have a pupil whose father is dead; he has only his mother to look after him. Now I will go and say good-bye to them, for I am soon starting on a journey to the mountains.[4]

译文中阿阇梨高僧，“山伏”都成了teacher，而且只是在寺院的私塾中任教的teacher。而原文中的“弟子”也成了一般的pupil。入山修行的行动只是轻描淡写地译成“journey to the mountains”。韦利在这故事开端的数行译文中，把整个故事都定了格。深刻的宗教故事成了一个冒险旅行记。紧跟着的对话中，韦利在词语的选择上，也出现了一种将特殊性一般化的倾向。

母　げにげに峯入とやらんは、大事の行とこそ承りて候へ、松若も御供にて候か。

先達　幼き者の供すべき道にてはなく候。

3 《谣曲大观》第三卷，明治书院，昭和39年，第1938页（以下引文均引自本书，中文为笔者所译。）

4 Arthur Waley : *The No Plays of Japan* ,George Allen and Unwin Ltd, London, 1921. p.230.

母　さてはめでたうやがて御帰り候へ

（母亲：此次你们入山，我想是非常重要的修行，请让松若也和你们同行。

先达：这不是幼小者可以同行的山路。

母亲：那么祝你们幸运地如愿返回。）

以上的对话，韦利译为如下:

MOTHER.

I have heard that it is a dangerous ritual, Shall you take my child with you?

TEACHER.

It is not a journey that a young child could make.

MOTHER.

Well, — I hope you will come back safely.

在此韦利将“重要的仪式”译成“a dangerous ritual”，可庆可喜的“めでたう”变成了平安归来的“safely”。具有神圣的宗教色彩的修行仪式变成了一个危险的旅行，大家只有祈求平安归来。

亚瑟·韦利在以上的翻译中，首先碰到的障碍就是原文存在而译文不存在的固有词汇的问题。韦利以词语转换的手法处理了这些障碍，实现了翻译的可能性。但是他在转换的过程中，采取了以20世纪西方人为中心易于理解的手法，也就是说，把日本的一种宗教活动中的难懂的固有词汇简易化。而这种简易化却把原本的宗教行为，变异为当今社会里常出现的冒险旅行。这一开场白译文为后续的故事奠定了一个基调，一直影响着往后译文的展开。原作所希望表现的诸如孝子情怀、师徒之情、宗教美谈等等内涵，都因基调已被固定，而面临着变异的危险性。

三、文化的变异

随着故事的展开，入山修行的行列中，同行的少年在登山的路上不幸得病了，按照规矩，少年将被抛落到山谷下去。在这一部分中，韦利的译笔下原文所表达的文化内涵完全被曲解变异。弟子生病，导师与少年进行了如下的对话:

いかに松若たしかに聞け、この道に出でてかやうに違例する者をば、谷行とて忽ち命を失ふ事。これ昔よりの大法なり。御身に代るものならば、何か命の惜しからん。進退谷まりて候。

仰せ承り候、この道に出でて命を捨てん事こそ、最も望む所なれども…

（“松若君哟，你好好地听着，入山修道的，像你这样得病，算是犯了规矩，会马上被抛下山谷，失去性命，这称之为‘谷行’。这是自古以来的大法。如若可以取而代之，有何可惜我的性命呢，不过这不可能啊。真可谓进退维谷啊。”

“您说的我都明白，入山修道舍其性命，这正是我最期求的。”）

从这对话中，我们可以感到师徒之间存在着的深厚感情，这包括了师徒爱，以及超凡脱俗的宗教心。通过舍身以求得比活在现世更重要的东西，这正是修行的目的所在，少年松若正因为具有这样的认识，所以他能做出“入山修道舍其性命，这正是我最期求的”这样的回答。但是，韦利的译文中却没能正确地把少年松若的心情表现出来。韦利将松若积极的对应翻译成这样：

“I understand. I knew well that if I came on this journey I might lose my life.”

这译文是非常消极的，少年松若强烈的宗教心没有表现出来，译文中笼罩着一种摆脱不了命运的控制，无可奈何、听天由命的消极气氛。把韦利的这段译文和前面出现的少年母亲的关于入山修行的看法的译文相比较，我们可以看出，问题早就发生在韦利对此次入山修行的行动的理解上。

在前面的开场白中，原文里少年的母亲称入山修行的行动为：“大事の行とこそ承りて候へ（入山是重要的修行）。”在母亲的这种认识上，少年松若的牺牲应该是一种庄严的宗教行为。

而“入山是重要的修行”，韦利的译文却是：“it is a dangerous ritual（这是危险的仪式）。”这种对母亲理解的变异，直接影响到了对少年的发言的理解上。在山谷上少年松若的“入山修道舍其性命，这正是我最期求的”的表现，韦利只译成“I might lose my life”。这样，母亲临行前的鼓励成了担心，少年充满勇气的宗教牺牲精神成了无可奈何的丧生。古典的宗教美谈成为了现代人无谋的冒险旅行记，而这旅行又是具有残酷性的。这所有的变异，都来源于韦利独断地改变词义的修辞手法。

入山修行是一项神圣的宗教活动，因此谁也不能违反它的规矩。尽管为师的表示“如若可以取而代之，有何可惜我的性命呢”，但也只能服从规矩。此时称之为“谷行”而将同行者抛下山谷的这一行为，具有巨大的宗教魅力。这并非寻常的无谓牺牲。导师和少年之间产生了复杂的心理矛盾。他们的对话已经超越了寻常的世俗之情。但是在韦利的译笔之下，这种文化心情没能正确地表现出来，而是向另一个方向变异了。

韦利在英译《谷行》的解说文中，称这部作品是“The ruthless exactions of religion（残酷的宗教迫害）”。他的译文和他的解说文，完全给《谷行》定了性。展现在现代英文读者眼前的，是一种残酷的宗教迫害行为。韦利的《谷行》译文一直贯穿着他的这一理解，甚至在翻译某些段落的过程中，单靠以上的遣词造句而不能自圆其说时，他采取了更为武断的手法——删除。

实际上，韦利没有忠实地把《谷行》译完整，为了证实他给予《谷行》的定性，他把故事中属于宗教说教的部分删掉了。故事中有这么一段合唱：“俗世间所有的行为，都如梦幻泡影，如露亦如电。”这充分地表达了人生的无常观，在故事中起着很重要的启示作用，把修行者视死如归的精神境界很好地表达了出来。而韦利完全把这段箴言删掉了。删掉了这重要的教诲之后，韦利马上把故事导入到人们是如何把少年推落到山谷下的。韦利很执著地强调了故事中的一段合唱，把故事推到了一个“残酷的宗教迫害”的高潮。下面是他的译文和原文的对比：

Chorus:
Then the pilgrims sighing
For the sad way of the world
And the bitter ordinances of it
Make ready for the hurling
Foot to foot
They stood together
Heaving blindly
None guiltier than his neighbour
And clods of earth after
Flat stones they flung

原文：
皆面々に思ひ切り
邪見の剣身を砕く
心をなしてかの人を
嶮しき谷に陥れ
上に被ふや石瓦
雨塊を動かせる
心を傷め聲をあげ
皆面々に泣きゐたり
皆面々に泣きゐたり

(人们狠着心，无情的利剑削骨切肉，将他推下山谷，盖上石块。大雨滂沱，人们伤心叫喊，面面相对，痛哭流涕。)

在以上的译文中，韦利无视原文中的慈悲表现，着意强调其行为的残忍性，词语选择上，他变换着使用原文中没有的“hurl（用力投掷），heave（用力举起），fling（猛投）”等表现强烈抛砸的字眼，用来证明世上没有比这些同行者更罪恶的（None guiltier than his neighbor）。同时韦利把充满同情心的词语“伤心叫喊，面面相对，痛哭流涕”完全删去。

不但这样，通过与原文的对比，我们还发现，韦利还把故事中最为重要的点睛之处删掉。而这一部分正是本作品之所以成为宗教故事的重要部分，是将读者高悬的心平抚下来的一部分。这部分是这样的：在故事的结尾处，由于师父和同行人的祷告、祈愿，感动了伎乐鬼神，伎乐鬼神显形使少年松若得以再生。

《谷行》原文所表达的文化内涵无疑是被曲解变异了。而引起这曲解变异的修辞手法，除了更改词义，将有倾向性的宗教词汇或对话，改为中性的一般词汇和对话以外，更甚的就是删节。可以说韦利在翻译的过程中，遇到了与其价值观相违的文字表现，需要进行翻译语言的调整与选择时，他采取了歪曲原著、转移概念的修辞手法。

四、文化越境的障碍

文化越境是一种非常困难的行为。亚瑟·韦利在翻译的过程中，通过语言的调整与选择，试图超越翻译过程中的障碍之一：原文与译文因不同的文化背景而形成的差异。但在其文化越境的过程中，韦利失败了，造成了太多的文化变异。

译者与原作者各有不同的人生经历，两者又处于不同的时代，带有不同的宗教观。韦利从现代人的角度对古典原文加以解释，赋予了一种西方现代人的价值观，这是文化越境失败的原因之一。究其深层的原因，可以追究到译者对文化的必然性与相对性关系的理解上。韦利在对《谷行》的理解上，没能从文化没有优劣之分，只有其成立的必然性这样的角度去看待不同的文化。没能相对地看待自己本身的宗教价值观，而把自己的价值观绝对化，以自己的判断去评价和翻译其他民族的价值观。因此他没能正确地把握《谷行》的真意，没能巧妙地把《谷行》中的日本文化元素译介到别的语言环境中去。

谣曲《谷行》所表现的是一个有关“牺牲”的题材。作为20世纪的英国人，韦利对《谷行》中关于“牺牲”的价值观缺少理解，因而他的翻译导致了极大的变异。牺牲，这个人类的自然现象，当它出现在文学作品中时，有时它是作为一种宗教题材出现，有时又是作为一种政治题材出现。因此对于临终前主人公的心情描写，或者对其牺牲的意义的解释也是因人而异的。处在不同时代或是不同文化背景的论者，理所当然会出现不同的议论。特别是当这牺牲是一种非自然的、特殊形式出现，具有一种特别含义的时候，对其的评价势必更深地显示出论者的价值判断。韦利也不例外，他在翻译《谷行》的时候，在语言的“调整与选择”中，充分地投入了他的价值观，译文中随处都能看出他对原著的抵抗情绪，他力图通过独自的修辞表现，构建新的英语版的《谷行》故事。

韦利的翻译重视译文的文体美和创造性，侧重于从现代人的角度对古典原文加以解释，赋予一种现代人的价值观，这种手法使韦利的文学翻译常常伴有很大的变异。由于时代的隔阂，对古典的解释，难免出现不同见解，本国人尚如此，更何况外国人呢。在将别国的作品介绍给不同时代、不同文化背景的读者的时候，确实需要一种解释性的说明，这种努力被称为“翻译创造性”。但进行这种创造性的努力时，需要特别慎重的态度、精确的修辞，以达到尊重原文、再现原文的目的。

亚瑟·韦利在《谷行》的翻译中，通过他的再创造，为今天的英语读者提供了一种文学的美。但同时不得不注意的是，过分的解释性的翻译，具有很大的危险性， 有时候甚至会让读者曲解异文化。在翻译文学作品的时候，难免会出现一种变异，我们指出这种变异，其目的是为了减少异文化间的误解，同时通过分析产生变异的原因，也可以加深对处于异文化范畴内的译者和读者的理解。而探讨翻译过程中的修辞手法，有利于探明翻译变异的原因。

参考文献

[1] Morris, Ivan. *Madly Singing in the Mountains: An Appreciation and Anthology of Arthur Waley*[M]. London, G.A & Unwin. 1970.
[2] 平子義雄『翻訳の原理—異文化をどう訳すか』大修館書店　1999年
[3] 平川祐弘『アーサー・ウェイリー「源氏物語」の翻訳者』白水社　2008年
[4] 張偉雄『比較文学考』白帝社　2012年

Rhetoric in Translation and Cultural Transmission

Zhang Weixiong
(Sapporo University, Japan)

Abstract: Translation is an act of transferring and changing two languages. We can give a new interpretation and a new expression to the original text through translating activities. The new interpretation and expression are called rhetorical practice of target language with which we will translate. Rhetoric is an art of using a language and the "adjustment and selection" of language. In the same way Thus translation is also a process of language "adjustment and selection". A large number of translators have their own theories on "adjustment and selection" of words in translation and put their thought into the translation. When we study a case of translation, we should pay attention to whether words and sentences in the translation are suitable to the context, whether the translation achieves its purpose of communication, how the translator uses different words and sentences to express the original text by translating, and etc.

This paper is a case study on an English translator Arthur Waley. Investigate his rhetorical translation; his adjustment and selection of words, and what kind effect of cultural transmission have caused.

Keywords: translation and cultural transmission; adjustment and selection of a language; cultural transformation; *Tanikou*

从道教的性别隐喻看道教的女性观及其当代价值

赵静

（[中国] 西南交通大学）

摘　要： 道教语言是充满隐喻性和象征性的语言，其传承的审慎性和隐秘性使得流传于世的众多道教典籍无不具有相当的隐喻色彩。本研究以自建的道教典籍语料库作为语料和数据来源，运用实证研究的方法，对语料中多次出现的性别隐喻关键词进行分析，建立词汇的共现关系以及词汇的分布特征信息。运用概念隐喻理论，以道教典籍中的性别隐喻为途径，对道教的女性观及其在当代社会的应用价值进行了考察。

关键词： 道教；性别隐喻；女性观

道教被认为是为数不多的尊重妇女的宗教。“在中国，在儒教、佛教和道教三种基本教义中，道教在观念上对女性最抱有善意”。[1] 道教女性观是道教区别于其他宗教的最为明显的标志之一，也最能体现出道教的特色。

道教以老子的理论为最高信仰。在论及《道德经》时，牟钟鉴提出《老子》“是真正的女性哲学，它推崇的是阴柔之性”。[2]《道德经》中载有大量雌雄阴阳的比喻，故李约瑟认为道家的思想是女性化的，“儒家知识属于男性化的，倾向于操纵和管理的知识；道家传统反对这种知识，寻求一种女性化的接受型的知识，它只能来自观察自然过程中的被动顺从的态度。”[3] 刘笑敢先生在《关于〈老子〉之雌性比喻的诠释问题》一文中肯定了《老子》中的雌性比喻之重要性，认为其不仅在先秦典籍中是独一无二的，而且在全世界古代哲学与宗教典籍中也可能是唯一的。同时也指出对于“如何理解和诠释《老子》中的雌性比喻，如何发掘这种比喻的现代意义，这种雌性比喻与当代风靡全球的女性主义运动是否可以发生关联或交涉，似乎讨论不多”。[4]

老子哲学的范畴是道，用以指宇宙、世界、社会以及人生的总根源和总根据。《道德经》花了很大篇幅来论述道是“无状之状无物之象”“道之为物惟恍惟惚”，而且“道之出口，淡乎其无味，视之不足见，听之不足闻，用之不足既”，

1 Immortelles de la chine ancienne. Tao'isme de alchimie feminine，门田真知子，《中国女性道教史》，女のタオイスム，人文书院，1996，第13页。

2 牟钟鉴：《老子的学说》，《道教通论——兼论道教学说》，齐鲁书社，1993，第161页。

3 李约瑟：《中国科学技术史》(第二卷)，科学出版社、上海古籍出版社，1990，第35页。

4 刘笑敢：《关于〈老子〉之雌性比喻的诠释问题》，《中国文哲研究集刊》，2003年第23期。

且不可“道”。正因为“道”无法言说，老子通过大量隐喻的方式来帮助人们多方面、多角度地理解和接近“道”。根据概念隐喻理论，典型的实体隐喻有容器隐喻（Container Metaphors）和视觉分野（The Visual Field）。《道德经》中的实体隐喻最典型的莫过于将“天地”视为一个“容器”，有一个里外的方位，有一个进出的方向，拥有内部和表面。“天门开阖能无雌乎”。“道”也是一个容器，所谓“道之为物，惟恍惟惚。惚兮恍兮，其中有象；恍兮惚兮，其中有物；窈兮冥兮，其中有精；其精甚真，其中有信”。同时，又将寻“道”之路视作“旅程”，因此，“道”又实体化作“道路”之“道”，“使我介然有知，行于大道”。

此外，老子又借用了“雌”“牝”“母”等一类的隐喻来描述“道”。所谓“在早期道教的宇宙观架构中，关于女性特质的明显观念构成就存在着。特别是在周朝的《老子》和《庄子》中，对于女性有‘天下母’‘谷神’以及‘阴阳’等多重的表达”。[5] 虽然“男女”二字在先秦典籍中并不鲜见，在春秋战国时期二字也已经普遍使用。但《道德经》全文五千余字并不见“男女”二字。老子用了很多代表性别的词语如“雌雄”“牝牡”“阴阳”等来区分物体的性质。在此基础上，道家建立了一套主阴的哲学体系。

一、“母”隐喻

美国学者爱德华·赫伯特在1960年发表的《道教笔记》（*A Taoist Notebook*）一书中，曾把老子的“道”同西方神话学和宗教史学中的“大母神”（The Great Mother）相联系，认为“道”是原始母神的抽象和隐喻表达。《道德经》始终贯穿着“以母为本”的主题，不论是本体道论，还是养生治国论，都体现了老子的主阴思想。[6]《道德经》直接言及“母”字的，通行本五章内共计七处，如：[7]

有名万物之母。(第一章)

我独异于人而贵食母。(第二十章)

周行而不殆可以为天下母。(第二十五章)

天下有始以为天下母既得其母以知其子既知其子复守其母。(第五十二章)

有国之母可以长久。(第五十九章)

“母”的一个引申义是“宗”，有“道冲，而用之或不盈。渊兮似万物之宗”；“母”的另一引申义是“先”，“吾不知谁之子，象帝之先”。老子以“母”用来比喻“道”，认为“道”是“万物之始”，是世界万物之所出，是万物和天下的根源。

“母”的重要区别性特征是“生”的概念。这是“道”与“母”对应的关键纽带。“生”的概念，是一个创造的过程，与“道”创生万物有异曲同工之妙。

5 Lindsay Jones, Editor in Chief, Encyclopedia of Religion (Second Edition). vol.5. Macmillan Reference USA, 2005. p.3342.

6 詹石窗：《道教与女性》，上海古籍出版社，1990，第47页。

7 孙洪卫：《〈道德经〉主阴思想的认知隐喻分析》，西南交通大学硕士论文，2010年。

“母”指“道”，“子”指万物。老子用母子关系来说明道和万物之间的联系，老子认为“生”是最伟大的美德，而且这种“生”的能力是普通人可望不可及的，只有万事中的“天地”，只有“圣人”才能习得其中的真谛，具有“生”之德的“天地”“圣人”则是“万物”“人”中的最高层次。“他用女性生殖原理和母子关系来形象化地解说大道与万物的关系。‘道’的最大特点是‘道冲，而用之或不盈’，道体虚空却能源源不断地生育万物。”[8]

“道”与“母”在养育模式上也极为相似，即“生而不有”。“子”出母体之后，便是独立个体，“母”并未对“子”名有，“子”却如何也脱离不了“母”而存在。这个重要的特点与“道”神似：“万物作焉而不辞，生而不有，为而不恃，功成而弗居。夫唯弗居，是以不去”“生而不有，为而不恃，长而不宰，是谓玄德”“大道兮，其可左右。万物恃之而生，而不辞功成不名有。衣养万物而不为主”。“生而不有”是通过“母”这一桥梁，渗透到“道”的概念中去的。如果说“生”是“道”之德的话，那么“生而不有”则是“道”之为，也就是“无为”之“为”。所谓“道常无为，而无不为。侯王若能守之，万物将自化。”[9]

二、“雌”“牝”隐喻

《道德经》直接言及“雌”的共有两次：

天门开合，能无雌乎？(第十章)

知其雄，守其雌。(第二十八章)

可以看出，“雌”这里更多地是指向“道”的一种特质，即阴性静柔的特质。

“牝”在《道德经》出现五次：

谷神不死，是谓玄牝。玄牝之门，是谓天地根。(第六章)

未知牝牡之合而全作。(第五十五章)

天下之牝，牝常以静胜牡以静为下。(第六十一章)

据史华兹分析，“谷神不死，是谓玄牝。玄牝之门，是谓天地根”。此处“谷”是一种象征，谷的空虚、接纳、被动、包容的特征意指女性的性别和生育的角色。[10] 王弼注：“谷神，谷中央无谷也。”“门，玄牝之所由也。”刘笑敢先生认为：“谷神”的“谷”其实也是指的女性生殖器，女性生殖器是中空的，所以称为谷。“谷神”的“神”有神妙莫测之意，如同“玄牝”一样，也是用来比喻道的玄妙莫测、幽深抽象的。可见谷神、玄牝都代表着母性和生殖本能，这种奇妙的母性和生殖本能也许具有持久的自然生养能力，而这种无形而永存的能力当然就是玄牝之门、天地之根，即天地万物的总根源，就是“道”。此外，萧兵、叶舒宪先生也用数百页的篇幅讨论了《老子》与女性和生殖崇拜的关系。[11] 陈张婉辛认为：

---

8 牟钟鉴、张践：《中国宗教通史》(上卷)，社会科学文献出版社，2000年，第30页。

9 孙洪卫：《〈道德经〉主阴思想的认知隐喻分析》，西南交通大学硕士论文，2010年。

10 史华兹：《古代中国的思想世界》，江苏人民出版社，2004年，第209页。

11 萧兵、叶舒宪：《老子的文化解读——性与神话学研究》，湖北人民出版社，1994年。

"我们强烈地感觉到《道德经》的思想形式来源于母系社会存在的启示。"她进一步把书中的某些观念与生殖崇拜联系起来："根据宗教与早期哲学的联系，我们相信'无''弱''黑''虚'等观念本来是与生殖力崇拜相联系的。"[12] 这些学者都认为，《道德经》体现了明显的女性生殖崇拜思想。

《道德经》中有很多概念如牝和牡、雌和雄、柔软和刚强等都是相对出现的。刘殿觉先生指出，这些相对的概念之间存在着令人吃惊的不对称的现象，而前者明显更受偏爱。从数量上看，《道德经》直接言及"母"字的，通行本五章内共计七处，直接言及"雌"的两章内两次，"牝"三章内出现五次，而"父""雄"一次，"牡"两次，且都缺乏独立性，皆为对举时连带而出。刘笑敢先生认为："《老子》中的'雌''牝''母'等词汇的出现和地位明显比'雄''牡''父'多而寓意深远，其'柔弱胜刚强'不仅是哲学和方法论的主张，而且也似乎有着某种性别暗示或性别取向。"[13] 在陈述次序上，陈鼓应先生曾在《道家易学建构》中指出："《老子》中'阴阳''牝牡''雌雄''静动'的排列次序，如'万物负阴而抱阳，冲气以为和''牝常以静胜牡，以静为下'等等。这种崇阴尚静的阴性词在前、阳性词在后的排列序次于先秦古籍中独见于《老子》。"[14] 而且，《道德经》还多次直接表明：

> 柔弱胜刚强。(第十章)
> 牝常以静胜牡。(第三十六章)
> 强大处下，柔弱处上。(第六十一章)
> 天下之至柔，驰骋天下之至坚。(第七十六章)
> 守柔曰强。(第四十三章)

这里更多地表现出老子对"柔"这种品质的偏爱与提倡。老子的哲学在很大程度上是将女性勤劳质朴、坚韧吃苦、慈祥亲和等美德哲理化，将女性所特有的一般属性升华的思想原则。台湾学者吴怡先生的《中国哲学的生命和方法》一书中说："中国哲学上有两本运用女性之德的经典之作，一本是易经，一本是老子。易经只用了一半，而老子彻头彻尾都是女人哲学。"因为老子"讲母，讲婴儿，讲玄化，讲水，讲柔弱，讲慈，讲俭，可说无一不与女人有关"。[15]可以说，《道德经》整个哲学体系是建立在女性隐喻之上的。

三、"胎"隐喻

与道教的生养模式相关，在道教典籍中，还经常出现一个和"母"有关的词"胎"，这里的"胎"常是隐喻用法。如：

---

12 Ellen M. Chen, Nothingness and the Mother Principle in Early Chinese Taoism, *International Philosophy Quarterly*, 1969 (9). p.391-405.

13 刘笑敢：《关于〈老子〉之雌性比喻的诠释问题》，《中国文哲研究集刊》，2003年第23期。

14 陈鼓应：《道家易学建构》，商务印书馆，2010年，第19页。

15 吴怡：《中国哲学的生命和方法》，东大图书公司，1981年。

人之受生，于胎胞之中，三元养育，九气结形。《云笈七签》

千龄胎化，中以驾羽之期；万岁岩者，献以华封之寿。《益州至真观主黎君碑》

神光流入于琼胎，瑞彩结成其金骨。《西川青羊宫碑铭》

三壬三乙之神，离胎于水木；六丙六辛之将，出孕于火风。《西川青羊宫碑铭》

有圣研极，镌胎剖魄，识其倪绪，取安诸隅，广宇泰宁。《成都府玉局观新建五符幢记》

上圣凝气为真，与道合体，非寓胎禀化之形，乃西华少阴之气也。《神女庙记》

岂非以水生于金，而西方为其胎息之地耶。《玄帝祠碑》

中有一二羽客，危坐胎息，何其逸也。《重修三台观碑记》

相此胎禽，浮丘著经。《瘗鹤铭》

且人生天地之间，处最灵之首，当受生于胞胎之中，三元育养，九气结形，戴天履地，莫不本乎道者也。《宣和御制化道文碑》

临目而万八千神，咽胎而千二百息。《御制叶真人碑》

此诚有生和合，二象匹对之要也，若以道交接，解脱网罗，推会六合，行诸节气，却灾消患，结精宝胎，上使脑神不亏，下令三田充溢。《真诰》

明朝伍冲虚在《天仙正理直指》里论述了“胎”并非真有婴儿：“胎即神、气耳，非真有婴儿也，非有形有象也。盖大丹之成，先以神入乎其气，后气来包乎其神，如胎儿在胞中无呼吸又不能无呼吸，生灭之相尚在，出入之迹犹存，若胎孕之将产时，故比喻之曰怀胎、移胎、出胎。”经过一系列的去阴气存阳气的过程，当修炼达到一定程度时，即“负阴抱阳”时，即达到了所谓有胎、有孕的程度。《道枢·契真篇》：“其六曰玄一炼神结胎。刘根曰：凝人丹田、成童而去，此结胎者也。故精有主焉，气有源焉，呼吸绵绵，合于自然，则胎结而真全矣。蚌饮月华之气，犹成珠于腹、况炼其神乎。是以炼气成形，其名曰仙人；炼仙以仙，其名曰真人：炼真成仙，其名曰至人；炼圣成形，其名曰神人。”

在道教语言中，“胎仙”指结圣胎之人。《海琼问道集·玄关显秘论》中有云：“先师陈泥丸学丹法，每到日中冬至之时，则开干闭巽……袖铅添汞，结成圣胎，十月既满，气足形圆，身外有身，谓之胎仙。”又如《性命圭旨·性命双修万神圭旨第六节口诀》有云：“陈泥丸云：男儿怀孕是胎仙。”“胎气”谓自然的正气。《黄庭内景经·百谷章》：“臭乱神明胎气零。”梁丘子注：“胎气，谓无味之味，自然之正气也。”这里“胎息”指道家的一种修炼方法。《后汉书·方术传下·王真》：“年且百岁，视之面有光泽，似未五十者。自云：‘周流登五岳名山，悉能行胎息胎食之方，嗽舌下泉咽之。’”李贤注引《汉武内传》：“习闭气而吞之，名曰胎息；习嗽舌下泉而咽之，名曰胎食。”晋葛洪《抱朴子·释滞》：“得胎息者，能不以鼻口嘘吸，如坐胞胎之中，则道成矣。”《胎息经·胎息铭》：“三十六咽，一咽为先，吐惟细细，纳惟绵绵，坐卧亦尔，行立坦然，戒于喧杂，忌以腥膻，假名胎息，实曰内丹。”

四、“天父地母”隐喻

在与自然的关系上，道教用“天父地母”的隐喻形象化地表述了人与自然和谐相处的基本方式。

> 乾，天也，故称乎父；坤，地也，故称乎母。《周易·说卦传》
>
> 圣人法天顺情，不拘于俗，不诱于人。以天为父，以地为母，阴阳为纲，四时为纪，天静以清，地定以宁。《淮南子·精神训》
>
> 天者主生，称父；地者主养，称母；人者主治理之，称子。父当主教化以时节，母主随父所为养之，子者生受命于父，见养食于母。为子乃当敬事其父而爱其母。《太平经》
>
> 天地之位，如人男女之别，其好恶皆同。天者养人命，地者养人形。今凡贼害其父母。四时之气，天之按行也，而人逆之，则贼害其父；以地为母，得衣食养育，不共爱利之，反贼害之。人甚无状，不用道理，穿凿地，大兴土功，其深者下及黄泉，浅者数丈。独母愁患诸子大不谨孝，常苦忿忿模困悒，而无从得道其言。……凡人为地无知，独不疾痛而上感天，而人不得知之，故父灾变复起，母复怒，不养万物。父母俱怒，其子安得无灾乎？《太平经》

道教认为：“今天下失道以来，多贱女子，而反贼杀之，令使女子少于男，故使阴气绝，不与天地法相应。天道法，孤阳无双，至枯，令天不时雨。女者应地，独见贱，天下共贱其真母，共贼害杀地气，令使地气绝也不生，地大怒不悦，灾害益多，使王治不得平。”[16] 在道教里，女性象征大地，对女性的迫害就是对地母不尊。如果地气断绝、地母发怒，就会有灾害发生。这说明道教认为不尊重女性，不给女性与男性平等的社会地位便不能“与天地法相应”。

对于男女平等的观念，道教不仅将其停留在理论层面，而且全面贯彻到制度修行中。在修炼行为和方式上，佛教认为女性是丑恶、罪恶的象征，把女性当作男性修炼成佛的重要障碍。《大般涅槃经》卷第九《大般涅槃经菩萨品》第十六即云：“一切女人皆是众恶所在之处。”与之相反，道教则将女性看作是修炼的伙伴、成仙的伴侣。这也是道教不同于其他宗教的一个特色。在道教的仪轨中，女性神职人员与男性神职人员一样，可以主持斋醮科仪，享有平等地位：

> 女官大法者为师。《要修科仪诫律钞》卷三引《太真科》
>
> 其人体道，含德厚淳，虽是女子，男亦师之。《洞真太上太霄琅书》卷四《择师诀第九》
>
> 俯仰之格，男女官通用。《黄书》
>
> 女真则称元君夫人，其名仙夫人之秩比仙公也。夫人亦随仙之小大，男女

16 王明：《太平经合校》，中华书局，1960年，第34页。

皆取所治处，以为署号，亦有左右。《太平御览》引陶弘景《登真隐诀》

天师道……立二十四治，署男职、女职二十四职。《玄都律文》

男女相度，智者为师。《太上洞渊神咒经》

不限师之多少，不格师之男女。《要修科仪诫律钞》

阴阳之施，男女更相过度。《上清黄书过度仪》

五、“阴阳男女”隐喻

道教从“阴阳平衡”的角度主张男女性别平等。“阴阳”最初并不是一种高度抽象的哲学概念，阴阳古义本指自然现象，《说文》解释为：“阴，闇也。山之北，水之南也。从阜，从侌。阳，高明也。从阜，昜声。”后逐渐引申成为宇宙间万事万物的一种相对属性。道教通过比附的手法将阴阳和合思想引申到两性关系当中：

男女者，乃阴阳之本也。《太平经》

男女各出半力，同志和合，乃成一家。天地之道，乃一阴一阳，各出半力，合为一，乃后共成一。《太平经》

道无阴阳，违天背元。《周易参同契》

有阴有阳而无和，不能传其类，亦绝灭。故有天而无地，凡物无于止；有地而无天，凡物无于生；有天地相连而无和，物无于相容自养也。故男不能独生，女不能独养。《太平经》

合夫妇之道，阴阳俱得其所，天地为安。《太平经》

牝，地也，女像之。阴孔为门，死生之官也，最要故名根。《想尔注》

男女者，乃阴阳之本也。《太平经》

男气白，女气黄……混沌黄白之气能相杀，能相生。《洞真黄书》

道教之“道”是以“一阴一阳谓之道”的阴阳相生思想为基础的，它所包含的“两为一合”“两两为合”思想深深地植根于道教教义之中。

阴阳合和生气。《黄书》

阴阳与合乃能生。《太平经》

阴阳各得其所，天下诸承负之大病，莫不悉愈者也。《太平经》

阳安即万物自生，阴安即万物自成。《太平经》

道无奇辞，一阴一阳，为其用也。《太平经》

天初一也，下与地相得为二，阴阳具而共生。《太平经》

夫天地之生凡物也，两为一合。今是上天与是下地为合。凡阳之生，必于阴中，故乃取于此地上人也。《太平经》

故纯行阳，则地不肯尽成，纯行阴，则天不肯尽生。《太平经》

阴气阳气更相摩砺，乃能相生。人气亦轮身上下，神精乘之出入。《太平经》

夫阴阳有对，否泰反用，二象既罗，得失错综，此皆往来之径陌耳。《真诰》

道教修炼过程所呈现出的女性与男性之间的相互依赖、相互帮助的关系，体现了道教所推崇的两性之间的和谐。构成“道”的阴阳二元素又可以相互转化，处于一种互动的关系中：

夫阳极者能生阴，阴极者能生阳。《太平经》

极上者当反下，极外者当反内；故阳极当反阴，极于下者当反上；故阴极反阳，极于末者当反本。《太平经》

阳变于阴，阴变于阳，阴阳相得，道乃可行。天须地乃有所生，地须天乃有所成。《太平经》

人复不可都绝阴阳，阴阳不交，则坐致壅阏之病，致幽闭怨旷，多病而不得寿也。《抱朴子内篇·释滞》

阴者，阴为无也，无则能变化，能无能有，出生入死，包容隐显也，如临军之用兵法也，六阴无形，用之则应。凡有道之士用阴，无道之士用阳，阳则可测，阴则不可穷也。《秘藏通玄变化六阴洞微遁甲真经》卷中《元阴隐秘要》

“阴阳相得，交而为和，与中和气三合，共养凡物，三气相爱相通，无复有害者”。这种“三一”观念所强调的两性和谐互动思想对提高女性在道教中的地位起了积极的作用。

在宗教构想的虚幻世界中，佛国中修成正果的基本上都是男性，而道教却认为男女同道，夫妇可以一同飞升。因此，女道士众多，《太上洞渊神咒经》第二十卷记载：“道言：自今以去至壬午辛已有女人道士多，有受三洞入山者亦多女道，男子反少也。”道教神仙谱系“三仙”“九品”中均有“成仙真”的女子的位置。众多的道教神仙故事和传说，有不少是关于女性的。刘向的《列仙传》、葛洪的《神仙传》，以及《汉书·汉武帝内传》、《太平御览》等就记载了众多女性神仙的事迹。唐代还出现了专门记载女性神仙的道书，像著名道士杜光庭所著的《墉城集仙录》就是专为女性神仙立传的。全书共六卷，收录了汉魏以来广为流传的三十八位女神仙的事迹，成为道教史上第一部较为系统的女性神仙谱系。宋朝张君房纂辑的《云笈七签》卷一百一十四、一百一十五、一百一十六都是专门为女性神仙而撰写的。而元代赵道一修撰的《历世真仙体道通鉴后集》则比较系统地记载了一百多位女仙的事迹。在道教碑文中也大量记载有关于女神、女仙和女道士的事迹。如：

颜真卿所撰《抚州临川县井山华姑仙坛碑铭》云：“华姑者，姓黄氏，讳令微，抚州临川人也。少乃好道，丰神卓异，天然绝粒。年十二，度为天宝观女道士。年八十，发白面红，如处子状，时人谓之华姑。蹀履而行，奔马不及。闻魏夫人仙坛在州郭之南，草木榛翳。结庐求之，不得。”

清乾隆二十四年巫山县令朱斐然在《神女记》碑文中写道：“治东神女祠，巫之胜迹也。古今艳称之。第泥于宋玉《高唐赋》寓言，毋亦以治西有高唐阳台旧基址，因群附会其说耶？自明张、马、范三公，据《集仙录》作《神女庙考》，世始知有授书开峡之事。三公可谓具卓识而有功于人心世道也。惟是祠止两层，年远倾圮颇失壮观。而土人又妄添置观音九子母等塑像于其中，不伦不次，岂专庙独尊之义乎！予为迁移诸像于各本祠，而此处独留神女一像。并略捐廉俸，修葺庙宇，既不没古迹而祠像亦庶乎独尊。至神之有功于三峡，而福庇于生民，则前人已言之，予不赘也。”

其中，“神女”，世人谓之仙人，道教尊之为神。“神女”“女仙”又作“玉女”，如：

仙人玉女，莫不敬经师。《太上洞渊神咒经》

阴娥假道，窥玉女于南轩；阳鸟回銮，昭青禽于北阁。《益州至真观主黎君碑》

玉女云衣，仙人露掌。《梓州道兴观碑铭并序》

王元林、孟昭锋在《论碧霞元君信仰扩展与道教、国家祭祀的关系》一文中详细考察了泰山玉女发展成国家祭祀神灵碧霞元君，经历了“立像”“建祠”“赐额”三个阶段，完成了从民间俗神到道教神仙，再到国家神灵的转变，成为国家“准正祀性”的神灵。其中特别提到“玉女”有一个从群体性的概念“仙女”到物化载体玉女池、再到玉女石像的个体化过程。这涉及一个通过概念的修辞转换，而达到女神信仰的确立问题。论文引用六朝时道教文献《太上九赤班符五帝内真经》：“（东岳青帝）常以立春之日，乘碧霞九龙云舆，从青腰玉女十二人，手把青林之华九色杖幡，游行东岳泰山。”又曰：“（泰山府君）乘龙驾舆，飞行太空，回灵曲映，下降我房……六丁侍卫，玉女扶将。”又引《洞真太上紫度炎光神元变经》之《西王母授经时作颂三篇》云：“东岳仙官乘碧龙碧霞，手把五芝，从玉女十二人，飞青羽裙。”稍后的《元始五老赤书玉篇真文天书经》载“（东岳仙官）天真下降，给青腰玉女九人，取东岳神仙芝草，不死之药”证明，此时的“玉女”仍是诗人意境中轻盈飘逸的仙女，只是一个群体性的概念描述，没有一个令人信奉的现实载体，并且是侍从身份，地位低下。由于泰山自古便是人们心目中的圣地，又是后代封禅祭祀之场所。因文求实，诗文在意境中对泰山玉女的描绘，对泰山泉水的讴歌，必定引起人们对泰山玉女的崇拜并从现实中寻找对其信奉的载体。而女属阴，水亦属阴，泰山中的圣水泉池正可作为玉女的代表，“玉女坤质，为水象，池固其所自来耳”，故人们自然将玉女池看作玉女的化身。这样，位于岱顶的玉女池自然成为人们追逐和求证的理想场所。于是，宋真宗东巡封禅时，亲临玉女泉（即玉女池），易玉女石像。石像的出现，为泰山玉女信仰的进一步扩展奠定了基础。[17]

道教的神仙世界一般都是男女对偶的局面，故称之为“对偶神”或“配偶神”。在各层次的神仙系列中往往也重视男女对偶。如梁陶弘景的《真灵位业图》第二等级中，玉皇大帝居中，左有30名道君，右有30名女真。男女班列，共享祭供，这是道教尊神的一个特点，包含了一定的男女平等思想。陈撄宁先生说：“在神仙家眼光看起来，男女资格是平等的。若论做工夫效验，女子比男子快，若论将

17 王元林、孟昭锋：《论碧霞元君信仰扩展与道教、国家祭祀的关系》，《世界宗教研究》，2010年第1期。

来的成就，亦无高下之分。至于普通重男轻女之陋习，乃是人为的，不是天然的。世界各大宗教，如佛教、天主教，中国内地种种密教，如某某门，某某堂，某某社，皆是男女不能平等，独有仙道门中，无此阶级。仙道不为陋习所拘，女子亦同样易修实证。”[18] 由于妇女与男人一样具有独立成仙的可能，因此在道教中出现了像《女金丹》、《灵源大道歌》、《樵阳经·女工修炼》等这样一些专论女性丹经的道书。“宋元以来，内丹家专述女子内丹修炼的‘女金丹’著述便有三十余种，包括《女金丹》、《壶天性果女功十则》、《坤道功夫次第》、《坤元经》、《女功炼已还丹图》、《女丹合编》、《孙不二女丹诗注》及《守一诗》等等。”[19] 这些都是针对女性生理特点而专为女子修道而作的女性丹法道书，这在其他各教中几乎是没有的。

在主阴思想的影响下，“由于主阴的思想本来就是女性崇拜的哲学化，当它成为道教的理论基础之一而被广泛宣传和应用时，必然反过来加强女性崇拜，促进女性崇拜的发展。”[20] 从刘向的《列仙传》、葛洪的《神仙传》到清代王建章的《历代仙史》，女仙的数量急剧增加，在道教教派中的地位和影响亦是与日俱增。西王母、九天玄女、谌姆元君等女神、女仙在各种典籍中频频出现，都可看出道教女性崇拜的普及和深入人心。

近年来，西方女性主义神学家们对父权制文化的代表——基督教进行了猛烈的批判，认为基督教是父权制宗教，基督教的女性观念直接影响到了女性的社会地位与生存状态。汉学家李约瑟在评述道家思想时曾专辟一节，题为“水与阴性的象征”。他认为不健全的现代社会在一定程度上是文化中阳性因素借助于父权制而过度发展的产物，纠正的策略在于发扬被压抑了的文化中的阴性成分，而老子思想正是这种成分。反观中国道教，其贵雌守柔的女性观念所体现的自然秩序和社会和谐，可以为我们重新认识当代社会和人类面临的各种问题提供新的思路，对当代的国际关系也有重要的启示意义。

18 陈撄宁：《道教与养生》，华文出版社，2000年。参见李素萍：《从道教成仙修炼看女性之地位》，《中国道教》，2001年第3期。

19 陈麟书、袁亚愚：《宗教社会学通论》，四川大学出版社，1992年，第265页。

20 詹石窗：《道教与女性》，上海古籍出版社，1990年，第49页。

Study of *Taoist* View on Women and Its Contemporary Value Based on the *Taoist* Gendered Metaphors

Zhao Jing
(Southwest Jiaotong University, China)

Abstract: The tradition of prudence and secrecy makes the *Taoist* classics full of metaphorical expressions. This paper studies the key gendered metaphors appeared in the *Taoist* classics as well as its vocabulary-building and co-occurrence relations based on self-built *Taoist* Corpus. Intended to examine the *Taoist* unique view on women and its value in modern society from the perspective of conceptual metaphor theory.

Keywords: *Taoist*; gendered metaphors; view on women

论当代中国电影韩国语译名的翻译品质[1]

罗敏球

([韩国] 韩国外国语大学)

摘　要： 本文对2000年以来上映的华语电影的韩国语译名进行了细致考察，并就此进行了翻译品质评价，以促使当前翻译的日臻完善、电影译名更加优秀。作者认为，为了迎接美好翻译时代的到来，韩国电影片名应译得正确、易懂，应适当地采用直译和意译，才能创作出雅俗共赏的片名，使之具有创意和审美双重意义。在韩流入华之际，研究电影译名以确保正确传递其中的民族文化和精神，具有重要意义。

关键词： 韩国语译名；中国电影；翻译品质；评价

维基百科对电影译名的解释是："把一个国家制作的电影介绍、引进到别的国家时使用的外国电影的译名。决定电影译名可以有多种战略。不经过特别的翻译过程，直接按照原文发音音读的方法（原语直接进口）、与原片名接近的翻译方法(直译)，以及不拘泥于原电影片名，创作有个性的译名(意译)等。"电影名称的翻译，关涉语言、社会、文化、知识背景等多种因素。这门学问可以叫作"沟通修辞学"，因为它主要解决由翻译导致的文化冲突问题，完全可以称得上是化解两门外语或两个国家间文化冲突的钥匙。为此，本文对中国内地、香港、台湾电影的韩语译名进行了分析，这些影片包括在韩国上映的或在韩国举办的国际电影节上参展的华语电影，并站在评价者[2]的立场上对这些译名进行翻译品质的评价(TQA)[3]，以期对今后的电影片名翻译有所助益。

一、韩国翻译品质评价 (TQA) 现状

韩国目前还没有对翻译作品确立客观的翻译品质评价标准，但是一直存在以"翻译批评"为论题的，针对文学作品的翻译品质进行讨论的工作。[4] 高丽大学的"法国名著小说翻译评价研究团"正在促进的项目就属于这种工作。"英美文学研究会翻译评价事业团"对英美古典文学进行翻译评价，经过4年的时间，对900多种英美文学作品的全译本进行了评价，整理出了推荐本。

---

1 This work was supported by Hankuk University of Foreign Studies Research Fund.

2 执行评价的评价者不仅要具备该领域的专业知识，而且应该以能够在语言层面上充分理解评价对象为前提。

3 TQA, Translation Quality Assessment. 译作"翻译品质评价"。

4 李香：《翻译品质评价的现况与课题》，《翻译学研究》，韩国翻译学会，2010年。

二、中国电影韩国译名TQA评价项目设定及分数分配

对字数还不到一行的电影片名设定评价项目并进行分数分配并非易事。必须考虑到，针对如何确保评价项目的客观性以及分数分配是否合理这两个问题，所有人的意见很难一致。忠实于原片名的直译和带有创意的意译之间必然出现难以把握尺度的问题。

这种逐字翻译（Literal Translation）和自由翻译（Free Translation）之间的选择和均衡是很重要的。[5] 这两种翻译方法各有优劣。逐字翻译是根据原来的片名进行直译，可以说"忠实而等价"地传达了原片名的意义。但是却无法摆脱在传达外国语言时所发生的文化模糊性、不完全性。自由翻译因为对原来的片名进行了变形，有无法对原来的片名做到"等价式"传达的弱点。但是，却可以创造出与读者产生共鸣的新译名。

最终这个问题的关键在于，在忠实性（Faithfulness）和内容（Content）之间更偏向于哪一方。本文赞同后者的做法。为什么呢？因为这种方法更能体现翻译精神以及为翻译者提供发挥创意的空间和机会。那么，我们可以说将二者有效结合的翻译才能称得上优秀的翻译。在此基础上如果能使观众产生共鸣(Pathos)[6]，才算完成了美学意义上的翻译。

这种既有效，又具有美学意义的翻译，就是本文在翻译品质评价(TQA)中所青睐的目标。因此，本文具体观察了中国电影片名的韩国语电影译名是不是逐字翻译的、是不是自由创作的以及是否为音译（音读）的。本研究设定的评价项目和分数分配如表1。

表1 中国大陆电影名韩国语翻译品质评价(TQA) 等级表

	评价项目	加分及扣分	评分	评价意见	星等级表示
1	创作出有效适宜的优美片名	+ 3	5	最优秀	★★★★★
2	对意译进行新的尝试的片名	+ 2	4	优秀	★★★★
3	通过直译有助于理解的片名	+ 1	3	良好	★★★
4	通过音译有助于理解的片名	0	2	普通	★★
5	把英文译名直接翻译成韩国语的片名	− 1	1	须监修	★
6	音译后无法理解的片名	− 1	1	须监修	★
7	误译	− 2	0	不良	☆

1. 创作出有效适宜的优美片名

这类电影的译名属于最理想的译名。我们以在韩国上映的美国电影的韩国语译名为例。

2007, 그 여자 작사 그 남자 작곡, Music and Lyrics

5 Finding the balance between literal translation and free translation is rational in the translation of film titles.

6 Pathos 指的是亚里士多德提出的数学式说服三要素，引发听众或观众共鸣的作用。

这部影片原来的片名是“Music and Lyrics”(2007)，如果直接翻译的话就是“音乐和抒情诗”。在门户网站的专题“我随意挑选的外国电影译名中的好例子”所开设的博客中观众评价道:“充分体现了浪漫喜剧的特点，文字对仗加上韵律，朗朗上口且散发浪漫气息，真是上乘之作。不仅如此，译名也压缩显示了电影的实际内容。即便如此，却没有让人产生显而易见的乏味感，反而让人对剧情产生了期待，更激发了人们想一睹为快的念头。”该电影译名也被选为深得观众之心的译名。再看一下下面这部中国电影的译名。

1999, 책상서랍속의 동화，一个都不能少, Not One Less

张艺谋导演的这部电影的译名激起了韩国观众对学生时代特有的美好回忆。如果照原片名翻译的话，就是“하나도 모자라선 안 돼”。单看这部电影的内容，“一个乡村女代课教师为寻找一名因家计困难而必须放弃学业到城市去打工的学生，在没有人帮助的情况下进了城。”那么，直译的片名很符合原片内容。但对于韩国观众来说，比起影片中中国乡村落后的教育环境，对自己小学时代的回忆更贴近他们的心。所以“책상”(书桌)、“서랍”(抽屉)、“동화”(童话)等感性的词汇更适合于译名。

对于这类能够创作出兼顾电影的背景以及内容甚至文化因素并且引发观众兴趣的译名给予最高加分3分，总分是5分。

2. 对意译进行新的尝试的片名

不参照英文译名，不对汉字进行字对字的音译，为帮助观众理解尝试意译的片名加2分，总分为4分。这种尝试是为了能够吸引观众或电影人的视线，更好地传达中国语的含义而进行的崭新尝试。即在进行直译的基础上，加入带有辅助意义的词汇增加新的内涵。

1967, 의리의 사나이 외팔이, 独臂刀, One Armed Swordman

直译这部电影的话，叫作“独臂刀”。但是为了体现电影主人公的侠义胆肝，并帮助说明剧情内容，译名改为“独臂大侠”。虽然不足以说它是具有美学意义的译名，但是却是有助于观众理解本片内容的新颖佳译。

2008, 적벽대전, 赤壁, Red Cliff

这部电影再现了《三国志》中的战争史话。此战役对于一般人而言已颇为有名，即使以“赤壁”原片名进行音译，也足以想象得到是“赤壁大战”。译名加了“大战”两个字更有助于观众对电影的理解。所以虽然只是简单的词汇，却没有沿用“赤壁”的英语片名，而是加了两个字作以辅助说明，为此加了 2 分。

3. 通过直译有助于理解的片名

进行直译的比照字数音译的片名多加了 1 分，总分是 3 分。虽然是比较简单的直译，但是比起照搬字数（借音）而来的片名来说，多了一层思考，付出了更多的努力，所以加了 1 分。

2007, 말할 수 없는 비밀, 不能说的秘密, Secret

这是直接将原片名翻译成韩国语的译名，属于最常见的类型。此部影片的英语片名是“Secret”，比较简单。韩国语译名因直译原片名而来，平淡无过。

4. 通过音译有助于理解的片名

这是最为普遍的韩国语翻译技巧，也很好地反映了中国人在日常生活中经常使用成语的语言习惯。例如：“英雄本色”（借音）直译为“영웅본색”，通过利用中国人喜爱的四字成语，强调异国印象和氛围。受中国人的这种语言习惯影响，韩国电影的译名也常用四个字来进行创作。如：“말죽거리 잔혹사”译为《高校往事》；“귀신이 산다”译为《幽灵鬼屋》；“홍반장”译为《艰难的爱》；“클래식”译为《爱有天意》等。还有美国电影“Transformer”译为《变形金刚》；“Matrix”译为《黑客帝国》；“Speed”译为《生死时速》等等。这种译名因为有了中国语的意境，观众通过音译能够理解电影，就算不加分，也得到了2分的基本得分。

2001, 소림축구, 少林足球, Shaolin Soccer

少林足球中的少林是少林寺的少林，暗示本片与少林寺武术有关。再加上足球两个字，可以推定本片是以和少林武术有关的足球为题材的。

5. 把英文译名直接翻译成韩国语的片名

照英文译名直接用韩国语音标翻译的片名也相当多。Liu Kelan 和 Xiang Wei 曾指出，中国电影偶尔出现的英文片名过分模仿了好莱坞 (Hollywood Blockbuster)大片的翻译模式。[7]

2005, 몽골리언 핑퐁, 绿草地，Mongolian Ping Pong

2008, 포비든 킹덤, 功夫之王，The Forbidden Kingdom

以上两部电影的韩国语片名既没有对中国语原片名进行直译，也没有音译。只是把英文译名直接用韩国语音标标注。即使是站在国内翻译者的立场上，也可以避免把“녹색초원”和“쿵푸의왕”进行直译，创作出更加出类拔萃的片名。当然如果是进行了直译，还可以说勉强完成了翻译的基本任务。只是这两个片名实在毫无概念可言。因此在基本分数线上扣了 1 分，同时判定必须进行监修。

6. 音译后无法理解的片名

对中国语原片名进行音译，也就是（借音）加深理解是最一般的翻译技法。如“金枝玉叶금지옥엽”“至尊无上지존무상”等。

1994, 금지옥엽，金枝玉叶, He’s Woman, She’s Man

1989, 지존무상，至尊无上, Casino Raiders

但是像下列几部影片一样，通过音译以后仍然无法理解其含义的也比比皆是。

---

7 “There are three main problems, the messy and low-quality situation, the argument between alienation and assimilation, and over-imitation to Hollywood blockbusters' translation modes.”

1996, 변검，变脸, The King of Masks

2007, 색,계，色·戒，Lust, Caution

对“변검”原片名直译就是“变化的脸”。用韩国语直译为“변검”的话，很容易让国内观众误以为是“变化无双的剑”，所以是不恰当的翻译。这样可能导致译名和电影内容及主题背道而驰。“색계”也是如此，若光看片名完全不知所云。

7. 误译

误译，顾名思义就是错误的翻译。创作译名后只有译者自己清楚是什么意思，类似的创作应该严加杜绝。我们偶尔还会看到这种致命的片名：

1992, 귀주이야기, 秋菊打官司, The Story of Qiuju

2003, 대척료, 大鸟, Running On Karma

2008, 황시, 黄石的孩子, The Children of Huang Shi

由张艺谋导演、巩俐主演的这部“귀주이야기”是典型的误译范例。原片名“秋菊打官司”(추국이 소송을 걸다)的含义有些模糊，所以就盗用了其英文片名“The Story of Qiuju”。但是，将“Qiuju”翻译成“귀주”简直匪夷所思。

“대척”不是指钓鱼时量鱼用的长度单位“大尺”，而是“大鸟”的意思。所以译名“대척료”和原片名“大鸟”以及英文译名“Running On Karma”所表达的内涵不尽相同，纯属误译。

“황시”实在令人无法明白其意。原片名为“黄石”，中国语发音是“황스(huangshi)”。片名的误译可能源自对中国语发音符号的错误理解。总之，归类到误译范围。

不管这种误译发生的理由是什么，对电影人和电影界来说，都是不应该发生的值得羞愧的事情。

三、结论

21世纪前10年在国内上映或参加电影节的作品共计106部。其中，中国内地制作的电影41部、香港制作的电影53部、台湾制作的电影12部。按照本文设定的评价指标，评出电影译名最优秀的8部，优秀的作品7部，良好的作品27部，普通的14部，须监修的48部，不良的2部。45.2%（48部）被判定须监修。详细数据参见下表：

等级 国家	★★★★★ 最优秀	★★★★ 优秀	★★★ 良好	★★ 普通	★ 须监修	☆ 不良	电影篇数
中国	4	4	14	2	16	1	41
香港	3	3	8	12	26	1	53
台湾	1	0	5	0	6		12
合计	8	7	27	14	48	2	106
占有率	7.5%	6.6%	25.4%	13.5%	45.2%	1.8%	100%

综上所述，韩国电影片名应译得正确、易懂，应适当地采用直译和意译，才能创作出雅俗共赏的片名，使之具有创意和审美双重意义。在韩流入华之际，研究电影译名以确保正确传递其中的民族文化和精神，具有重要意义。

参考文献

[1] 罗敏球.中国映画题目、字幕翻译研究[J]. 中国言语研究14，韩国中国言语学会，2002年. 罗敏球. 中国映画翻译的修辞学——以题目与字幕为主[J].中国学研究30,中国学研究会，2004年.

[2] 南哲镇. 中国映画翻译研究的现状与课题[J]. 中国语文学论集54,中国语文学研究会，2009年.

[3] 李香. 翻译品质评价的现况与课题[J]. 翻译学研究,韩国翻译学会，2010年.

[4] Larose, Robert. Méthodologie de l'évaluation des traductions[J]. *Meta* 41(2):1-24，1998.

[5] Liu Kelan & Xiang Wei. On English and Chinese Movie Translation, La traduction des titres des films Chinois et Englais[J]. *Canadian Social Science*, Vol.2 No.2 June，2006.

On the Translation Quality of Korean Titles of Chinese Movies

Na Mingu

(Hankuk University of Foreign Studies, Republic of Korea)

Abstract: Regardless of who a translator may be or how he may translate, he should not make a mess of the title of a movie, which is a cultural icon of global era. It has been long since Korean movies also took their places in Chinese-speaking countries as a representative genre of Hanryu. The titles of Korean movies are faces that symbolize and represent Korean culture. Likewise, the titles of Chinese movies also imply Chinese culture and tradition. We must make the titles of the movies frequently introduced from other countries accurate and, furthermore, more aesthetic.

If the targets of movie translation are set to Korean titles of Chinese movies and Chinese titles of Korean movies, we — Chinese majors — must provide correct guidelines in regard to such translation tasks and, at the same time, are obliged to promote correct translations by means of performing fair evaluations over the results of translations. In that respect, this paper will suggest proper ways of translation by analyzing the aspects of Korean titles of the Chinese movies — mainland China, Hong Kong, and Taiwan — introduced to Korean international film festivals or released in Korea, by analyzing their aspects, and by determining the quality of existing translations from the viewpoint of an assessor.

Keywords: TQA; Movie Titles Translation; Chinese movies

第五部分

文艺修辞研究

台湾新诗的反讽技巧表现

林于弘
（［中国］台北教育大学）

摘　要： 诗歌的功能除了咏物、抒情、纪行、赠答之外，还具有赞美和讽刺的积极功能。然而对一个讲究“温柔敦厚”的民族来说，直言其恶、直指其非的方式，毕竟很难被大家接受。因此通过间接委婉的方式、包装修饰的手法，以达到积极的讽喻目的，也变成一种不可或缺的表达技巧。台湾新诗发展的历史虽然不长，然而在不同时代与不同族群的创作中，以反讽为主要书写策略的作品也不在少数。本论文以台湾新的反讽技巧表现为分析对象，一方面梳理不同时代的反讽书写意识，另一方面分析不同族群的写作内容，最后整合分析台湾新诗在反讽技巧所达成的成就与所呈现的意义。

关键词： 新诗；修辞；反讽；写作技巧；族群

一、前言

孔子曰：“诗可以兴、可以观、可以群、可以怨。”诗歌的功能除了咏物、抒情、纪行、赠答之外，当然也具有赞美和讽刺的积极功能。郑玄《诗谱序》云：“论功颂德，所以将顺其美；刺过讥失，所以匡救其恶。”欧阳修《诗本义・本末论》亦曰：“诗之作也，触事感物，文之以言。善者美之，恶者刺之，以发其揄扬怨愤于口，道其哀乐喜怒于心，此诗人之意也。”可见从孔子以来的传统文学观，都充分肯定了诗歌的功能。

诗歌虽然兼有颂扬与讽刺的作用，但是对一个讲究“温柔敦厚”的民族来说，直言其恶、直指其非的方式，毕竟很难被大家接受。因此通过间接委婉的方式、包装修饰的手法，以达到积极的讽喻目的，也变成一种不可或缺的表达技巧。所谓“上以风化下，下以风刺上，主文而谲谏，言之者无罪，闻之者足以戒”的精神，始终是诗歌文学极重要的表现方式。

台湾新诗的发展虽然已近百年，但衡诸其艺术表现，究竟能达到何等高度？在此我们所提出的检测标准，是对修辞技巧的细部考察。反讽在讽刺体（Satire）的文学作品中，不仅能运用于陈述，也能运用在事件、情况、结构等方面。而在批判现实的基本创作意图下，是否运用“反讽”手法及运用的优劣，也足以成为台湾新诗发展成就的一项具体指标。

二、反讽的意义与价值

反讽（Irony）也称“反语”“倒辞”“倒反”，是修辞学的一种手法表现。它是把表象和现实相对比，然后采取一种“以是为非、以非为是”的修辞方式；即把正反相互颠倒表现，然后在其中蕴含讽刺的意思。历来台湾论及反讽的学者，也大体有相似的看法，如沈谦即明言：“反讽，即表象与事实相反的方式。[1]”黄庆萱也表示：“粗略地说：反讽指表象与事实的对比。包括：表面上讲的是一件事，骨子里指的是另外一件相反的事；以及事与愿违的矛盾事实。”[2]

另外，张春荣与严蔼珠亦曾归纳：“论及反讽分类，大抵依D.C. Muecke《反讽》（Irony），主要分‘言辞反讽’（Verbal Irony）、‘场景反讽’（Situational Irony）两类。而后亦译称‘词语反讽’、‘结构反讽’；或‘口头反讽’、‘处境反讽’。”[3]

颜元叔曾表示：“一个人的智力经验多寡可由他辨认反讽的能力决定。反讽出现时总有一种冷酷的幽默，作者须有‘不动感情的超然’（Unemotional Detachment），即便感情激动时也只作冷漠的表达。其特有的方式就是在责骂的文字中假作赞赏之意，而在赞赏之中真含责骂。”[4]张春荣也曾归纳：“反讽，偏于语调的表里不一。在欲张故敛、似抑实扬、明褒暗贬中，往往自我调侃，砍散发幽默诙谐的情味。”[5]

反讽（Irony）一语，不必一定有强烈的情感与道德意味。我们可以把“反讽”看成一种认知的原理，“反讽”原理延伸而为矛盾的原理，进而扩张成为语象与语象结构的普遍原理——这便是文字作新颖而富于活力使用时必有的张力。[6]

“反讽”这种文学技巧的高度表现，不仅可以提高文学的艺术性，更能彰显创作者反思的情怀。“反讽”对作者的创作技巧与读者的解读功力，都是相当程度的考验，如果没有足够的文学素养，便不容易明了“反讽”的真义。我们依据“反讽”的运用来评断台湾新诗的成就，也正是基于这样的思维与检证。

三、台湾新诗中不同时代的反讽类型与实践

诗虽有新旧之别，但其作为文学的本质却无差别。五四以后，白话诗逐渐蓬勃兴盛，除了在语言、格律、用韵等形式为主的革命之外，诗所讲究的艺术手法也一如传统，因此反讽精神与技巧的继承与发扬也未曾中辍。而在1950年代以后的台湾

1 沈谦：《修辞学》（上），台北芦洲：空中大学，1991年，第260页。

2 黄庆萱：《修辞学》，台北：三民书局，2002年，第455页。

3 张春荣、严蔼珠：（〈西洋电影的反讽修辞〉），台北大学古典文献学研究所，《第八届中国修辞学国际学术研讨会会议论文集》，台北三峡：台北大学古典文献学研究所，2007年，138页。

4 颜元叔：《西洋文学辞典》，台北：正中书局，1991年，第400页。

5 张春荣：《修辞新思维》，台北：万卷楼图书有限公司，2001年，第97页。

6 卫姆塞·布鲁克斯：《西洋文学批评史》，颜元叔译，台北：志文出版社，1975年，第692页。

诗坛，也有不少精彩的创作，痖弦（1932～）就是堪为代表的个中好手。

赫鲁晓夫是从烟囱里
爬出来的人物
在俄国，他的名字会使森林发抖
他常常骑在一柄扫帚上
吓唬孩子和妇女
他常常穿过高尔基公园
在喷泉旁洗他的血手

但上了年纪的爷儿们
都知道赫鲁晓夫实在是个好人
虽然他拧熄所有教堂里的灯
虽然他以婴儿的脂肪擦靴子
虽然他用穷人的肋骨剔牙齿
但他的的确确是个好人

是的，赫鲁晓夫，一个好人
他的衬衣被农奴们洗得
比古代彼得堡的雪还白
他大口喝着伏特加
他任意说着俏皮话
在夜晚他把克里姆林宫的铁门紧闭
大概是不忍听外面的哭泣
他如此有慈心
他是一个好人

一个好人，是的，赫鲁晓夫
他是患着严重的耳病
因此不得不借重秘密警察
他爱以铁丝网管理人民
他爱以鲜血洗刷国家
除了顺从以外
他从不过问小百姓的事情
他实实在在是一个好人

赫鲁晓夫，好人，是的，好人
他扼紧捷克的咽喉

为的是帮助他们的国家呼吸
他以刺刀和波兰握手
又用坦克
耕耘匈牙利的土地
他的的确确是个好人

没有人把他赶出莫斯科
没有人把他赶出阴冷的红场
所以乔治亚人永远啃黑面包
所以高加索人永远戴枷锁
所以乌克兰人永远流血……
就是因为他们有了像赫鲁晓夫那样
那样好的好人[7]

这是1960年前后的创作，时值抗俄的时代背景，而以反讽作为“政治诗”的表现方式，的确颇为特殊。这首诗的首段，先从正面描写赫鲁晓夫（Khrushchev Nikita）的可怕与恐怖，但是从第二段开始，却不断反复使用“他是一个好人”的相似语句，反讽其种种暴行。诸如“虽然他拧熄所有教堂里的灯／虽然他以婴儿的脂肪擦靴子／虽然他用穷人的肋骨剔牙齿”以及“他是患着严重的耳病／因此不得不借重秘密警察／他爱以铁丝网管理人民／他爱以鲜血洗刷国家／除了顺从以外／他从不过问小百姓的事情”。而叙述对待其附庸国的“善意”行为，则是更为强烈的反讽。如：“他扼紧捷克的咽喉／为的是帮助他们的国家呼吸／他以刺刀和波兰握手／又用坦克／耕耘匈牙利的土地”如今苏联虽然已经解体，但是通过这首诗作的内涵，以及其反讽的表现技巧，我们就可以深刻地体会出，当年苏联民众在极权专制下所受的折磨与苦难。

除了战后迁台的大陆诗人之外，台湾的本土诗人也有以反讽为主轴的书写。如桓夫（陈千武，1922～2012）的《不必·不必》。

不必让给我位置
小姐　车子开得很快
我的终站马上会到达
在这么拥挤的人群里
你怕我这个老头儿
站不住脚吗？

不必，不必可怜我
虽然我的年纪这么大

7　痖弦：《痖弦诗集》，台北：洪范书店，1985年，第161-164页。

但年龄不是经过我的努力获得的
不做过什么
也会自然这样丑老
老并不值得令人尊敬的特权
不必优待我　不必

不必同情我的皱纹这么多
我吃过历史
吐出了好多固有道德
使脸上的皱纹越多越神气
不过我知道　我是一个败家子
连一篇新潮红楼梦也未曾写过

不必　不必捧我场
在这么拥挤的人群里
在这么摇动的公共汽车里
能够站得住脚
我才感到安慰
谁也不必扶我下场
我的终站马上会到达[8]

这首诗在1974年10月发表于《笠诗刊》第63期，描写了一个老头儿搭上公交车却无人让座的窘境，全诗以“不必”为关键词，至于如：“小姐　车子开得很快／我底终站马上会到达”“虽然我的年纪这么大／但年龄不是经过我的努力获得的”“老并不值得令人尊敬的特权”“不必同情我的皱纹这么多”都是非常犀利的刻画。至于两次出现的“我的终站马上会到达”，更有丰富的双关意涵，反讽的意味尤为深长。

迥异于痖弦对于国家世界政治的批判，桓夫回到“小我”，感慨社会个人年迈体衰，以及年轻人一代的冷漠，不同的环境背景造就不同的思维与作品，痖弦和桓夫正好可以互为参照。

到了更年轻的一代，其写作范围更为宽广，取材也可以更为辛辣，面对各式各样的议题，他们有的人主张直接呐喊，也有的人执着于技巧的表现。方群（1966～）即采取“以负为正”的反讽手法，表达出对“核四厂”的不同意见。

给我一座核四厂
让我解决能源缺乏的长期恐慌
厚重的西装才能抵御办公厅的低温冷气

8　陈千武：《陈千武全集》，台中：台中市文化局，2003年，第35-37页。

地方的父老为何还是肝火上扬?
给我一座核四厂
让我发展神秘的武器不再困难
昂贵的外线交易总是不切实际
我们需要一把MIT的核能保护伞

给我一座核四厂
让围标的工程早日开张
让回扣的成数随经济成长
让国际友人对我们的勇气刮目相看
亲爱的全体国民啊!
我们绝对需要核四厂

给我一座核四厂
安全的问题大家不必紧张
高级的官员每年都会来定期巡视探访
除了人为的疏失之外，理论上
是不会发生任何的故障

给我一座核四厂
牺牲小我总是无法避免的创伤
但是只要大家肯稍微点头转向
关于地方建设回馈医疗保健服务的补助金额
一切都可以慢慢慢慢地好好商量

给我一座核四厂
适量的辐射对人体绝对不会有任何损伤
权威的说法必须虔诚信仰
大家的福利才不会受到影响

给我一座核四厂
找不到理由还是得坚持主张
假设的民意虽然有所顾忌
现实的利益绝对不能屈服沦丧
伟大的理想需要你我来共同护航

给我一座核四厂

早早晚晚你们还是得投降
听不听是你可笑的权力
做不做是我一贯的主张
在最后通牒的草稿完成之前
请你请你请你请你请你请你仔细考虑之后
赶快，给我一座核四厂[9]

台湾地狭人稠，又缺乏各种能源，于是“核能”便成为1970年代以后重要的电力供给来源，然而核能所暴露的危险与后续处理问题相当棘手，于是正反双方的意见持续交锋。方群的此诗发表于1994年，以“给我一座核四厂”作为每段开头反复呼告，但是详观其后文的叙述，却都是些“似是而非”的牵强理由，文字表面的意义恰好与诗人心中的意念背道而驰，“给我一座核四厂”真正的涵义却是“不要给我一座核四厂”。这种“以非为是”的表现手法，也正是反讽批判的核心精神。杨昌年曾表示：“方群的诗作艺术，贵在能以客观笔触表现反讽、批判，诗句冷冽，常能予人以清明的鉴照而引发鸣应。”[10] 向阳也表示：“方群的这本集子，更可观的部分在于他对台湾社会、政治现象的嘲弄，而又多半出以反讽方式写作的诗作。”[11]这都是相当深刻的评析与见解。

相对于政治环境封闭的时代，反讽的作用也就相对具有意义。德国作家海涅（Heinrich Heine）就曾表示：“在精神压抑与文章检查制度下的受苦作家，不能违反自己的良心，于是特别需要依赖反讽与幽默。因为这是保有诚实的唯一解决之道，在幽默、反讽的掩饰下最能动人地显示事实。”[12]

四、台湾新诗中不同族群的反讽类型与实践

除了一般的语言写作之外，不同族群的写作修辞表现，也是写作技巧成熟的明确指标。以下将以台湾最主要的三大族群——闽南、客家与原住民为对象，观察其在反讽诗作的具体表现。

以创作台（闽南）语闻名的诗人向阳（1955～），在《土地的歌》这部母语诗集中，开创了写作路途的里程碑。其中如《乡里记事·显贵篇》系列，就是以反讽技巧呈现当时现实状况的浮世绘。

村长伯仔欲造桥
为着庄里的交通收成的运送

9 方群：《给我一座核四厂》，引自《文明并发症》，台北：文史哲出版社，1997年，第130-133页。

10 杨昌年：《七彩与一白——评方群诗集〈文明并发症〉》，引自《文明并发症》，台北：文史哲出版社，1997年，第V页。

11 向阳：《摆荡在美学与生活的两峰间一白——读方群诗集〈文明并发症〉》，引自《文明并发症》，台北：文史哲出版社，1997年，第XI页。

12 林爱华：《浪漫反讽诗人：海涅》，引自《文学中的幽默与反讽》，吴锡德主编，台北：麦田出版社，2003年，第89页。

犹有团仔的教育
溪沙同款算未完的理由

村长伯仔每一家每一户撞门
讲是造桥重要爱造桥
村长伯仔实在了不起
旧年装的路灯今年会发光的存一半
今年修的水管旧年也已经修过两三遍
只有溪埔虽然无溪水也爱有一条桥
有桥以后都市人会来庄里就发达
造桥重要收成运送也顺利

造桥确实重要否则庄里就无脚
出租车会得过不过小包车想欲过不赶过
咱的庄里观光资本有十成便利无半成
造桥重要请村民支持这亦不是为我自己
虽然我有一台金龟车，桥若无造
同款和各位父老步轮过溪埔

村长伯仔讲话算话
每一日自溪埔彼边来庄里走纵
为着全庄的交通村民的利便
他将彼台金龟车锁在车库内
村长伯仔讲是桥若无造他就不开锁
哎！造桥确实重要爱造桥[13]

这首诗从头至尾一直通过叙事者的陈述来强调造桥的重要，但这些“似是而非”的理由却是令人发噱的。表面上村长伯仔“实在了不起”，但实际上是“旧年装的路灯今年会发光的存一半／今年修的水管旧年也已经修过两三遍”，如此低劣的工程质量，在经由陈述者的反讽之后，可以让读者有更深一层的体会。因此“只有溪埔虽然无溪水也爱有一条桥”和“溪沙同款算未完的理由”，都只是种种障眼法，村长伯仔为了自己的那台金龟车，才是最重要的关键。这些地方土豪劣绅的卑鄙作为，实在令人不齿，而通过反讽的手法来对比呈现，意义尤其深刻。张汉良先生就曾针对“村长伯仔欲造桥”提出批评说：“在这种情形之下，读者的认知与叙述者的认知发生冲突，村长伯仔的原形毕露，而‘实在了不起’便成为反讽，张力于焉产生。”[14]这也就是反讽所表现出来的最重要精神。

13 向阳：《村长伯仔欲造桥》，《土地的歌》，台北：自立晚报社，1985年，第39-41页。
14 张汉良、萧萧：《现代诗导读——导读篇三》，台北：故乡出版社，1979年，第277页。

除了上述的作品之外，在《土地的歌》里，类似的反讽诗作还有不少。整体来看，向阳这一系列以方言（台语）为写作工具所完成的社会写实诗，每首诗都是以一位被讽刺的核心主角所架构成的人物素描，在反讽的表现下，这些乡里人物的行为举止乃至心灵活动，都无所遁形了。王灏先生曾说："用闽南语方言来写诗，非始自向阳，但用一种更严肃的态度，更精确的方言语汇，有计划而有系统性的处理方法来经营方言诗，而卓然有成者，则非向阳莫属。"[15]他又说："向阳的方言诗创作，俨然而有着导正的勇气及自期，他想更自觉地使用乡土方言，表达真正的人性，在以乡土为表的同时，更能以文学为质，以人性为本，发而为真正的乡土声音。"[16]在今日台湾新诗发展方兴未艾之际，如何在现实与艺术的天平上，维持动态而和谐的平衡，这确实是每个创作者所必须费心考虑的问题。

客家（Hakka）族群在台湾虽号称有四百万人口，却必须面对漳、泉等强势的闽南族群的同化；而与占总人口2%不到的原住民相比，客家人又缺乏被积极保护的理由。长此以往，不论是政治、经济、文化、艺术，都早已习惯沉默的客家人，也让他们专有的族群文学相对沉默。

在台湾的新文学运动发轫之后，客语文学并未被刻意标举，直到1987年解严以后，才逐渐点燃火种。而在现今的客籍作家中，杜潘芳格（1927～）是其中的佼佼者。

年年都系太平年，年年都作平安戏，
就晓得顺从个平安人，就晓得忍耐个平安人，
围着戏棚下，看平安戏。

个系你兜侪肯佢作个呵！

尽多尽多个平安人
情愿啮菜铺根
K甘蔗含李仔咸。
保持一条佢个老命
看，平安戏。[17]

平安戏是客家传统农业社会非常重要的一项活动，客家乡亲通过这种仪式，除了慰藉一年来的辛劳，更重要的是为了感谢天地神明，并祈求来年的平安。杜潘芳格以客家思维与客语词汇表现这个特属于客家族群的节庆活动，更能彰显诗句的感染力。然而这首《平安戏》的重点并不是在表现平安戏的节庆欢乐，反而是站在一种相背的角度，以反讽的笔法传达在平安戏的背后，其实是经过人为操控的结果。

15 同注14，页157。

16 同注14，页162。

17 杜潘芳格：《平安戏》，《青凤兰波》，台北：前卫出版社，1993年，第131-132页。按：此诗有诸多版本，用字、排版或有差异，此处所据为《青凤兰波》版本。

之所以会造成这种现象，除了过往的政治氛围，诗人也点出客家乡亲是一群只晓得忍耐、顺从、明哲保身的人，借着平安戏的意象，达成其讽刺的目的。

诗言志的传统是毋庸置疑的，不论古典诗或现代诗。同样的，诗的兴、观、群、怨，也有着亘古不变的诉求。因此以文学作为一种思想的传播，或是理念的倡导，必须先谨慎确立自我的定位，才不致迷失错乱。所以“语言是文学创作的主要媒材，作家以他的知识、心性、才情去感受他生活的时空万象，然后把感受、思索之所得，采用他最能驾驭的语言，或最能贴切地表达那个时空万象的语言表现出来。”而综合以上的诗作来看，反讽虽然只是讽刺诗体中的一种修辞技巧，但是它所表现出来的张力（Tension），与对现实的反映与质疑，却呈现了更为深切的省思与批判。

五、结论

新诗是一种新生的文体，在打破诸多限制之后，反而失去客观公允的评判标准，由于“矫枉过正”的情形产生，不少诗作只是平铺直叙的呐喊或控诉，甚至与标语口号无异，如此“鱼目混珠”又有什么价值？文学的内容固然重要，但是其艺术性也不可轻视，因为没有艺术性的文学作品，犹如失去双翼的鸟，根本无法振翅高飞；而修辞技巧的提升，更是文学水平高低的评判标准。

对人、对事，或是在文学的表现上，有时使用正面而直接的指责与批判，倒不如采用旁敲侧击的“反讽”来得实际且有价值。特别是在诗歌文学的表现上，本来就偏重于间接隐讳的方式，“反讽”技巧的产生与应用，都是基于对人、对事、对物等现实问题或理念所产生的深刻感动，再加以“倒反”处理。因此反讽的使用及其技巧呈现，也代表着一种文学的成熟与发展。

龚敏律曾指出：“反讽在西方文化语境中虽然历经了几千年的演变和发展，但是它依然焕发着一种强烈的生命活力。也正是通过这样一种矛盾的、对立的意义，德国浪漫主义、英美新批评、再到20世纪后现代主义，把反讽这一最为基本的内涵不断地扩大、延展、扩充，最终发展为一种反思意识和批判精神，一种主题人格意识和自由价值观念，以及最终对于存在本身的质疑和思考。”[18]由此可见反讽所继承的精神意义与使命。在台湾新诗发展日新月异、方兴未艾的同时，我们通过对台湾新诗在“反讽”技巧方面的考察，可以管窥台湾新诗的实际成就，并给台湾新诗整体的发展提供另一个值得期许的思考方向。

托马斯·曼（Thomas Mann）曾称许“反讽”是“世界上最深刻、最迷人的东西。”[19]反讽不仅可以提高文学的艺术性，更能彰显创作者的反思情怀。进入新世纪以后，台湾新诗以这种技巧来表现的作品日趋兴盛，但仍有待努力。我们相信诗歌必须兼具主题意识与艺术价值前提，以“反讽”作为主体呈现的理念与作品，仍需要所有的创作者去努力加以实践。

18 龚敏律：《西方反讽诗学与20世纪中国文学》，北京：人民出版社，2011年，第83页。

19 D.C. 米克：《论反讽》，周发祥译，北京：昆仑出版社，1992年，第117页。

参考文献

[1] 陈千武. 陈千武全集[M]. 台中：台中市文化局，2003.
[2] 杜潘芳格. 青凤兰波[M]. 台北：前卫出版社，1993.
[3] 范文芳. 方言与文学[A]. 摘自木麻黄的故事[Z]. 新竹：新竹市立文化中心，1993.
[4] 方群. 文明并发症[M]. 台北：文史哲出版社，1997.
[5] 龚敏律. 西方反讽诗学与20世纪中国文学[M]. 北京：人民出版社，2011.
[6] 黄庆萱. 修辞学[M]. 台北：三民出版社，2002.
[7] 林于弘. 台湾新诗分类学[M]. 台北：鹰汉文化企业股份有限公司，2004.
[8] 沈谦. 修辞学（上）[M]. 台北芦洲：空中大学出版社，1991.
[9] 台北大学古典文献学研究所. 第八届中国修辞学国际学术研讨会会议论文集. 台北三峡：台北大学古典文献学研究所，2007.
[10] 王浩威. 重返原乡寻找祖先的名[J]. 联合报·读书人，1997年6月16日.
[11] 吴锡德主编. 文学中的幽默与反讽[M]. 台北：麦田出版社，2003.
[12] 向阳. 土地的歌[M]. 台北：自立晚报社，1985.
[13] 颜元叔. 西洋文学辞典[M]. 台北：正中书局，1991.
[14] 原住民族委员会.（来源：http://www.apc.gov.tw/portal/docList.html?CID=6726E5B80C8822F9，2012.08.31）
[15] 张春荣. 修辞新思维[M]. 台北：万卷楼图书有限公司，2001.
[16] 张汉良、萧萧编. 现代诗导读——导读篇三[M]. 台北：故乡出版社，1979.
[17] D. C. 米克. 论反讽[M]. 周发祥译. 北京：昆仑出版社，1992.
[18] 瓦历斯·尤干. 想念族人[M]. 台中：晨星出版社，1994.
[19] 卫姆塞·布鲁克斯. 西洋文学批评史[M]. 颜元叔译. 台北：志文出版社，1975.

The Rhetoric of Irony in Taiwanese New Poetry

Lin Yuhong

(National Taiwan University of Education, Taiwan, China)

Abstract: In addition to object-chanting, lyrics, travel-recording and reciprocation, new poetry positively functions as praise and irony. However, for an ethnic group of ceremonies, direct critique is not proper and acceptable. Therefore, it is necessary to apply euphemism and rhetoric in order to accomplish the positive function of irony. Although Taiwanese new poetry has a relatively short history, there are a high number of works of irony in different time periods and among different ethnic groups. Accordingly, this paper aims to examine the rhetoric of irony in Taiwanese new poetry. It first addresses the intention of irony in different time periods, and then explores the content written by various ethnic groups. Finally, it analyzes the achievement and meanings of Taiwanese new poetry in light of the rhetoric of irony.

Keywords: new poetry; rhetoric; irony; writing strategy; ethnic group

从《生死疲劳》看莫言的魔幻语言风格与摹绘修辞[1]

江南　孙进芳　张璐

（[中国] 江苏师范大学）

摘　要： 莫言是中国第一位诺贝尔文学奖获得者，是中国当代文坛上东方魔幻现实主义的杰出代表。莫言深得拉美魔幻现实主义精髓，从继承和模仿拉美魔幻文学到后来自成一家的创作，其作品已经成为文坛一道独特的风景。长篇力作《生死疲劳》是“魔幻语言”运用极致的范本，它留给读者深刻印象的不是狂欢恣肆的情节，而是那种流畅奔放、幻影憧憧的语言和激情澎湃的感情倾诉。莫言魔幻语言实验的重要贡献之一是运用摹绘修辞策略，并注重突出摹绘的主观性一面，以此来表现自己沸腾的情感与躁动不安的内心世界。在《生死疲劳》中，莫言一方面利用摹声偏离和摹声隐喻制造充满神秘、诡异、朦胧、空灵的氛围，另一方面利用奔突异样的色彩书写，构造了一个魔幻的意象世界；修辞是一种复杂的话语优化过程，如果从单一的摹绘格方面来解读这部小说未必能切中肯綮，必须结合更复杂的修辞手段——隐喻、象征，并将之放置在魔幻现实主义的语境中加以理解，变异的声、色词语成了宣泄作者现实情感的象征性符号，使读者感受到其弦外之音，色外之色。

关键词： 《生死疲劳》；魔幻语言；摹声摹色；　隐喻象征

魔幻现实主义兴起于20世纪的拉丁美洲，它着眼于客观现实，对其进行荒诞、虚幻的描写，在似假似真、虚实交错中，营造出光怪陆离充满魔幻色彩的世界，在超脱现实的描写中淋漓尽致地剖析现实生活。西方的魔幻现实主义使中国作家开辟了新的写作视角，莫言曾坦言：“魔幻现实主义对我的小说产生的影响非常巨大。我们这一代作家谁能说他没有受到过马尔克斯的影响？”[2] 2012年，莫言获得诺贝尔文学奖，得到的颁奖评语是“他创作中的世界令人联想起福克纳和马尔克斯作品的融合”。[3] 在自己的众多作品中，莫言向诺奖组委会推荐其获奖长篇《生死疲劳》供全世界大学生阅读，“因为这本书比较全面地代表了我的写作风格，以及我在小说艺

1 本文系教育部人文社科基金项目“变异修辞视角下的新时期小说语言”（编号：12YJA740029）阶段性成果。

2 《著名作家莫言做客新浪实录》，新浪网，http://book.sina.com.cn ，2003年8月6日。

3 《莫言让中国教育哑口无言》，搜狐网，http:// learning.sohu.com，2012年，第74期。

术上所做的一些探索”。[4] 在语言上，《生死疲劳》“力争用一种最自由、最没有局限的语言来表达我内心深处的想法”。[5]

对于拉美魔幻现实主义，莫言并不是在一味模仿，《生死疲劳》就是其深得拉美魔幻精髓之后而创作的东方魔幻文学的重头长篇，其独具一格的“魔幻语言”首先是借助奇幻的感觉描写取得的。莫言有着十分敏锐的感受力，“我的长处就是对大自然和动植物的敏感，对生命力丰富的感受，比如我能嗅到别人嗅不到的气味，听到别人听不到的声音，发现比人家更加丰富的色彩”。[6] 阅读《生死疲劳》小说，如同步入了一个色彩斑斓的童话世界，万物莫不有声，万物莫不将自己最丰富的色彩展示给读者。在新时期的文坛或许没有任何一个作家像莫言那样大量使用了摹绘格，摹绘格是对客观事物声、色、形状、景象与情态的描摹，而莫言摹绘手法的使用总带有很强的主观表现色彩，在基本尊重现实的基础上，他常将自己的想象与感觉投射到现实之上，让主体赋予客体以感性形态。鉴于《生死疲劳》具有丰富的解读性（如六道轮回的东方想象力，每一种动物都是人类自身生物本性的一种隐喻；如病态、畸形、怪诞的蓝脸, 西门闹等人物形象，作为一类人物代表具有很强的象征性等），因此，如果从单一的摹绘格出发，其解读未必能切中肯綮, 必须将之放置在魔幻现实主义语境中加以理解。本文拟立足摹声、摹色修辞方式并结合更复杂的修辞手段隐喻、象征，分两大部分简要解读拉美魔幻现实主义对《生死疲劳》“魔幻语言”风格的影响。

一、《生死疲劳》的魔幻语言与摹声偏离及隐喻

在《生死疲劳》小说中，许多变异的象声词语充满力度，穿透纸背, 直抵人的心灵。象声词是对客观世界中存在的各种声音的一种摹拟，其本身就带有变异性。因为“人的耳朵并非录音机，对自然界的声音只能模拟，无法如实记录”。[7]也就是说，象声词这种摹拟本身无法自足，既像又不像，必然有一个艺术变异。在《生死疲劳》中，作者对声音的捕捉主要存在着三种形式：第一种是叠音摹声偏离，反逻辑的描写声音，造成词语搭配的异化，创造一种非现实的荒诞怪异气氛使人有闻声临境之感。第二种是异化摹声词——拟声摹音，循声得情，主要指摹拟某种声响形态，与语言所特有的语义符号相结合使所呈现的声音意象里倾注了人的超验感知与情感色彩，这是最精彩也是最具特殊意味的一种摹声方式。

第三种是指代神秘的摹声“隐喻”。隐喻是“比喻性语言”，在“魔幻化”中扮演了非常重要的角色。对于人类情感的细密微妙、复杂深沉，隐喻借助一定的形象进行烘托、类比、暗示，使象声词语表现出绵长深远的艺术化审美特征。现代语言学家J. R. 塞尔有这样的表述：“我们使用隐喻恰恰是因为没有任何准确表达我们

4《莫言推荐〈生死疲劳〉：全面代表个人写作风格》,《扬子晚报》，2012年10月15日。

5《莫言推荐〈生死疲劳〉：全面代表个人写作风格》,《扬子晚报》，2012年10月15日。

6 [日]大江健三郎、莫言：《文学应该给人光明》，《南方周末》，2003年2月28日。

7 叶国泉、罗康宁：《语言变异艺术》，广东教育出版社，1992年，第53页。

所意谓的字面的表达式。”[8] 由于意义的怪诞、荒唐，读者也许一时体会不出其中的况味，尽管这种况味可能正是作者想表达的。总之，摹声偏离及摹声隐喻在《生死疲劳》小说中的作用非常广泛，概括起来主要表现在以下三方面：

1. 叠音摹声偏离与魔幻文学语言

现代汉语主要构词方法之一是音节的重叠，无论是叠音的单纯词，还是重叠语素的合成词（本文均称叠音词）都可以借声音的复叠，加重形象的摹拟，使繁复的感情与语气得以恰当的表达。在《生死疲劳》中，莫言超常组合叠音摹声词或叠音词反常规地修饰声音，使听觉感官在特定的情境中产生超验感知，营造了荒诞氛围，加强了读者的听觉印象，让读者在品味怪异的言语表达的过程中接受词语背后隐含的真实情感。我们来分析下面两种情况。

（1）AABB式的叠音摹声偏离。莫言通常使用AABB式的叠音摹声格式，其中的叠音词不管是作谓语、定语还是状语，呈现在读者面前的都是对声音的反现实逻辑的描写，造成词语搭配的异化，共同制造出了非现实的表达效果，给读者一种荒诞、怪异、玄妙的感觉。即使侧重于所谓“逼真”的声音摹写，也主要是创造一种非现实的荒诞怪异气氛，使人有如闻其声、如临其境之感。例如：

[1] 我的身体滴油淅沥，落在台阶上……头颅似乎随时会从脖子处折断，冒出一簇簇黄烟……。我焦干地趴在油汪里，身上发出肌肉爆裂的噼啪声，……我听到自己的皮肉发出噼噼啪啪的细微声响，感受着血水滋润焦煳的皮肉……

[2] 吹鼓手们手忙脚乱地跳起来，铿铿锵锵地敲了三通锣鼓，又呜呜哇哇地吹奏起迎宾的乐曲。

例[1]写鬼魂西门闹下油锅后，鬼卒高高举着西门闹，一步步走上通往大殿的台阶。两边的鬼卒撮口吹哨，如同成群的吸血蝙蝠鸣叫。油炸后西门闹的酥脆皮肉被驴血浇灌发出“噼噼啪啪”的声音，这一情节本身就是超现实的存在，带有强烈的魔幻色彩，所以，被滋润的皮肉发出的“噼噼啪啪”的声响实质上却是对神鬼世界一切情景的玄幻描写，是为了通过违反现实，使得魔幻化的形象效果更加具体。例[2]对于“咚咚锵锵”的“三声锣鼓”，作者选用“铿铿锵锵”来修饰，而迎宾的乐曲也不可能是“呜呜哇哇”的，这些脱离常规的描写把吹鼓手的手忙脚乱，场面的滑稽不堪透过听觉意象呈现在读者面前，极具嘲讽意味，同时也为迎宾场面的描写蒙上了荒诞的色彩。

另外，AABB式的叠音词反常规地修饰声音，夸张变形地处理出了非现实的表达效果，为小说蒙上了魔幻色彩。例如“我的声音悲壮凄凉，传播到阎罗大殿的每个角落，激发出重重叠叠的回声”。（《生死疲劳》）“重叠”本是一个双音节动词，通常用来指称事物的层层堆叠，该例通过AABB式的叠音形式把它作为形容词用

8 [美]A. P. 马蒂尼奇：《语言哲学》，牟博、杨音莱、韩林合等译，商务印书馆，1998年版，第840页。

来修饰“回声”，“回声”本是无形的声音，通常给人的听觉印象是“空谷传响，哀转久绝”，即声音响亮、长久不绝才是对“回声”最常规的描写。但是作者却打破了常规的语用规范，用超常短语使得“回声”具有了意念上的实体形态，仿佛在大殿里“层层堆叠”着悲壮苍凉的声音。这看似荒诞，但是通过超验的音响效果，生动形象地向读者展示了“我”的凄惨状态，更衬托了“我”因为冤屈得不到申诉的不屈服状态。

（2）配合比喻意象的叠音摹声偏离。声音的反复渲染之所以具有描绘性，是因为通过节奏的回环表示节奏的加深。但语言的法则并不允许所有的词语和结构都有重叠的资格，即使在能够重叠的大类中，也还有习惯、语义、语序上的种种限制。文学是有韵律的语言艺术，为了追求美的节奏、美的情绪，配合比喻意象，有时不免要“违反”既定的规则，让韵律取代一部分语法，从而形成了叠音摹声偏离。例如：

[3] 北风呼啸，河道中巨冰开裂，发出惊天动地的响声，梆梆梆梆，犹如命运在深夜里敲门。

例[3]中，巨冰开裂的声音一般是“咔嚓咔嚓”，显然“梆梆梆梆”是对冰层断裂声进行了变异描写，而且把ABAB式的重叠语词变成单音节“梆”的连续重叠，通常摹声叠音两次足矣，作者却连用四次，重叠的音节无异于一个声音的气息延缓，重叠的部分在发音上必然轻重相间，自成节奏使语言充满音乐的动感；同时，此例更多的是为了配合“命运在深夜里敲门”这个比喻意象，就为读者构造出了一种魔幻化的氛围，同时正是这种变形的意象，把冬天的干冷、北风的强劲凸显在读者眼前，让读者借助听觉和想象完成了别样的审美体验。

2. 摹声异化与魔幻文学语言

“拟声词不仅包括对客观存在的人和事物声音模拟，还包括对客观上不存在的想象的声音的模拟，即便是对客观实有声音的模拟，主观故意或无意地对它进行放大、缩小、误听等，对修辞主体来说也是常有的事。”[9] 小说《生死疲劳》叙述了地主西门闹经历了六次轮回看破生死的故事，分别从人的角度和牲畜的角度反映了北方农村自建国以来的发展变化。书中对声音的许多摹拟在现实中是不存在的，因为作家的目的不在于真实地传达驴和狗的叫声，而是主观地临时赋予这种声音以某种思想内容，将它变异为具有理性意义的语言，以成为西门闹轮回为牲畜时宣泄情感的真挚话语，即拟声摹音、循声得情，同时为小说情节的展开蒙上一层魔幻色彩。例如：

[4] 呜噢……呜噢……这是我西门闹的女人啊。

[5] 啊噢……啊噢……但是被打到畜生道里的却是我正人君子西门闹。

[6] 闹闹，啊噢；花花，嗯哼；我们永远在一起，天公地母也休想把我们分

9 段曹林：《论拟声词、叹词、语气词皆“摹声”》，《湖北师范学院学报》，2009年第6期。

离，啊噢好不好？嗯哼非常好！

例[4]中，历经困苦轮回为驴子的西门闹（下称西门驴）见到了曾经的二姨太迎春，思绪万千，各种心情和思想汇集交杂一起，当西门驴想去安慰他的二姨太迎春时，才发现自己的声音只是驴叫；其内心情感无法宣泄，更无法用人的话语倾诉，所以它呜咽，它激动，它在内心叫唤迎春："呜噢……呜噢……"，"呜"声似"我"的发音，仿佛是"我噢……我噢……"的叫唤，寓情于声，以声托情。这完全是一种扭曲变形的人的心声，对自己被打入地狱又轮回为驴的荒诞做法的无奈、惆怅和恐惧。例[5]中，接触迎春之后，进一步看清现实的西门驴内心的仇恨和冤屈的种子茁壮成长，身为驴子的西门闹需要大声嚎叫、宣泄："啊噢～～啊噢～～"，叹词"啊"声音响亮，发音较长时能表达出悲痛或忧伤的情感，而"啊噢"连用后都是开口呼音节，发出的声音都是响亮的，摹拟西门驴的吼叫并宣泄出西门闹极度的愤怒和不甘。例[6]通过摹拟两头驴的不同的对话声音，真正升华了驴子的语言。"啊噢好不好？嗯哼非常好！"情从声发、声由情生，具有魔幻色彩的一问一答，既是对前几次驴子言语表达的证明，也是对西门驴和花花内心情感的完美描绘。

现实中驴子的叫声类似"欧啊～～欧啊～～"或是"嗯昂～～嗯昂～～"，西门闹后来接受了驴子身份，作为一只即将践行自我价值的公驴，西门驴第一次发出的自豪叫声是"昂噢～～昂噢～～"，"昂"的发音粗重又响亮，表达出驴声的欢快。莫言对驴子的叫声多次进行变声摹写，正是通过异化摹声词，制造出一种荒诞怪异的表达效果，同时也把西门闹到西门驴的思想情感变化恰当地表达出来。在对话新作《生死疲劳》时，莫言说："第一轮转世为驴，但他认为他仍是一个人，对人世的仇恨时时控制着他，他以人的目光体察人间的一切，即使是驴还是以人的思考方式来介入一切……但转世为狗时，他已得意于作为主席狗的身份，狗性越来越浓，控制着他的其他所有行为。"[10] 例如：

[7] 哐！哐！哐！——我的叫声震得梧桐叶子哗哗响，吓得南邻家院里那两只鸵鸟嘎嘎叫，我的意思是说：没——问——题——！

例[7]是狗小四对蓝开放的回答，在这里，莫言不仅采用对话的方式，把狗作为言语交际的一方，而且对狗的叫声进行了变形。狗叫声应该是"旺！旺！旺！"但是为了符合小说描写的荒诞性，作者却选用"哐！哐！哐！"相比较"旺"的发音，"哐"为平声调，多了送气过程，音响效果变得粗重雄壮。此时，转世为狗的西门闹以大声回答的方式把急于表现、意欲让对方信任的心理活动活灵活现地表现了出来。

3. 摹声隐喻与魔幻文学语言

隐喻作为一种思维方式不能算是比喻，但是"在传统文学作品中隐喻通常是以修辞的方式出现的，它更多的是停留在语言的层面上，有着相对稳定的本体与喻体

10 曹雪萍：《莫言VS李敬泽：向中国古典小说致敬——对话新作<生死疲劳>》，《新京报》2005年12月29日。

的关系。"[11] 在《生死疲劳》中，存在一种没有明确本体、喻体且指代神秘的"摹声隐喻"，总之，是在没有真实声音提供摹拟的情况下一种人为想象的声响，这些主观臆想出的声音或许是为了营造虚幻、神秘的氛围，或许是借突兀的声响摹拟人对特定场面的心理感受，或许是在揭示一种声音和某些象征意义之间的关系。莫言小说语言正是借助了"摹声隐喻"的力量才充分显示了魔幻艺术的效果，下面就以最具代表性的"魔幻意象"的建构来说明"摹声隐喻"在其魔幻语言的构筑中所起到的特殊价值。例如：

[8] 金色的草帽划着美丽的弧线飞向已经远去的月亮，一曲动人的草帽之歌的旋律在空中轰然响起：啦啦啦～啦呀啦啦呀啦～～妈妈的草帽飞啦～～妈妈的草帽飞向了月亮～～啦呀啦啦呀啦～～

[9] 啦呀啦～～啦呀啦啦呀啦～～妈妈的草帽丢了～～猪们有的拍爪子，有的跺脚，合着节拍，齐唱草帽之歌。

[10] 啦呀啦～～啦呀啦啦呀啦～～三哥，好样的～～我感到火烧心头，恨不得扑上去……但依然头晕。

例[8] [9] [10]中"啦呀啦～啦呀啦啦呀啦～～"的草帽之歌是凭空产生的，并且每次出现都配有不同的场面描写，或是群猪起舞歌唱，或是西门猪与刁小三（猪名）的打斗，或是西门猪的心里自白等等。总之，草帽之歌没有明确的意指对象，充满难以明示的隐喻意味："啦呀啦～啦呀啦啦呀啦～～"成了冥冥之中的一种预言、一种指引或者是暗示，使小说情节扑朔迷离、变幻莫测，给人一种神秘莫测的感觉，充满神秘和魔幻色彩。莫言或许是有意识地规避了明确的意指对象，用神秘的隐喻流畅地描绘出猪群的动态，西门猪和刁小三的打斗场面及各自的心态，使整个叙述话语充满了神秘虚幻及陌生化的意味。

"真正的艺术就是一种原始语言，它既唤醒情感，又引起呈现，而不带来概念性意义。"[12] "有时我们感到我们准确地知道隐喻所意谓的东西，然而却不能确切表述一个字面的释义语句，因为没有任何传递它意谓的东西的字面表达式。"[13] 中国古代的先贤也早已注意到言不能尽意或只可意会不能言传的矛盾，"恒患意不称物，文不逮意。盖非知之难，能之难也"（语出陆机）。隐喻表达思想感情不是荡漾在字面上，而是蕴藏在字里行间，蕴藏在言外之意的空间，使语言表现出绵长深远的诗性的审美特征，从而揭示出文本的内在意味和深层意蕴。

二、《生死疲劳》的魔幻象征与主观色及摹色的语义偏离

色彩词语作为视觉表象的信号而被作家广泛运用于文学语言中，用以描绘对象的某种特征，实现其指称功能。但许多作家在指称对象的需要之外，大量使用色彩词，就像印象派绘画一样，有意通过色块的涂抹去表达一种情绪与感受；这种涂抹

---

11 洪志纲：《守望先锋——兼论中国当代先锋文学的发展》，广西师范大学出版社，2005年，第120页。

12 [法]米. 杜夫海纳：《审美经验现象学》（上），韩树站译，文化艺术出版社，1996年，第167页。

13 [美]A. P. 马蒂尼奇：《语言哲学》，牟博、杨音莱、韩林合等译，商务印书馆，1998年，第810页。

又通常是夸张的、变形的，在许多情况下它们的功能仅仅就是为了创造某种情绪氛围，根本就不是及物的，根本就不指涉对象的某种外部特点。正所谓“以我观物，物皆着我之色彩”[14] 在先锋作家中，莫言对颜色词似乎有一种特殊的偏爱与倚重，他对色彩的超常感知和攫取极具个性特点。其代表作《生死疲劳》用奔突异样的色彩书写，构造了一个魔幻感觉的意象世界，许多颜色词的使用不再具有传统意义上的指代，色彩词语往往带有某种神秘的暗示和象征意味，变异的色彩词语成了宣泄作者现实情感的象征性符号，让读者在现实与虚幻之间徘徊。

从中国古典小说中吸取经验，莫言将西方的“魔幻现实主义”和中国古代“志怪”传统结合，《生死疲劳》对人物的摹绘描写许多都兼有象征的意义，即其一方面确实是在摹写人物，但另一方面又明显具有一定的象征意义。如小说中全中国唯一的单干户蓝脸心智极其偏执而奇特，这个怪诞形象的怪诞言行就是一种纯粹的人类孤独的象征。约翰·拉塞尔曾说：“色彩对直觉来说是一条热线，色彩所能传递的信息甚至优于语言传递的信息。”[15] 所谓语义偏离，也可以说是搭配的偏离，因此，从变异的角度来看，《生死疲劳》中许多超常搭配的颜色词表现的不是事物原色的物理意义，也不仅是体现汉民族文化一般的象征意义，而多是具体语境下的临时变义。莫言曾经谈到：“变异的色彩，是作家情感的印记和艺术灵感爆发的契机，是他对历史和现实深深思考的结果，也是最简便、最自然、最有艺术效果和艺术表现力的途径。”[16] 结合《生死疲劳》对颜色的铺展描写，下面从三个方面试作分析。

1. 涂抹色块于景物以凸现情绪感受，实现魔幻文学象征

物理世界的颜色词同文化世界的颜色词具有不同的品格色彩，而“色彩作为文化的载体往往代表着某种象征，承担着特定的含义”。[17] 因此，颜色词具有浓郁的象征意味，色彩语言就成了特定情绪的象征性符号。在莫言小说中，那些带有夸张变形特点的色彩词伴随着他对生活的原初印象从他笔下汩汩流出，那些色彩浓重的画面通常既是他某种主观情绪的反映，同时又是作品整体氛围的暗示与象征。莫言曾说过：“我的家乡有红高粱但却并没有血一般的浸染，但我要她有血一般的浸染，要她淹没在血一般茫茫的大水中……那血红中第一位的是你自由的感觉，你千方百计地描述，千方百计地渲染，不过是为了你心中的那个真实。”[18] 在整个色谱中，红色无疑最具有刺激性，它令人振奋与激动。先锋作家，尤其是莫言笔下的月亮、太阳常为大红色，具有血腥之灾的红色与自然现象相结合，在刻画环境的同时，营造了一种非比寻常的气氛与表达一种象征义。请看《生死疲劳》小说的描写:

[11] 这月亮同样是胖大丰满，刚冒出水面时颜色血红，仿佛从宇宙的阴道中分

14 王国维：《人间词话》，上海古籍出版社，1998年，第26页。

15 [美]约翰·拉塞尔：《现代艺术的意义》，陈世怀、常宁生译，江苏美术出版社，1996年版，第60–61页。

16 殷相印：《莫言小说色彩词的超常运用谈片》，《修辞学习》2000年第1期。

17 [日]滝本孝雄：《色彩心理学》，成同社译，科学技术文献出版社，1989年版，第73页。

18 赵玫：《淹没在水中的红高粱——莫言印象》，《北京文学》，1986年第8期。

娩出来的赤子，哇哇地啼哭着，流淌着血水，使河水改变颜色。

例[11]写道，在猪十六和小花猪坎坷的逃亡路上，月亮成了“从宇宙的阴道中分娩出来的赤子，哇哇地啼哭着，流淌着血水”，这是通过比喻制造出荒诞恐怖的声音和色彩，制造出月亮的魔幻意象。这轮怪异的“血红”月亮从某种意义上昭示着一种灾难与不祥，中国人一向认为自然界的反常现象会意味着灾难来临。在中国传统文化中，月亮、太阳都是经常用于承载主体思想感情的意象，蕴含丰富的意蕴。而《生死疲劳》中“很少写到太阳，但月光下的世界写得极为诡魅华美，白昼属于人和历史，黑夜属于灵，属于大地”。[19] 与莫言的这种写法类似，前苏联作家肖洛霍夫的小说《静静的顿河》中，主人公麦列霍夫在阿克西尼亚死了以后，太阳在他的眼中也变成了黑色。

2. 敷色着彩于人物以凸现色外之色，实现魔幻文学象征

文学作品描写中心是人，小说常常以色彩描摹人物肖像、心理，塑造在特定的社会背景下，被压抑、被扭曲的人物形象，同时利用人物的面部色彩变化来表现其心理活动。莫言善于运用色彩词对人物绘色赋形，并在浓墨重彩的色彩意象中艺术地埋进了一层深义，“透过色彩的表面，可见色外之色，可闻弦外之音，从而形成他自己的一种色调和追求，实现文学象征”。[20] 如描摹人物的蓝色词意象较为独特，作为中国人，自然生长的蓝色脸庞，蓝色胡子、蓝色眼眶实属罕见，再加上流出的蓝色泪水及鬼火样的蓝色月光恰能烘托小说中诡异神秘的气氛。例如：

[12] 我瞥着两个鬼卒的蓝脸，恍然觉得他们很像是舞台上浓妆艳抹的角色，只是人间的颜料，永远也画不出他们这般高贵而纯粹的蓝脸。

[13] 我打了一个滚爬起来，举爪抹了一下鼻子，爪子沾着蓝色的血迹。我低声骂：“你奶奶个熊！”刁小三打了一个滚爬起来，举爪抹了一下鼻子，爪上沾着蓝色的血迹。它低声骂道：“你奶奶个熊！”

[14] 你爹手扶着门框，蓝色的脸抽搐不止，蓝色的胡子哆嗦不停，蓝色的泪水流出蓝色的眼眶。中秋的月亮已经放出蓝色光辉。

蓝色是语言中基本颜色词之一，其最易联想到的三个词为：典雅、理性、悠闲，正如莫言在例[12]中所言，蓝色是“高贵而纯粹的”。该例选自小说第一部第一章《受酷刑喊冤阎罗殿 遭欺瞒转世白蹄驴》，背景为：西门闹大闹阎王殿，追问真相、捍卫清白为冤死抗诉，受尽煎熬而被阎罗王放回人间，于是鬼卒送“我”到人世轮回：为驴，为牛，为猪，为狗，为猴，最终为人。鬼卒本身的非现实性决定了他们拥有高贵蓝脸皮的虚拟性，尽管两位鬼卒名叫“牛头”和“马面”，但他们并不像我们在有关阴曹地府的图画中看到的那样，真的在人的身躯上生长着牛的头颅和马的脑袋。他们的身体结构与人无异，所不同的只是他们拥有闪烁着蓝色光芒的

19 曹雪萍：《莫言VS李敬泽：向中国古典小说致敬——对话新作〈生死疲劳〉》，《新京报》2005年12月29日。

20 徐怀中：《有追求才有特色——关于〈透明的红萝卜〉的对话》，《中国作家》，1985年第2期。

肤色。例[13] 借畜眼看人道，融现实与虚幻于一体。靠劳动致富、智慧发家并好善乐施、有万贯家财的西门闹，冤死后魂魄离体依次附着在驴、牛、猪、狗、猴以及大头儿身上，无论是重生为驴、牛、猪还是狗和猴，始终保持着理智，都在冷眼旁观，或是讽刺挖苦嘲笑着人类的无耻和愚蠢，所以轮回的“动物”具备蓝色的品质，体内燃烧的火焰是纯蓝的，这种品质延伸到托生动物身上，流出的血也是蓝色的，这是因为动物缺少人类的钩心斗角，没有物质欲望。例[14]中的“蓝脸”是小说主人公之一，因为半边蓝脸而得名，蓝脸是冷漠、凶悍、莽撞、执拗的，虽然“蓝脸”木讷，没有远大的理想，缺乏进步的思想，但是他可以说是整部小说人物中，最单纯、最没有功利心和物质欲望的人，他是唯一固守内心信念、固执地坚持单干的农民，无论出于何种风气下、何种运动中，内心的一份坚持始终不变，而这也未尝不是一种纯粹，一种冷静和理性，是一种大智若愚，而拥有蓝色特征的人或物都不约而同地具有冷静、理性的特征。同时，狂热和疯癫也是小说中具有蓝色特征的人物身上或多或少具有的性格标签，用蓝脸儿子蓝解放的话说：“我爹的存在，既荒诞，又庄严；既令人可怜，又让人尊重。”[21]

黄色类色彩词在人类的心理联想上，同灿烂、快乐、权威和希望等美好的象征意义密不可分。在传统文化中，“黄色”寓意着高贵与神圣，代表了华夏民族五千年的古老文化传统，但在莫言笔下，描摹人物时却象征着环境的恶劣、现实的邪恶、人性的肮脏和鄙俗。虚伪、贪婪的黄瞳是《生死疲劳》中令人十分讨厌的一个角色，他“忘恩负义”“满肚子坏心眼”等等，没做一件为人称好的事。在《生死疲劳》中“黄色”似乎成了对黄瞳性格的定义，黄瞳似乎就是“黄色”的代表，而他卑劣的人性也就成了“黄色”或“金黄色”的象征。例如：

[15] 这小子黄头发黄面皮，黄眼珠子滴溜溜转，似乎满肚子坏心眼。

[16] 他的金黄的瞳仁那么亮，宛若两颗金星星。

[17] 黄瞳在洪泰岳面前点头连连，脸上全是虚笑，两只细眯的眼睛射出金光，咧着嘴，龇着黄牙，露出紫色的牙龈。

例[15] [16] [17]中，黄瞳皮肤是黄的，牙齿是黄的，头发也是黄的。此外他的眼珠是黄的，且瞳仁金黄：“宛若两颗金星星”“射出金光”，虽然中国人的肤色是黄色，但是“黄色”不可能是人物身体各个器官的颜色，显然这种描写是超越现实的，明显带有虚幻、荒诞感觉色彩的，而这种色彩的怪诞描写使“黄色”成为卑劣、贪婪和虚伪的象征，带给读者新奇的视觉印象。

3. 颜色词的语义偏离与魔幻文学象征

所谓摹色的语义偏离，也可以说是颜色词搭配的偏离。色彩本来是视觉形象，用于视觉描写是其正途，如果用于听觉、嗅觉、味觉、触觉，那显然是一种知觉的“移位”；而如果将色彩词用之于某种抽象的思想、情感、意念，则是一种表意领

---

21 莫言：《生死疲劳》，作家出版社，2012年，第188页。

域的“移位”，即将一种表意领域中的词用于另一个表意领域中。总体来说，它们都偏离了特定词语本身的意思，本文概括地称之为“语义偏离”。在《生死疲劳》中，色彩词的这种语义偏离很多，使用起来也很有特点，主要有以下两种情况：

（1）魔幻语言与颜色词的知觉移位。莫言语言感觉中有色彩，而且有极具个性的色彩感受。因此，《生死疲劳》小说世界中的听觉、触觉都有色彩。例如：

[18] 迎春的惨叫像一条银蛇在月光中飞舞，而迎春的身体却像一团人形的棉絮一样往后倒去。你们不要以为俺是一头猪就不懂得什么叫高速摄影，呸，这年头，谁还不能当个导演呢！

[19] 你们的嘴巴和鼻孔里喷吐着粉红色的热气，你嘴边的毛上、我爹的胡子和眉毛上，都结着霜花。

例[18]“迎春的惨叫”在物理世界中是客观存在的，没有具体的形态，也没有颜色，只能通过听觉感知，无法看到。但上例中，莫言故意通过喻体“银蛇”将色彩加之于声音，由无形到有形，并且借助虚构出来的“飞舞”意象表达出声音的传播状态，为小说情节涂抹上了玄幻的色彩。其效果，可以说是一种比喻性通感，也可以说是一种极富创意的诗性连接。从作者的角度看，是要表达对声音的丰富感受，而对读者来说，则可以创造陌生化的阅读效果。例[19]为了充分调动读者的知觉，使之更深刻地感受作品主题和人物的情感，莫言还以色彩词来描写触觉。如该例中的“粉红色”似乎是没有实用价值的冗余信息，剥夺了话语的实用性，但在虚拟的审美意向中，在这个尖锐刺眼的早晨，牛嘴巴和鼻孔里喷吐的“粉红色”更突兀地显示其感性特征——温馨、浪漫、美好，给主人公身心带来了措手不及。读者能够感知到人物微妙的心理：“西门屯通往公社与县城的电话线被大雪压断，那时县里的有线广播使用的是电话线路，电话不通，广播也就成了哑巴。道路被雪封住，报纸更没人来送。西门屯成了与世隔绝之地。”[22] 色彩与温度的联结形成的色彩冷暖感，实际上是人对色彩的情绪感受。以上知觉的移位还是在知觉内部，其实《生死疲劳》中的“语义偏离”，更多的则是跨越某个领域或范畴进行的表意领域移位。

（2）魔幻语言与颜色词的表意领域移位。“在情感强烈时，人们对人和事物的认识往往很难出现原来的客体，而是由新的一种变形客体来代替。”[23] 大自然是客观的、冷漠的，但是人可以赋予自然以情感，用移情的方式创造人化的自然，在这个方面，色彩词在莫言手里发挥了很大的作用，作者可以跨越某个领域或范畴，用色彩词突显事理的某种特殊状态以表达一种情绪与感受。例如：

[20] 几近全圆的月亮面孔青白，好像因水银中毒而死者的脸孔，同样青白而阴森的光辉照耀着凝滞的水面。

[21] 我看着半个月亮爬上来，红红的脸膛，像一个怕羞的农村大姐。

小说《生死疲劳》通过各种动物的眼睛观察世界、体现了魔幻现实。轮回的动物是假的，不存于现实，而动物眼中的形形色色，五味陈杂的大小诸事却是活脱脱

22 莫言：《生死疲劳》，作家出版社，2006年，第151页。

23 骆小所：《艺术语言学》，云南人民出版社，1996年，第28页。

的真事，“假作真时真亦假”，徘徊于真实与虚境之间。在金龙的婚宴上，西门猪眼中的月亮又大又圆而且是那样的多情：高密东北乡西门屯村的杏园里成了地球上最佳的赏月地点。当西门猪决定与一群人决一死战，为已被杀害的同胞复仇时，它眼中的月亮又大不相同了，所以在例[20]中，西门猪眼中的月亮变成了阴森的、有毒的、死了般的。例[21]中，同一物体——月亮的变化，是因为主体不同（西门猪换成狗中领袖西门狗），环境不同、心境不同，西门狗初来乍到，新环境、新主人、新任务，月亮的红脸膛是此时西门狗在害羞心情之下，眼中的主观色。与西方印象派类似，莫言笔下的色彩大多带有强烈的主观印象。作者不循常规，以甲物的色彩着色于乙物，或给无色物着色，“青白面孔的月亮”“红脸膛的月亮”，这些均是主观印象之色而非客观物象之色，这样的主观色彩描写给读者造成一种视觉与常识的强烈反差，使其内心受到震撼之余，领略到作者深刻的用意与独特的象征。

综上所述，莫言从继承和模仿拉美魔幻文学到后来自成一家的创作，《生死疲劳》是一部有中国特色的魔幻小说。“重建宏大叙事确实是每个作家内心深处的情结。所有的作家都梦想写一部史诗性的皇皇巨著，而我既不想落入窠臼，又舍不掉情结，还想独树一帜，所以《生死疲劳》只是另辟蹊径的一种努力”。[24]《生死疲劳》努力开掘着中国的魔幻资源，荒诞的故事情节、离奇的主观想象、夸张和变形的感觉描写，奇崛的比喻充斥其间，带有穿透力的似真非真、似假非假的荒诞语言将社会现实生活笼罩在魔幻氛围中，营造出荒诞怪异魔幻化的审美效果，使读者处于现实与虚幻之中。《生死疲劳》已形成蔚为大观的魔幻系统即“感觉魔幻小说”；从某种意义上说，幻影憧憧的语言正是莫言在这部小说中艺术上最突出的贡献。

莫言是一位高度重视语言创新与技巧的世界级作家，他拥有新时期最具个性特点的小说语言，他说过：“一个写作者所使用的语言，应该是属于他自己的、能够使他和别人区别开来的语言。”[25]“好的小说也应该提供丰富的解读性，越是让评论家无法打包、归类的小说，就越是好作品”。[26]立足修辞学作解读，既有利于透视和把握莫言中小说中语言“魔幻”修辞的规律、模式和动因，以及由此体现出来的作家的魔幻语言风格，有助于更好地为修辞理论研究提供新佐证，这正是文学作品语言研究的新方向。作为魔幻现实主义的一个典范性文本，《生死疲劳》在很大程度上代表了中国魔幻语言实验小说的最高成就，而这位作家对语言使用的任何一个单项突破都很有价值，对其作任何新的探讨都是很有意义的。

---

24 曹雪萍：《莫言VS李敬泽：向中国古典小说致敬——对话新作〈生死疲劳〉》，《新京报》2005年12月29日。

25 莫言：《坚持独立与个性》，第二届“华语文学传媒年度杰出成就奖”颁奖典礼获奖感言，2004年4月18日。

26 《等待被作品撞倒的那一刹那——毕飞宇访谈》，《河北日报》2005年12月2日。

Study on Mo Yan's Magical Language Style and Isography Rhetoric: Taking *Life and Death Are Wearing Me Out* as Example

Jiang Nan　Sun Jinfang　Zhang Lu
(Jiangsu Normal University, China)

Abstract: Mo Yan, the first Chinese winner of the Nobel Prize for literature, is the outstanding representative among oriental magic realists in China's contemporary literary world. He grasps the essence of Latin American magical realism, inherits from it, imitates it and has eventually developed his own unique style. The masterpiece *Life and Death Are Wearing Me Out* serves as the modal for fantastic magical language usage, which impresses readers not with unconstrained plot, but the most inner feelings, passionate pouring and fluent and imaginative language. One important contribution of Mo Yan's magic language is the using of G painted rhetorical strategies, highlighting the subjective side and expressing their boiling restless emotional world. In this novel, he on the one hand creates mysterious, strange, hazy, and ethereal atmosphere by making use of onomatopoeia deviation and onomatopoeia metaphor, and on the other hand constructs a magical imagery world via marvelous color writing. Rhetorical discourse is a complex optimization process, only interpreting the aspects of the novel from a single copy painted areas may be hard to get to the point, it must be combined with a more complex rhetorical device of metaphor, symbolism.what's more, it must be placed in the context of magical realism to be understood. The sound and color words variations become symbols of author's emotional catharsis, so that readers are able to feel the overtones and color outside.

Keywords: *Life and Death Are Wearing Me Out;* magical language; onomatopoeia G color, metaphoric

方言在马来西亚华文小说中的表达效果
——以原上草小说为例

潘碧丝
([马来西亚]　马来亚大学)

摘　要: 马来西亚华文文学（简称马华文学）自1919年以来，在当地生根、发展，形成非常浓郁的地域色彩。华语虽然是马来西亚华人的沟通语，但是大部分当地华人还是以方言为母语。因此，华人在沟通时，华语与多种方言交叉使用的现象非常明显。这种现象亦反应到了文学作品当中。原上草的小说运用了大量的方言土语，尤其是客家方言，使其作品呈现浓郁的客家风味。小说中方言土语的适当运用不仅强化和凸显了作品的主题，也在塑造人物形象方面起到了一定的修辞效果。方言土语的运用造就了原上草小说的独特性和地域性，也显示了马华文学发展的历程。
关键词: 马来西亚；马华文学；小说；原上草

原上草，原名古德贤（1922～1999），出生在广东省梅县，4岁时随父母到马来亚（今马来西亚），从此在当地发展。原上草只受过初中教育，当过文员、小贩、教师等。1959年后，先后担任《学生周报》、《建国日报》、《马来亚通报》、《写作人》季刊等主编。1978年，马来西亚华人写作人协会成立，原上草被选为第一届会长。他从1941年开始写作，写作生涯长达50年，所用笔名除原上草外，还有沙风、古迹、虱虫等。原上草善于写散文和小说，结集出版的散文有《万家灯火》（1976）和《原上草散文集》（1991）；小说则有《韭菜花开》（1961）、《诗人方如梦》（1963）、《房客》（1964）、《迷途》（1975）、《水东流》、《榴莲风雨坑》（2001）。由于作品丰富，对马华文坛贡献巨大，1998年，原上草荣获第五届马华文学奖。

2012年6月，马来西亚华人作家协会与台湾秀威资讯出版原上草小说选集《水东流》。编者从原上草的4本小说集中选出了20篇小说，结集出版。这些作品是：

篇名	小说集/出版年份
韭菜花开	《韭菜花开》（1961年）
搬家	
疯子	
带工	
后来娘	
五块钱	
开张大吉	

（续）

篇名	小说集/出版年份
栽培	《房客》（1964年）
房客	
蒙面人	
冷暖人间	
诗人方如梦	《迷途》（1975年）
迷途	
浮沉	
妈妈哭	《水东流》（1981年）
水东流	
一夜	
一缕青烟	
微尘	
不了局	

原上草的小说以写实著称，对小市民困苦生活的描绘和对社会问题的探讨是他小说的特色之一。原上草对他成长和生活过的地方，发生的事情和人物所面临的问题都了如指掌，通过小说娓娓道来，逼真而写实。他的小说带有强烈的乡土味和地域色彩，充分反映了当时的社会现象。然而，其小说最大的特色还是在于语言的应用。原上草的小说蕴含丰富的方言土语，特别是客家方言。他把生活中的经验和积累起来的客家方言，运用在小说中，使他的小说客家味十足。

乡音乡语：不变的客家方言

原上草4岁随父母移民到马来西亚，在当地成长，接受教育。和其他第二代、第三代华人作家一样，他的作品体现了马来西亚本土的面貌，更具特色的是作品里运用了大量的客家方言，字里行间穿插了许多客家方言土语，营造出浓郁的客家氛围和当地客家村的生活面貌和特征，形成小说语言的一大景观。这与他的生活有密切的关系。早期南来华人的居住模式与他们语言籍贯息息相关。为了互相照应，相同语言籍贯的人会聚居在一起，因此形成了不同的方言群。另一方面，方言群的形成也与他们的工作有联系。那些已经居住在当地的移民，一般会把同乡招揽过来工作，形成同样籍贯的人进行同样的工作。比如闽南籍贯多集中在城市，进行商业活动；广东人与客家人则多集中在矿区或橡胶园从事劳动工作。这样的居住和工作模式使得这些华人都以祖籍地的方言交谈，即使是其他籍贯方言的人，也会受到该地方的主流沟通交际方言的影响而学习并运用该方言。

大部分的学者认为马来西亚的新式华文教育可以从1904年开始算起，并认为1919年五四运动后华语替代了方言作为马来西亚华人的华文教育媒介语。然而，在40～50年代的马来西亚，老一辈的华人多数没有受过教育，即便有也是在方言私塾里接受方言教育，只会说方言，因此方言依旧是许多华人家庭的沟通交际语。而方言群之间的交流，也以方言为主，或者方言与华语交叉运用，形成非常独特的语用现象。小说创作最能反映社会现象，也最能体现人民的生活习性，因此方言的使用渗透在文学作品的字里行间，使得小说呈现出非常浓郁的方言色彩。

原上草祖籍广东梅县，是地道的客家人。在他成长、生活的那个年代还是以方言作为主要交际语，方言群的居住模式依旧非常明显。他从小与客家人生活在一起，说客家话，用客家话思考。因此，客家人的生活习俗、歌谣小调、语言习惯早已深深地融入他的生活中。曾有一位作家说过，地域文化是作家的精神母乳，而方言也是这些作家的母语，因此他们的作品都离不开地域文化和方言。同理，作为一个写实作家，原上草的小说背景离不开他的生活，小说主题是发生在他身边的事，而小说的人物也与他身边的人息息相关。他熟悉作品中的人物，也熟悉该族群的风俗习惯，更熟悉作品里人物所用的语言—客家话。他把这些他最熟悉的元素都运用到作品中，他曾经说过："我有一个原则，创作小说必须要从真人真事入手，写起来才觉得兴致盎然。所以收在我这本集子里的各篇小说，不是我亲眼见到和经历到的事实，就是从旁的地方听来的真人真事。如《水东流》中的主角，本来就是我当年的一名同事。《微尘》中的崩牙朱邓几个角色，我家乡老一辈的人，无不认识的。《爸爸怨》中的老人家是我所熟悉的叔辈人物，他的不幸遭遇是一位老朋友告诉我的。"[1] 因此，他的小说是生活的真实写照，从小说背景到人物的塑造，再到语言的运用，都是他最熟悉不过的元素，而这一切决定了他的小说话语以及叙事视角的选择。客家方言土语的大量运用，使他的小说有着强烈的客家味道，给人留下深刻的印象。

翻开原上草的小说，客家方言土语的运用俯拾皆是。丰富的客家语言资源，大大增强了小说语言的艺术表现力，也让人感受到了客家语言的魅力。很多时候，原上草是直接引用客家方言，引领读者进入故事语境，并渲染环境氛围，生动和深入地刻画小说人物和情景，显现了客家人的行为方式和思维观念。

> "三次？好家伙！三次？——阿龙古！死畜生！是不是？是不是？ 你行过来，快！"（《韭菜花开》）
>
> "加班？加你的死人头班！我到工厂去看过，哪里有人在？"（《水东流》）
>
> "听他车的死人大炮！"（《水东流》）
>
> "打斋念经用不着那样死命敲呀！我看不大对。"（《风雨榴莲坑》）

这些词语、句子凸显了客家人骂人时的用语和口吻，再现了客家人骂人惯用"死"字的特点，"死人""死鬼"和"死命"都是客家人常用的骂人语。文中"阿龙古"的"古"字是客家方言里一个常与名字组合起来，以表示长辈（或平辈）对晚辈（或平辈）男性的称呼。原上草通过这些地道的客家方言，将故事置放于一个非常真实的客家地域中，使小说情节、人物形象更加深刻，可信度更高，让读者读起来更有亲切之感。

1　原上草：《水东流》，马来西亚写作人（华文）协会出版，1981年，第162页。

除了直接引用客家方言，原上草的小说也大量运用了富有客家特色的词语或词组，不论是名词、动词、形容词，还是俚语、惯用语，都生动形象、表现力强。比如：

"何止打官司，我要劏了他！"（《迷途》）

"睡得不知南北东西。"（《韭菜花开》）

"二胡也拉过两下子，靠这日中走走山芭小埠，捞它一块几毛吊吊命。"（韭菜花开））

"不砍下他的头来我就是四脚爬的。"（《迷途》）

"叫他们行开！叫他们行开！莫等吃多了变作阿吉灵无人爱负责。"（《韭菜花开》）

从表达效果来看，用"劏"比"杀"来得形象，"睡到不知南北东西"比"睡到什么都不知道"来得生动，用"吊吊命"也比"养家糊口"更能突出穷困的程度。至于"四脚爬"（禽兽）、"阿吉灵"（印度人，指说话不算数的人）这些俚语虽然可以用华语中其他词语代替，但却不及客家方言俚语的简练精当、形象生动，表达效果更理想。此外，这也是重要的地域文化现象之一，出自底层社会客家人的口语，充分地显示了客家气息和氛围。

方言土语：鲜明的人物形象

方言在原上草所处的时代是主要的沟通语。随着人们的交际往来，单一方言群聚居的现象越来越不明显，各种方言的混合使用成了非常普遍的现象。原上草生活的环境，身边的人虽然大部分都说客家话，但是方言混合运用，词语相互借用的现象常见。原上草将这些方言土语适度地运用在小说中，使他作品的语言独特，表达效果强。

老舍曾经说过："小说中人物的话语要一方面负起故事发展的责任，另一方面也是人格的表现。"[2] 原上草与他小说里的人物关系密切，那些人物是他熟悉的人，尤其是那些跟他一起生活和工作的人。他清楚他们的生活状况，更了解他们的心理变化。除了文字的描述，原上草也让小说里的人物说属于自己的话语，用自己独特的方式去表情达意，他让什么样的人说什么样的话，什么时候说什么话，做到了人物的言语符合他们的身份、地位、心态、环境，准确地刻画和凸显了人物的性格形象。

胡适当年也说过："古文里的人都是死人，方言土语里的人物是自然流露的人。"[3] 这说明了要更突显人物的性格形象，方言土语的运用是少不了的。原上草生活在小说人物的生活圈子里，运用他的语言能力，将小说人物的语言再现，使其人物言如其人，人如其言，个性鲜明，形象丰满生动。

"怪不得我的运气这么衰，就是你，驼衰家的，好快去死呀！"（《房

2　老舍：《我怎样写小说人物的描写》，文汇出版社，2009年，第150页。

3　胡适：《海上花列传·序》，载《胡适文集》第6卷，人民文学出版社，1998年，第263-284页。

客》）

拍！她把罐子用力顿在桌面上，那一对火红的眼睛死瞪着我："一百你都没有吗？"（《房客》）

说话的人是"财富娘"，一个养得白白胖胖，天天打扮得花枝招展出门，半夜静悄悄地回来的女人。她嗜赌如命，从不顾家，对唯一的女儿时常恶言以对，女儿桂芳身上更是被她拧得伤痕累累。这些话出自她这样一个好吃懒做、滥赌成性的女人之口，真是再贴切不过了。原上草通过典型的客家话语，将女赌徒的嘴脸、性格特色活生生地再现了。

"好呀！洋琴伯，你很威风，今晚上我们又碰着了，大家也好算一算账，是好汉的不要走，走的是老妓仔！"（《房客》）

"我打你也不过打只老狗！你这鬼样还是我的手脚？"烧火秋一拍胸口。（《房客》）

洋琴伯接受了人家的好处而在"甲巴拉"（主管）面前中伤烧火秋，使烧火秋被辞退。当烧火秋出现在工地帮助阿龙劈柴时，被早到的洋琴伯发觉了，于是一场口舌之争也就开始了。烧火秋这一骂，他那粗鲁强横的性格立即展现眼前，而洋琴伯老奸巨猾的形象也烘托出来了。小说通过人物话语中客家方言的运用，强化了人物的形象，凸显人物的性格，使读者更容易与作品产生共鸣，留下深刻印象。

王希杰曾经说过："方言成分的适当采用，可以增添作品的地方特色、乡土气息，有利于塑造人物形象。"[4] 方言在文学作品中用以塑造人物形象的效果明显，而用方言外号别称来刻画人物更是小说作品中不可缺少的元素。一个富于形象化的别称或者外号，不论是褒义还是贬义的，往往给读者留下深刻印象，也提高了作品的艺术性和趣味性。所以，许多作家绞尽脑汁为人物取名字，选外号，择别称，以概括其外貌长相、性格特征、工作身份等。一般这些外号别称都源自日常生活，带有浓浓的乡土味，反映出特有的地域色彩和民风民情，同时也表现出当地人民的精神面貌和人生态度。

原上草的小说取材于客家人聚居工作的地方，这里有小贩、矿工、橡胶工人、管工、教师等。原上草的小说在典型、真实的客家环境中，用朴实、平凡的语言书写他们的生活，并赋予他们客家方言里的外号或者别称，勾勒出带着客家乡土气、形象鲜明的人物角色，使读者倍感亲切、真实。原上草小说人物的外号别称，精彩丰富，俯拾即是。他善于捕捉人物的某些独特、具有代表性的特征加以概括，并采用风趣、诙谐、生动的词语来确定外号别称。这些别称，有的是根据人物的外貌特征，比如四眼仔、高佬福、大头福、射牙秋、朱红鼻、傻仔贤、半唐番等。一看这些外号，浮现在读者脑海里的是戴着眼镜的小伙子"四眼仔"；个子高的"高佬福"；脑袋较大的"大头福"；一口龅牙的"射牙秋"；皮肤黝黑，长相不像华人的马来族和华族混血儿"半唐番"等鲜明的人物形象。有的外号别称则与人物的工作职位有关，如豆芽婆、车衣妹、卖菜荣、黄金仔、屋主婆等。根据人物品性态度

4 王希杰：《汉语修辞学》，商务印书馆，2004年，第85页。

而取的外号，如老实伯、毒婆娘、老鸡婆等。有的外号带有强烈的贬义成分，如“毒婆娘”让人想到的是心肠坏透的女人；“老鸡婆”则让人联想到了像母鸡一样咯咯叫，说个不停的老女人。原上草所选取的外号别称平凡纯朴，但很形象化，不用加以描绘，即能联想出其人其貌，具有非常明显的表达效果。

粗言秽语：现实生活的反映

原上草长期生活在客家人的生活圈子中，他的小说取材于客家人的社会生活，反映的是客家人的现实生活。由于原上草所接触的都是比较底层的客家人，因此，他小说里的语言有平实质朴的一面，也有比较粗俗的一面。对许多文学家来说，文学作品讲究语言的美，然而对原上草来说，他更重视的是能反映小市民真实生活，表现他们的心态和感情的语言。所以，他笔下的人物各有各的谈吐和话语，不同场合不同语境下说话的语气和用词特点，原上草都能捕捉到，并贴切地将它们呈现出来。因此，即使是那些不堪入耳、不便说出来的粗言秽语他都毫无顾忌地运用在自己的小说作品中。

在原上草的小说《带工》里，黄金仔一夜之间突然被升为“带工”，意气风发，为了显示他的权威，对原来是难兄难弟的那班工友大声呼喝咆哮，连难听的粗话也派上了用场。

> “集合！集合！点名啦！漏了不关我卵事。”
>
> “啡！喂！这里来，拍拍拍！丢那妈，还想捞世界吗你们？”

“卵”“丢那妈”都是粗话，说粗话原本就是没受教育或者底层小市民的习惯，有些人甚至把粗话当成口头禅，常以粗话为开头，结束话语时也不忘再来一句粗话，说者无心，听者无意，大家早已习以为常。

> “铜茶壶，我丢那妈昨晚输——输——阿肥，你讲衰不衰，昨晚一连断三庄！在这里。”（《韭菜花开》）
>
> “我丢那妈的同茶壶，还想捞么？——开始！”（《韭菜花开》）

原上草毫无节制地将这些粗言写进作品中，虽然粗俗和不雅，但却显示了人物的身份和地位，同时也凸显了故事氛围，无形中提高了小说的表现手法，增强了艺术效果。

无可否认，真实地原上草的小说具有强烈的现实主义，记载了20世纪40年代至70年代马来西亚华人的生活状况。小说中方言土语的适当运用不仅强化和凸显了作品的主题，也在塑造人物形象方面起到了一定的修辞效果。方言土语的运用造就了原上草小说的独特性和地域性，也显示了马华文学发展的历程。

第六部分

话语修辞研究

庭审语篇的态度研究
——修辞视角

张鲁平
（[中国] 中国政法大学）

摘　要： 合理运用介入资源有助于在法庭中实现说服。本文探讨庭审各方如何通过引用观点来源展示自己的看法，归纳可采取的说服策略。本研究发现，介入资源在法庭辩论中得到广泛应用，论辩双方均可通过构建事实表明立场来支持己方、反驳对方，进而实现说服法官作出有利于己方判决的目的。

关键词： 庭审语篇；态度；法律事实；评价理论

一、研究问题

1. 简介

语篇同事件紧密联系，庭审语篇也离不开相关事件。法庭中，各方当事人不同的陈述体现案件的不同侧面。由于立场不同，诉讼各方在看待同一案件时会从不同角度考虑，同时采取利于己方的言语行为以确保自身的利益。在庭审交际中，法律事实的建构依赖于不同态度的互动。

建构主义者提出人通过语言可以建构世界，而建构即意味着人对语言所包含信息的主观选择、积极利用与带有针对性的增减。在庭审中当事人会出于不同的立场，运用修辞方式论证事实。当事人对争议论点的构建必然要依赖修辞，使目的具有可接受性，并提供可供论证的知识，从而使得命题具有说服功能。

案件事实的认定关系到法官的判案。当事人修辞论证的出发点必须围绕事实，而法官对法律事实的认定和阐述也必然依赖修辞。本文探讨语言中的态度因素是如何建构概念世界的。换言之，法官如何从当事人庭审的话语总结出案件事实并据此进行法律论证从而做出裁判。为使这一研究具有可操作性，我们以庭审语篇为语料，以马丁提出的评价理论和佩雷尔曼新修辞学理论为框架，从语类特征入手，探究庭审语篇中相关法律人用“态度”建构“法律事实”的过程。

2. 相关概念

(1) 庭审语篇

廖美珍认为，庭审语篇是对所涉案件事实的言语再现，是在特定地点，按照特定程序和规则，由具有不同目的参与者参加的，各自取得一个符合自己目的和利益的结果，以互相说服的方式而进行的活动。庭审语篇所要表达的能够基本确定的规定性内容，可变性较小，一般围绕案件事实及法律适用等话题展开，通常围绕以下三方面的内容：一、案件事实的时间、地点、起因、发展、结果等可能影响责任划分和法律适用的事实要素；二、案件中的证据材料的真实性和证明力，包括证据来源和证据收集、认定、保全及其合法性，证据与事实的证明关系，对证据的判断、运用等；三、适用法律情况，包括对依照法律认定责任、适用的法律条款，对诉讼者行为的法律定型、对法律和法令的理解和解释等。

(2) 庭审语篇中的态度

庭审交际中由于立场的不同，各方对同一事实会产生不同的态度。例如，在刑事案中，法官的职责是按照法定程序查清事实做出公正的判决，实现所代表的机构的职能；公诉人要证明被告人触犯了法律，应受到法律的制裁；被告人及其律师想澄清指控，争取利于己方的判决或混淆事实，逃脱或减免法律制裁。由于三方立场不同，导致态度的不同。简言之，控辩双方描述事件时有差别的原因之一就是双方所持立场的差异。“一般而言,立场是指认识和处理问题时所处的地位和所持的态度。……出发点不同，我们看待问题的态度、方法以及视域就会存在很大的差别，有时甚至会得出截然相反的结论。”

(3) 评价理论

评价理论认为评价系统分态度、介入及级差三个子系统。语篇中的态度分为情感、判断与鉴赏三个系统。情感系统关注积极或消极感情的表达；判断系统根据伦理、道德和社会规约评论人的行为，得出是该赞美、表扬还是批评、谴责的判断；鉴赏系统涉及对符号和自然现象的评价，依据的是场域内评价的方式和标准。介入涉及态度的来源，展示表达各种观点的不同声音。级差表示语言的分级，用于调节态度与介入的程度。

(4) 法律事实

法律事实是法律规定的，能够引起法律关系发生、变更和消灭的现象。换言之，法律事实是在法律程序中围绕原告、被告、被诉行为、损失程度以及如何赔偿之间的法律关系。

法律事实作为一种社会事实离不开人的主观价值判断与评价，法律事实的认定或解释不能脱离体题的价值选择与判断。法律事实应定义为“在法定的程序空间内，由多方诉讼主体依据既定的规则建构起来的一幅案件事实图景，它是某种法律裁决据以做出的事实依据”。

语篇同事件紧密相联系。庭审语篇也离不开相关事件。法庭中各方当事人的态度发端与对法律事实的陈述，不同的陈述体现案件的不同侧面。由于立场不同，诉讼各方在看待同一案件时会从不同角度考虑，同时采取利于已方的言语行为以确保自身的利益。庭审交际中法律事实的建构依赖于不同态度的互动。

1 胡旭晟：《作为一种立场和方法的法律文化》法学家，2004年第6期。

3. 语料来源与案情回顾

本文选取了从2006年年底至2007年上半年在国内引起广泛关注的小商贩崔英杰杀死城管队员的刑事案件，材料包括本案一审判决书、公安机关的起诉意见书、检察院起诉书、庭审实录、两位辩护律师的辩护词，法庭外由法律专业人士提供的一些辩护意见和案件评论，以及媒体报道。该案基本情况如下：2006年8月11日，北京市中关村科贸大厦楼下，城管与小商贩崔英杰发生冲突，导致一名城管队员李志强死亡，崔英杰被逮捕并起诉。

本案的基本线索如下：2004年初崔英杰来到北京，2006年崔英杰在中关村无照摆摊，2006年8月11日崔摆摊受到阻止后与对方纠缠，城管队员李志强被崔手中的刀刺中，李送往医院后死亡。构成本案的核心事件如下：（1）崔英杰是进城务工的农民，被雇主拖欠四个月的工资，生活陷入困境；（2）崔英杰借钱购买了三轮车等工具，在中关村路边售卖烤香肠，没有营业执照；（3）2006年8月11日17时左右，海淀区城管大队队员到崔英杰摆卖地点查处无照小商贩；（4）第一批到达现场的城管没有穿制服，没有出示任何书面证件和文件，没有任何口头说明；（5）崔为了三轮车与城管纠缠，当时崔手里握有小刀；（6）三轮车被没收，崔离开现场，与一同摆卖的赵某失散；（7）崔返回现场，手握小刀跑进人群；（8）城管大队副队长李志强被崔刺伤颈部，送往医院后死亡。

二、理论框架

庭审语篇中的态度

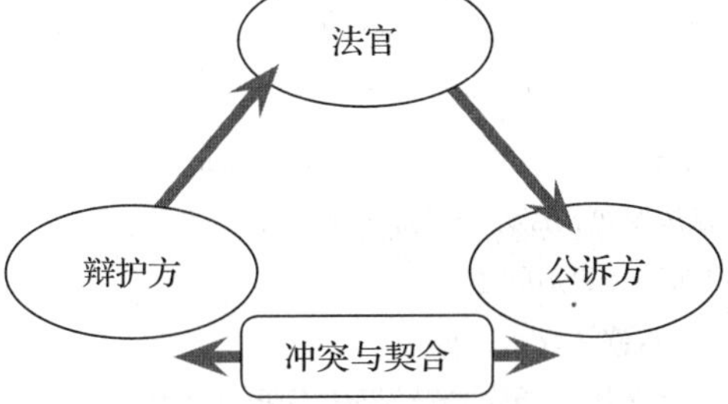

图1 态度互动构建法律事实

分析框架

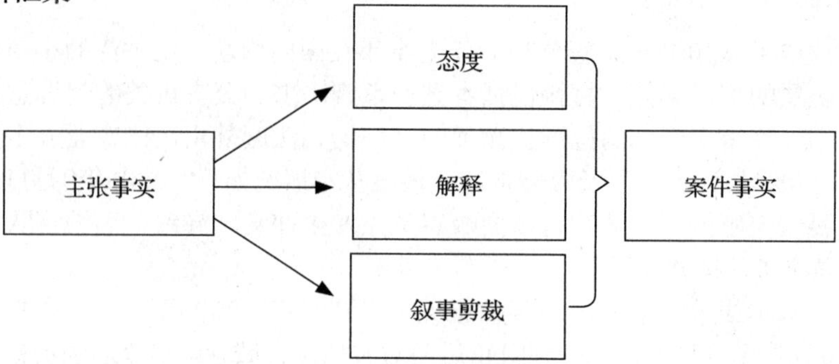

图2　庭审语篇的评价资源

唐纳德·布莱克指出："一般而言，法律原则本身不足以预测或解释案件如何处理……法律上相同的案件——关于同样的问题、拥有同样的证据支持，常常得到不同的处理，换句话说，法律是可变的。它因案件的不同而不同。它因情况而定。"

庭审语篇的各构成要素与评价系统的各种评价资源之间存在一定的对应关系。各要素都不同程度地使用多种评价资源。事实呈现不可避免地要使用态度系统中的判断和鉴别资源，因为事实的认定不仅要考虑当事人行为的常态、能力和韧度，更要判断事实或证据的真实性和适切性。

三、描写与分析

庭前准备：传唤当事人→宣读法庭纪律

庭审阶段：宣布开庭→核实当事人身份→询问当事人相关事宜

法庭调查：当事人陈述→举证→质证→认证

法庭辩论：控方→辩方→第三人

* 被告人最后陈述

* 合议庭评议

当庭宣判：宣读审判结果/告知择日宣判

图3　刑事庭审的阶段和过程

各种争论恰恰是审理阶段参与诉讼者以书面和口头的形式陈述案发当时的事件和情景。他们运用各种叙事技术、修辞方法试图诱导不同的判决结果，"原告和被告各讲一个故事——实际上是把他们'真实的'或原始的故事翻译成法律认可的叙事或修辞形式——然后陪审团从中选择自己更喜欢的故事"。

从零碎事件向叙事文本转变的过程是一个修辞过程，只有通过修辞，这种转变才能实现。这一过程中最为重要的修辞策略有三种：态度、解释与事件剪裁。

1. 态度

判决书的“事实”部分包括当事人的事实主张和法院认定的法律事实。在刑事判决书中，公诉方的事实主张通过“原告称”和“被告辩称”来表述，而法院认定的事实通常表述为“经法院审理查明”。

北京市人民检察院第一分院在起诉书中认定：

> “犯罪嫌疑人崔英杰于2006年8月11日17时许，在本市海淀区中关村科贸大厦西北角路边，无照摆摊卖货时，因被本市海淀区城管大队查处，即怀恨在心，持刀将执法的海淀城管队副队长李志强（男、36岁）颈部扎伤，造成李伤及右侧头臂静脉及右肺上叶被刺伤，致急性失血性休克死亡。
>
> “本院认为，被告人崔英杰无视国法，以暴力手段妨害城管执法人员依法执行公务，并持刀行凶，致人死亡。犯罪性质极其恶劣，情节、后果特别严重，社会危害性极大。”

辩护词中，辩护律师认为：

> “事件的起因：本案来看，被告崔英杰与被害人李志强素不相识、无冤无仇，只是因为现场混乱，城管在追赶被告，被告担心不止是三轮车被没收，自己的人身也可能受到强制，急于脱身的情况下随便挥了一刀。而且从公诉人提供的视听资料来看，被告第二次进入现场时曾经经过李志强的身边，并没有对李志强实施任何行为。在这种情况下，指控被告具有杀害李志强的故意，于理不通，于情不合。
>
> “被告所使用的刀：必须注意到，刺中李志强的刀是用来切香肠的、一把从西苑早市上花一元钱买的刀，质量如何可想而知，这把刀并非管制刀具。而且混乱之下、情急之中刺到了什么位置，被告并不清楚。被告崔英杰身高一米七八，李志强身高一米七五，以崔李二人的身高、相对位置和被告的反手握刀姿势分析，由上而下斜划一刀就是当时被告最顺手的姿势，并非刻意为之。被害人受伤的部位并不是被告追求的结果。”

公诉书用语极其简洁，但是在最后几句话中，还是不可避免地用上了修辞语句“被告人崔英杰无视国法，以暴力手段妨害城管执法人员依法执行公务，并持刀行凶，致人死亡。犯罪性质极其恶劣，情节、后果特别严重，社会危害性极大”。以上言语直接表明了公诉方的态度。这种措辞严厉的修辞方法，如果没有获得律师的另一方措辞，是很容易进入法官的主观心态，影响法官对案件的判断的。辩护律师针锋相对地回应，强调并不具有主观故意，竭力弱化被告人具有主观故意的形象，提出其（1）与被害人素不相识，没有冤仇；（2）没有杀人的故意，只是随意挥刀伤及被告。（3）解释细节，提出其所使用的刀并非管制刀具。

庭审语篇的建构是分阶段、有目的性的社会过程，庭审中控辩双方态度的冲突和契合共同作用于审判长的态度，三方态度形成一种合力，建构法律事实。这种建构的过程兼具进行性和未完成性。合力主要源自三个方面，一是对同一法律事件的不同态度之间的冲突；二是这些不同态度之间的契合；三是不同态度之间的相互影响。正是这种合力使不同的态度互动起来和法律事实交织在一起，构成完整的庭审语篇。也就是说，态度互动的方式具体体现为控辩双方之间态度的冲突与契合，以及他们对审判长态度的影响。这种冲突表现为正负面态度的冲突，阶段性建构相应的法律事实；契合表现为对于案件的一致性态度，并最终认定一个法律事实；影响表现为审判长受控辩双方一致态度的影响，根据认定的法律事实进行定性、宣判。

2. 解释

庭审语篇中对过去所经历事件的陈述并不能反映客观世界的全部，而是被建构的、修辞的、充满假设的，并且是解释性的，有选择的。个人怎样叙述——他们要强调或省略什么、作为当事人或受害者的立场、叙述要确立的叙述者与听众之间的关系如何——都会影响到叙述者怎样叙述。解释的方法分为两种：以叙事诠释证据以及情节故事化发挥。

(1) 以叙事诠释证据

事件（7）发生的时间是从崔英杰离开之后又重返现场直到李志强被刺伤之前，情景为崔手握小刀跑进人群。有关该事件最直接的证据是一段视听资料，由海淀区城管大队宣传科工作人员王金波现场拍摄，当时城管的面包车和卡车停在镜头左边，李志强站在面包车旁。崔英杰从镜头右边往左跑向卡车的方向，并且从李志强身边经过，李志强跟上去，接下来发生的情况被面包车挡住，没有拍摄到。此处证据形式是视听资料，能够显示的内容仅仅是被告人从镜头一侧跑向另一侧的简短举动。然而，叙事化的案件事实却没有这么简单，北京市公安局的起诉意见书写道：

> 犯罪嫌疑人崔英杰于2006年8月11日17时许，在本市海淀区中关村科技大厦西北角路边，无照摆摊卖货时，<u>因被本市海淀区城管大队查处，即怀恨在心，持刀</u>将执法的海淀城管队副队长李志强（男、36岁）颈部扎伤。

“因被查处，即怀恨在心，持刀将……”的措辞一来是对崔的情况的描述；二来将证据中显示的单纯身体举动转换为心理活动，并添加了因果关系。

作为对立方的辩护人则回应如下：

> “崔英杰第二次跑出来是为了找跟他在一起干活的小女孩，而并不是为了实施报复……他第二次返回，根本不是为了杀死李志强，就是为了讨回自己的谋生工具……从被告人崔英杰第二次跑出来，向货车的方向冲过去，到他去事发现场仅仅几秒钟，那么，从受害人以及其他城管工作人员向第二次跑出来的崔英杰围上去，到崔英杰把水果刀推向受害人的时间仅仅几秒钟，这几秒钟能说崔英杰是要报复而实施杀人吗？”

从证据中我们只能看到单纯的身体举动，但公安局、公诉人和辩护人言说的都是崔的心理活动以及导致这样心理活动和身体举动的原因——或者因为被查处所以怀恨在心，企图报复或者只想寻找失散同伴、夺回三轮车——它们都属于叙事者的想象发挥。这样的想象发挥带有推测性质，但推测所依据的不是确凿证据，而是日常生活的经验，且“报复”和“寻人”两种截然不同的推测显然在经验常识上都能自圆其说。

(2) 事件的情节化发挥

从身体举动到心理活动的想象，可以看作叙事者对观察到的现象的解释。当阅读事件（6）（7）（8）的时候，读者会有一种断裂感，进而产生一系列疑问：为什么崔已经离开了现场又要返回，目的何在？他是否跑向一个特定的目标？手中握着小刀是有意还是无意？他在什么情况下刺伤李志强，原因是什么？诉讼程序中的叙事者都在试图回答这些问题。

在公安局和公诉人的文本中，崔英杰因为工具被没收而怀恨在心，返回现场的目的就是报复杀人，他的目标是城管队员。辩护方则竭力提供另一种回答。崔英杰在庭上说返回现场是为了寻找一起摆摊的女孩赵某，辩护人在陈述辩护意见的时候也采用了这一说法，崔并没有报复的意图，他跑向货车是想追回被没收的三轮车。李劲松律师的辩护词称，崔英杰跑回现场的初始目的是寻找失散的赵某，同时看见他的三轮车正在被装上卡车，因为曾经听说其他小商贩在最后关头抢回被没收的工具，所以崔也打算做这样的尝试，“他第二次跑出来，根本不是为了杀死被害人李志强或其他任何一个城管……就是为了保住自己的谋生工具，想为自己借钱新买的一个三轮车，做最后一次努力。”

在叙事中，控辩双方均在事件的基础上进行情节化发挥。例如事件崔的离开与事件崔的返回由于“报复”或“寻人”获得关联，而在事件与事件之间的空白处，叙事者制造了情节想象，虽然我们看不到崔用刀刺向李的那一刻，但控方的解释显然在诱导读者或听众想象一个歹徒直奔城管队员、毫不犹豫地取其性命的场面，辩方的言辞则企图让读者或听众想象一个置身残酷环境的小贩偶然丧失理智的景象。经过解释之后，原本单调枯燥的事件出现了人物的思想活动、情感演变、行动发展乃至命运突转的同时，内部的情节推进也具有延伸效果，通过关联上下两个事件，使其在整体故事中得以定位。

3. 事实剪裁

本案一审判决认定崔英杰故意杀人罪成立，判处死刑，缓期两年执行。判决书陈述的案件事实如下：

> 被告人崔英杰于2006年8月11日17时许，在北京市海淀区中关村一号桥东南侧路边无照摆摊经营烤肠食品时，被北京市海淀区城市管理监察大队的执法人员查处，崔英杰对此不满，以持刀威胁的手段抗拒执法，当执法人员将崔英杰经营烤肠用的三轮车扣押并装上执法车时，崔英杰进行阻拦，后持刀猛刺该城市管理监察大队海淀分队的现场指挥人员李志强（男，殁年36岁）颈部一刀，致刀柄折断，后逃离现场。李志强因被伤及右侧头臂静脉及右肺上叶，致急性失血性休克死亡。

这一陈述与起诉书相差无几，和上文分析的各叙事文本一样，具有以下特征处于案件基本线索的序列之内，构成事实的素材没有脱离文章第二部分罗列的八项事件，并且娴熟地运用事实剪裁和解释两大策略。事件（1）被忽略，叙事从事件（2）

崔英杰非法经营小摊档起始，且对事件（4）只字未提。由此将崔摆摊的原因、城管的行为失当都排除在事实之外，一方面，展示在读者面前的是一个形象十分单一的人物，除了违法犯罪没有别的特征，另一方面，既然没有事件（1）和（4），那么读者便丧失了就这两项事件思考或提问的能力，事实也呈现出一种毫无疑问的状态。

接下来的故事删去了崔离开又返回的情节，从崔持刀威胁直接跳到阻拦三轮车被装上卡车以及刺伤李志强。通过裁剪情节，崔的“威胁”“阻拦”“猛刺”三个动作被衔接在一起，其表面效果连续、递进地出现三个攻击性动作给读者造成压迫感，仿佛行为者对自己的暴力举动态度坚决而且凶狠。在读者看来，这三个动作如此紧密地连续出现，也暗示了三者之间的关联，崔用刀猛刺城管队员的举动是他暴力抗法的一部分，也是他先前持刀威胁、阻挠执法行为的推进发展——读者不大可能再去想象，崔是在无望夺回合法财产之后的逃跑途中因为过度惊恐或者认错人才失手刺伤李的，也没有机会提出崔主观上是否属于过失而非直接故意的疑问。此处，两种修辞策略融合在一起，叙事中对事件的挑选也暗含了叙事者对事件背后诸多问题的解释。

四、结论

庭审语篇属于机构语篇的一种，受到法庭规则的制约。尽管庭审语篇力求客观、真实，但各方当事人由于立场、思维模式、文化程度等影响，在语言中几乎不可避免地融入了各自的态度，使法庭会话呈现出主观性表述的特点。本文以评价理论的态度、介入系统为分析框架，指出各种资源可用于阐述、证明己方观点及揭示对方论述武断、证据证明力不足。通过对庭审语篇的分析，进一步提出在构建事实、表明立场时应注意运用介入策略。

参考文献

[1] 程微.庭审语篇中“态度”对法律事实的构建[J]. 西安外国语大学学报，2011年第1期.

[2] 胡旭晟.作为一种立场和方法的法律文化[J].法学家，2004年第6期.

[3] 焦宝乾.西方修辞学知识传统及其对法律论证的意义[J].山东警察学院学报，2005年第2期.

[4] 廖美珍.法庭问答及其互动研究[M].北京:法律出版社, 2003年.

[5] 廖义铭.佩雷尔曼之新修辞学[M].台北: 唐山出版社, 1997年.

[6] 刘燕.案件事实的人物建构——崔英杰案叙事分析[J].法制与社会发展，2009年第2期.

[7] 彭中礼.论法律事实的修辞论证——以“崔英杰案”为例[J].西部法学理论，2010年第1期.

[8] 杨波.法律事实辨析[J].当代法学, 2007年第6期.
[9] 唐纳德·布莱克.法律的运作行为[M].唐越、苏力译，北京:中国政法大学出版社，2004年.
[10] 波斯纳.法律与文学[M].李国庆译,北京:中国政法大学出版社,2002年.
[11] 波斯纳.超越法律[M].苏力译，北京:中国政法大学出版社,2001年.
[12] Conley, J. M. & O'Barr, W. *Just Words: Law, Language and Power* [M]. Chicago: the University of Chicago Press, 1990.
[13] Perelman, Chaim. The New Rhetoric and the Rhetoricians: Remembrance and Comments, in *The New Rhetoric of Chaim Perelman*, Chicago: University Press of America, 1989, p249.
[14] Walker, David M. 牛津法律大辞典[M]. 李双元等译. 北京：法律出版社，2003年.

A Study on the Attitude of Trial Discourse: A Rhetoric Perspective

Zhang Luping
(China University of Political Science and Law, China)

Abstract: Effective application of engagement resources may help one to present facts and persuade audience during trial. This paper probes into how to demonstrate one's opinions through the quotation of information sources, and aims to find out applicable persuasion strategies during trial. The research shows that engagement resources play a vital role during courtroom debate. Defense lawyers and prosecutors both resort to engagement resources to present evidence and construct arguments, so as to persuade judge.

Keywords: trial discourse; attitude; legal facts; appraisal theory

转述的忠实类型及建构性和顺应性转述研究[1]

黄　友

（[中国]　上海大学）

摘　要： 以原话语和转述话语内容一致为忠实标准，我们把转述分为忠实转述、非忠实转述和介于两者之间的带忠实性转述；根据忠实再现动因、建构动因与顺应动因，把忠实性转述分为直接引述、建构性转述和顺应性转述。由于篇幅限制，本文只着重对建构性转述和顺应性转述加以详细分析，具体分析了转述者的视角、详略度、突显、心理扫描和主观情感对转述话语的建构；以及转述者顺应转述对象、情境、语体和代码的情形及转述策略。

关键词： 转述；忠实性；修辞动因；建构；顺应

引言：转述的忠实性类型

"转述话语"即学界常说的"引语"，目前学界对引语的分类跳不出"（自由）直接/间接引语"等框架。在实际转述中，转述话语往往不能或不必与被述话语保持高度忠实。本文旨在从忠实性角度来重新划分转述的类型。

我们设想：

（一）以原话语和转述话语内容一致为忠实标准，可以把转述分为忠实性转述、非忠实性转述和介于两者之间的带忠实性转述。

（二）对于忠实性转述，根据转述者如下三类转述动因，或称修辞动因①，可作相应分类：

1. 忠实再现动因：原原本本再现被转述的话语的动因，主要是"直接引述"；

2. 建构动因：转述者尽量保持转述话语的忠实性，但往往会自主选择转述策略（改变视角、详略度、突显、心理扫描、主观情感）对被述话语从积极意义上重新编码，一般只承诺对被述内容负责而不确保被述话语形式的原本再现，此类转述可称为"建构性转述"；

3. 顺应动因：转述者尽量保持转述话语的忠实性，但为顺应通讯系统诸客观要素（转述对象、场合）的制约而选择相应的转述策略（替换、删略、增添）的动因，此类转述可称为"顺应性转述"。

---

1 修辞动因：即使用语言的意图。如主观化编码的动因，言语行为以言表意、以言行事、以言取效的动因，认知关系变化的语言编码动因，交际互动中各种关系的协调等等。

（三）对于非忠实性转述，根据转述者是否意欲保证忠实，即是有意还是无意违背忠实性，可分两类，分别称为“曲释性转述”（有意曲解，故意歪曲，简称“曲述”）和“误释性转述”（无意误释，由于记忆、理解、表达能力等的制约，转述者在客观上无法保证忠实，简称“误述”）。

（四）对于带忠实性的转述，则可从信息增值、减值和变形的角度分为“增值性引述/转述”“减值性引述/转述”和“转值性引述/转述”。

由于篇幅的限制，本文将只对建构性和顺应性转述加以分析。

一、建构性转述

心理学家曾做过一个试验：要求16位受试者把一段电影台词背出来，等这16个受试者都能逐字背出来后，将16人分成两组，每组8人，要求其中8人把台词复述得“越准确越好”，结果99%的句子是逐字背出来的；对另外一组8人，只要求把台词告诉另一个人，结果只有62%的台词是逐字背出来的。可见人们在复述过程中的主观建构。

建构性转述往往与认知识解有关。“识解”（Construal）是指说话人心理形成和建构一个表达式的语义内容的方式，是“说话人（或听话人）与其所概念化和描绘的情景之间的关系”。一个特殊的情景可以用不同的方式“识解”，并且编码情景的方式构成了不同的概念。这充分表明，语言使用者在组织和构建其世界过程中发挥了更积极的作用。下面主要从视角、详略度、突显、心理扫描、主观性几个识解维度加以说明。

1. 视角

视角（Perspective，也译为视域、视点、眼光）这一概念是认知语言学家用来强调观察者在情景中的重要作用的，尤其是观察者的视点以及所注意的焦点成分的选择。间接转述实质上是视角转换。一般而言是从被述者的视角转移到转述者的视角，从转述者的视角出发，对被述话语重新加以表述。

间接转述一般要求根据转述者所处的时空变动人称和时态等等，时地状语以及具有被述者特点的语言成分（如语气、语调、情态、话语标记语等）根据需要可以转换也可以保留。学界根据引导句的有无把保留这些成分的间接转述语区分为“带特色的间接引语”和“自由间接引语”。因此，对于间接转述而言，可以采用多种转述策略。

如：父亲被激怒了，说“才多久的事？我会记错？”

可以转述为：

→（a）父亲被激怒了，**说才多久的事？他会记错？**

→（b）父亲被激怒了，<u>厉声反驳说</u>**才多久的事，他不会记错。**

→（c）父亲被激怒了，**说才多久的事**，他不会记错。

→（d）父亲被激怒了，说没过多久的事他不会记错。

这样的转述都是可以接受的，也保留了原有话语的不同层次：（a）仅仅改变人称，原有的语气语调、主观情态词都得到保留；（b）不仅改变人称，而且原有的疑问语气变为陈述语气，但是用描述语对其语气加以补充说明；（c）同时改变人称、语气语调；（d）在（c）的基础上还去掉了表达“父亲”主观情态的副词“才”。此外，还可能有以上几个叠加使用的情形。

2. 详略度

情景描写的详细程度（Different Levels of Specificity）是指说话人可以用不同的精细程度对同一情景进行描写。如，我们可以说一个人在“笑”，或者更精确地描写他在“放声地开怀大笑”，或“笑得肚子都疼了，笑得直不起腰来，笑得前仰后合”等等。对于一个复杂的话语，转述时可以采用不同的详略度，通过删减或添加，形成详略度不同的转述语。

略述：是对被述话语（一般相对复杂的话语）的删略叙述，一般是直接删略文本中不重要的隐含信息或枝节信息。文章缩写、摘要、摘录、节选等都是略述的实例。

概述：是用自己的话概括被述话语（一般相对复杂的话语）的主要内容。

详述：是指对被述话语加以扩充，补充具体细节的过程，是略述的反向运用。最典型的代表是文章扩写。

3. 突显

我们在对情景的识解过程中，情景的许多方面被忽略了，这是因为我们只会把焦点放在引起我们注意的那些部分上。我们有确定注意力焦点和方向的认知能力，这是形成突显原则的认知基础。

如：“猫在垫子上。”→她说垫子在猫下面。

前者是参照垫子（背景）确定猫（图形）的方位，而后者所表达的关系正好相反。转述者看到前者，然后在其心里形成表征，如果他转述成了后者，则说明他把“图形”和“背景”调换了位置，注意焦点发生了改变。

勾勒（Profile）也是一种突显方式，是突显某一情景中的某个或某些成分。如一个典型的及物事件图式应该是“施事凭借工具作用于受事”。在该行为链中，说话人可以选择勾勒任何一部分，至少有三种可能性，如：

（a）王刚用护宝锤砸碎了仿制品。

（b）她说护宝锤砸碎了仿制品。

（c）她说仿制品砸碎了。

转述者在转述时，就有可能采用以上不同的勾勒方式显示其注意焦点。

转述者略述时，往往会保留其感兴趣的注意焦点，哪怕这些注意焦点是不重要的信息，这也是突显原则在起作用。

4. 心理扫描

心理扫描（Mental Scanning）也是一种认知过程，是说话人为了描写事件而采用的一种构建情景的方式通常可分为序列扫描（Sequential Scanning）和概括扫描（Summary Scanning）。序列扫描就是把一个过程看成是事件成分的一个序列；概括扫描就是把一个过程看成是一个完整的单位，其中所有事件成分被看成是一个整合的整体。它们之间的差别体现在语法的许多方面，其中包括说话人在描写一个事件时是决定用名词还是用动词。序列扫描就好像是观看一个运动图像序列，而概括扫描就好像是观看一幅静止的照片。动词在此所勾勒的是一个过程，而名词所勾勒的是一件东西或事物。如：

把鱼切成片，然后用料酒腌几分钟。

→把鱼片用料酒腌几分钟。

上例中被述者采用的是序列扫描，而转述者采用的是概括扫描。

5. 主观情感

主观性（Subjective）是指语言的这样一种特性，即在话语中多多少少总是含有说话人“自我”的表现成分。也就是说，说话人在说出一段话的同时表明自己对这段话的立场、态度和感情，从而在话语中留下自我的印记。主观性研究主要集中在三个方面：一是说话人的视角（Perspective），二是说话人的情感（Affect），三是说话人的认识（Epistemic Modality）。这里主要说说说话人的“情感”“情感”包括感情、情绪、意向、态度等。语言中的韵律变化、语气词、词缀、代词、副词、时体标记、情态段都可以用来表达情感，涉及语音、构词、语法、篇章结构等各个方面。总之，对一段话而言，很难将它的表述命题内容的部分跟它表述情感的部分区分开来。以下转述实验就说明了这个问题：

“清晨我给妈妈准备好早餐和水果，然后带些蒸的小鱼给楼下的猫猫，结果它的小爪把我的手划了一条红线。”

受试者1：“小王说清晨她给妈妈做了早饭准备了水果，然后带了点鱼给楼下的猫吃，但是被它的爪子抓伤了手。”

受试者2：“小王说早上她给妈妈做了早饭还准备了水果，再带了一些鱼给楼下的猫当早饭，但是它居然用爪子抓伤了小王的手。”

实验者用的是“把”字句，而受试者1用了表示不如意的被动句，表示其对小王的同情和对猫的厌恶；受试者2则使用了典型的“施事+工具+动作+受事”的及物构式，而且添加情态副词“居然”，表示出乎意料，暗含对猫的谴责。此外，试验者表述的“小鱼”和“猫猫”都含有对小动物喜爱的情感，受试者改成客观冷静的“鱼”和“猫”则与其对猫的批评态度一以贯之。

二、顺应性转述

池上嘉彦探讨了通讯结构（如图1），并指出理想的信息传递是指发讯者使之符号化的传达内容与收讯者解译的传达内容完全一致，既不多余也无不足，理想的通讯只能是机械的机器传递。现实中，人们之间的通讯则十分复杂而灵活，讯息中常常包括了脱离代码的表现。

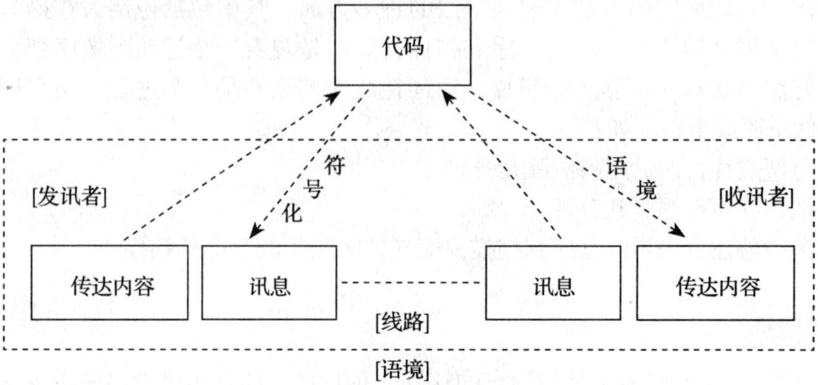

图 1　通讯结构图

因此，从通讯系统来看，系统中的每一个要素都有可能影响信息的正常传递，从而产生信息偏差。转述至少进行了两次讯息传递，出现信息偏差的概率更加增大。根据对通讯结构各要素的分解，需要顺应的制约因素有：转述对象、情境、语体、代码、被述话语、噪音干扰等等。

1. 顺应转述对象

言语交际必须以一定的共知话题为依据，才能得以顺利进行。这些共知话题涉及说话人和听话人双方的思想基础、文化素质以及共同的背景知识。转述往往要根据转述对象的年龄、学识、文化背景等条件，对转述话语做相应的改动。如行业中的行话、术语对于行业外的人来说，有可能是比较陌生的，需要改用日常用语或者添加说明用语；“新新人类”的网络语言对于中老年人来说则是非常陌生的；而成人的话尤其是隐喻的表达在幼小的儿童那里或许是不能理解的。因此：

如果要使针对A的被述话语也能被B理解，而A、B之间又存在较大的认知差异，那么转述者应根据B的认知能力做相应的改变。具体说来有四个方面：

（1）转述对象无法理解的信息需要替换或添加；

（2）转述对象熟知的信息可以删略；

（3）转述对象未知的背景信息需要添加；

（4）必要时替换语码。

2. 顺应转述情境

情境包括时空、社会文化情境等。

（1）时空

时间、空间维度对转述的影响至少体现在两个方面：

A. 由于转述本身占用一定的时间和空间（书面），因此，在时间、空间紧张的情况下，转述者往往进行简要介绍；而时间、空间充足的情况下，则有可能详细转述。这在大会发言时常见。电报和文章标题往往有字数的限制，常常要对原文进行高度的概括。

B. 随着时间的推移、空间的改变，转述也可能出现相应的变化，如古代的故事改写成现代的白话；在某处说普通话比较方便在另一处则改说成方言比较自然。关于这一点，我们将在顺应代码时详述。

（2）社会文化情境

典型的受社会文化情境影响的转述现象是隐语和跨文化交际。

隐语，又叫暗语、黑话、密语等，是一种特殊的社会方言，是各种行帮、组织或集团因内部交际需要而约定和使用的带有保密性质的语言变体，如江湖隐语、帮会隐语、盗匪隐语、流氓集团隐语、特务集团隐语等。隐语的突出特点是封闭性和隐秘性。战争时期的情报传递往往要采取暗语的形式，这就意味着要对被述话语进行改变。如1996年台海危机关键时刻，台商情报员周天祥接到广东省汕头市澄海机场一通公用电话后，自厦门回报台湾军情局的暗语：

有演习，但没有发射导弹

→工厂有生产，但没有出货。（《战云密布：台湾特工倾巢出动 将这样暗语发往对岸》中华网）

跨文化交际对转述的影响不仅体现在语言上，也体现在体态语上。一方面，表示同一语义，运用的体态语不一。如大多数民族都以摇头表示反对、不同意，以点头表示赞成、同意；但保加利亚人、尼泊尔人以及我国的独龙族则相反，摇头表示同意，点头表示反对。另一方面，同一体态语，有时也会因民族文化的不同而具有不同的含义。如翘起大拇指语，在中国表示赞扬；在希腊表示让对方“滚蛋”；在英国、澳大利亚、新西兰等地不仅有“搭车”之意，还是一种侮辱人的信号。因此，存在体态语差异的民族之间的转述，需要用到三个策略：

策略一：如果体态语只是起辅助作用，可以省略；

策略二：如果体态语具有表义的作用，补充说明体态语在被述话语情境中的含义；

策略三：改用转述对象民族的体态语。

3. 顺应语体

转述者往往要根据转述对象、情境选择不同的语体和语码，并受语体和语码的限制。

对语体的顺应典型地表现在散文体与韵文体之间以及口语与书面语之间的转述。

散文的特点是形散神不散，一般用白话的形式写出；而韵文则讲究结构的匀称、对仗的工整、相同的字数、讲究平仄和押韵。把一首唐诗换成现代白话文来表述，必然要替换、增删。

口语和书面语的联系在此毋庸赘述，书面语对口语的转述有会议记录、口供笔录、根据即兴表演整理而成的剧本、根据实况整理而成的访谈录、根据别人的口述写成的报道、课堂笔记等等。口语对书面语的转述，主要有以下情形：朗读、演讲、讲述书面故事、作报告、播报新闻、吟诗等等。口语与书面语之间的转述在以下情况下需要换述：

（1）照实转述会产生歧义，加以改变

A. 口语中没有歧义，书面语中会产生歧义

如："我当你说过多少次了。"

→她说她当Dāng着我的面说过很多次了。

→她说她当（Dàng，以为）我说过很多次了。

B. 书面语中没有歧义，口语中有歧义

如：我喜欢《秋夜》。

→她说她喜欢《秋夜》这本书。

（2）口语中的方音、口误、吞吐等现象，书面转述时往往规范或修正

书面转述口语中的语误等信息时，可以采用以下策略：

策略一：原样转述口误等信息，同时修正；

策略二：直接修正，隐蔽口误等信息。

4. 顺应代码

转述者对代码的顺应最典型的体现在被述者使用A代码（即语言）表述，转述者为顺应转述对象或由于使用A代码表述的能力不强，转用B代码换述。

来自不同语言或方言社团的人往往用通用语进行交流，而来自同一语言或方言社团的人，用方言交流更为亲切自然，"语码选择"（Code-Switching）指说话人根据时间、地点、内容、对象等因素的变化而换用不同的语言或语言变体。这一交际策略在转述过程中常被使用。

（1）不同语言之间的转换

他兴奋地说："Wonderful！"（太棒了！）

第二天一早，英迪拉向他告别，她双手合十，默默祝愿道："印地秦尼帕伊帕伊。"（印度同中国是兄弟）。（《人民日报海外版》1993-12-29）

他用韩语和她打招呼："你好！"

其实，翻译也是一种转述，翻译中相关的理论完全可以纳入到转述研究之中。

（2）不同语言变体之间的转换

不同的地域变体即方言之间或方言与通用语之间的转述，如：

其中一个又说话了："该（解）放军同志，她爸爸是富农。"（《北京晚报》1992-10-28）

不同的时间变体，即现代语言与古代语言之间的转述，如下面小学语文教材对《刻舟求剑》的转述：

楚人有涉江者，其剑自舟中坠于水，遽契其舟，曰："是吾剑之所从坠。"舟止，从其所契者入水求之。舟已行矣，而剑不行，求剑若此，不亦惑乎！（《刻舟求剑》）

→从前，有个人坐船过江，他一不小心，把挂在身上的宝剑掉进江里去了。那个人一点儿也不着急，拿出小刀在船舷上刻了一个记号。

有人催他："还不赶快捞！在船舷上刻记号有什么用呢？"

那个人不慌不忙地指了指刻的记号，说："不用着急，宝剑是从这儿掉下去的，等船靠了岸，我就从这儿跳下去，准能把宝剑捞上来。"（人教版小学语文教材《刻舟求剑》）

不同社会方言社团之间也存在语码转换现象。如：

一个学生在题为《我的理想》的作文开头中这样写道："偶8是美女，木油虾米太远大的理想，只稀饭睡觉、粗饭，像偶酱紫的菜鸟……"（我不是美女，没有什么太远大的理想，只喜欢睡觉、吃饭，像我这样子的新手……）如果你不是她那个年龄段的网民，真的很难理解这段文字的真实含义。（《人民日报》海外版）

此外，还有模糊的被述话语，如模糊字迹、模糊音，转述者自然无法原样转述，加以变换。口语转写规则中就有模糊音的记录规则，在此不再赘述。

不同语码之间的转换可以采用三个策略：

策略一：引述用语言A表述的原话，同时用语言B表述（翻译）；

策略二：模仿用语言A表述的发音，同时用语言B表述（翻译）；

策略三：直接用语言B表述。

三、余论

本文通过实验数据和语料分析，发现很多转述都不是原样再现的，其中所占比重较大的一部分是建构性和顺应性转述。转述者会依据自己的理解对转述话语进行主观建构；转述者往往还要根据转述对象、情境选择不同的语体和语码，并受语体和语码的制约。本文还分析了相应的转述策略，这些策略可以归结为：替换、删略、添加、换序、重新赋义等。由于篇幅所限，其他转述以及转述在对外汉语教学中的应用情况与策略，将另文研究。

参考文献

[1] 何自然.语用三论：关联论·顺应论·模因论[M]. 上海：上海教育出版社，2007.

[2] 刘大为.自然语言中的链接结构及其修辞动因[J]. 修辞学习，2008（5）.

[3] 彭建武.转述现象的认知语用分析[J]. 外语教学与研究，2001（5）.

[4] 申丹.对自由间接引语功能的重新评价[J]. 外语教学与研究，1991b（2）.

[5] 沈家煊.语言的主观性与主观化[J]. 外语教学与研究，2001（4）.

[6] 陶红印.试论语体分类的语法学意义[J]. 当代语言学，1999（3）.

[7] 王艺.言语行为和引语[D]. 华东师范大学，2004.

[8] 张传枝.朗读口误心理分析[J]. 湖北师范学院学报（哲学社会科学版），2007（6）.

[9] [美]纳尔逊·古德曼，姬志闯译.构造世界的多种方式[M]. 上海：上海译文出版社，2008.

[10] [日]池上嘉彦，张晓云译.符号学入门[M]. 北京: 国际文化出版公司，1985.

[11] Carrol，D.W. *Psychology of Language*（3rd）[M]. 北京：外语教学与研究出版社，2000.

[12] Langacker，R.W. *Foundations of Cognitive Grammar: Theoretical Prerequisites* [M]. Stanford：Stanford University Press，1987.

Research on the Fidelity of Language Reports and Volitional, Adaptional Language Reports

Huang You
(Shanghai University, China)

Abstract: This paper aimes at researching on the fidelity of Language Reports . It classifies the Language Reports into fidelity, not fidelity and with fidelity according to the consistency of the original discourse and the speech reporting. It points out that there are direct speech, volitional speech and adaptional speech because of different rhetoric intention. Due to space limitations, this article only focuses on the volitional speech and adaptional speech, including detailed analysis of the perspective, elaboration, profile, mental scanning and subjective affect to the volitional speech and the object , context, stylistic code to the adaptional speech.

Keywords: language reports; fidelity; rhetoric intensions; volitional; adaptional

第七部分

传统修辞研究

论表比喻的“仿佛”[1]

李胜梅

（[中国] 河北大学 南昌大学）

摘 要： 考察客观语料和实际语感，“仿佛”可分解为：①副词，“似乎”，表示不确定判断，主观推测。②动词，“像”，表示比喻关系。③动词，“差不多；类似”，表示比较关系。本文分析与比喻有关的“仿佛”的词汇意义、句法功能、修辞意义和语篇特征，并指出，用在比喻句中的“仿佛”有两种情况：1.直接充当比喻词；2.充当其他比喻词的修饰成分。二者词汇意义、语法意义和修辞意义皆不同。由“仿佛”充当比喻词和谓语中心语的句子，其句法结构的特殊性及与后续句的衔接连贯，与“仿佛”的宾语（同时也是喻体）的语义和结构密切相关；上下文有时出现其他比喻词可形成同义强化，有时出现说写者的比喻自述可强化句子的比喻特征。此项研究对“仿佛”一词及现代汉语其他比喻词的全面探讨、词典释义、对汉语教学的比喻词研究具有理论意义和应用价值。

关键词： “仿佛”；“仿佛+是/成/像”；比喻词；比喻关系；不确定判断

修辞学所论“比喻词”，指联系本体和喻体表示两者相似关系的词，也称“比喻语词”。（陈望道《修辞学发凡》称为“譬喻词语”，列举了“好像”“如同”“仿佛”“一样”“犹”“若”“如”“似”等。）其中，“像”是现代汉语中一个典型的表示比喻关系的词，“仿佛”也是常用比喻词之一。而词汇学所论“比喻词”，指以比喻的方式构成的复合词，如“龙眼、木耳、纸老虎、鸭舌帽……”。两个“比喻词”，同音同形异义，本文讨论的是前者，不讨论后者。

本文对现代汉语中的“仿佛”进行客观描写，不研究古代汉语中的“仿佛”（当然，由古代汉语发展而来，可能略有论及）。“仿佛”是联绵词，在文言中有多个异体（如“彷佛”“髣髴”等），本文不讨论。也不讨论其不沿用于现代汉语中的义项。如晋代陶渊明《桃花源记》：“林尽水源，便得一山。山有小口，髣髴若有光。”此“髣髴”，“似有若无貌；隐约貌”，意思是“隐隐约约，形容看得不真切的样子”，此义项本文不讨论。

本文根据实际运用情况和普通使用者的语感，分析“仿佛”的词汇意义、句法功能和修辞意义，充分描写表比喻的“仿佛”句的句法特点和语篇环境。此项研究

1 [基金项目]江西省社会科学研究“十一五”规划项目（08WX83）；江西省高校人文社会科学重点研究基地2010年度招标项目（S01015）。

有助于我们进一步探讨：如何系统考察现代汉语各具体比喻词的含义及所构成的比喻句的特点，如何系统考察面向对外汉语教学的现代汉语比喻词，如何更好地统一处理作为一种词语类聚的比喻词的词典释义。

我们曾对《现代汉语词典》和学习型（外向型）词典的“仿佛”释义提出具体修改建议并作了示例调整（李胜梅，2011）：

【仿佛】①副似乎：他干起活来～不知道什么是疲倦。｜春天的风非常温和，～是母亲的手。②动像：微风过处，送来缕缕清香，～远处高楼上渺茫的歌声似的。｜他的注意力全部集中在胸前的那个布包上，～抱着一个几世单传的婴儿。｜这两棵树靠在一起，～一对正在恋爱的年轻人。③动差不多；类似;近似：他的模样还和十年前相～。

但限于篇幅，“仿佛”不用于比喻句的情况，本文不讨论。具体说来，作为副词的“仿佛”（表示“似乎”，不确定判断，主观推测），有的用于不表示比喻关系的动词前（如“他干起活来仿佛不知道什么是疲倦”），本文不讨论；有的用于表示比喻关系的动词（如“是”“成”“像”“变成”“变作”等）前，在句中充当其他比喻词的修饰成分（如“春天的风非常温和，仿佛是母亲的手”），本文重点讨论。作为动词的“仿佛”，有两种情况，一是用于表示比喻关系，本文重点讨论；一是表示“差不多，类似，近似”，在句中出现时有特殊搭配条件（要与“相”组合），使用频率不高，语体要求明显（一般仅用于书面语），本文不讨论。（至于作为动词的“仿佛”与作为副词的“仿佛”在义项和句法功能方面的历时演变关系及在现代汉语共时层面的并存联系，本文仅略有涉及，也不重点讨论）

一、“仿佛”的句法功能

用在比喻句中的“仿佛”，有两种情况：1.直接充当比喻词，作动词；2.充当其他比喻词的修饰成分，作副词。

1.1 作动词：“仿佛”直接充当比喻词

1.1.1 从现代汉语语料和实际语感看“仿佛”表示比喻关系

无论是从语料所反映的运用事实看还是从人们的语感看，“仿佛”可以表示比喻关系的情形都是很常见的。如：

［1］微风过处，送来缕缕清香，仿佛远处高楼上渺茫的歌声似的。

［2］他的注意力全部集中在胸前的那个布包上，仿佛抱着一个几世单传的婴儿，裹得太紧怕压了它，太松又怕凉了它。

这两个比喻句因收进《语文》课本而几乎人人熟知。前一例是“‘仿佛’+喻体（NP）+‘似的’”格式，后一例是“‘仿佛’+喻体（VP）”。

［3］负责这项工作的机械工程师沃里斯比喻说，“勇气”号伸开“两腿”就仿佛婴儿出生后，首次尝试依靠自己的腿来站立。（本文语料凡引自北京大

学CCL语料库的，不再一一说明出处）

该例更是直接点明了“仿佛”可用来表示比喻关系。这是普通语言使用者的语感。

[4] 李嬷嬷对袭人的嫉恨，可想而知。但又无法按“宋太祖灭南唐之意”行事，因为作为奶母，随着宝玉的长大，她必须隐退，而作为贴身丫环中的首领，袭人的地位则在冉冉上升，倘硬作比喻，那么她倒仿佛南唐，袭人倒颇具宋太祖的架式。因而她的斗争矛头，便率先瞄准了袭人。

例中普通语言使用者对“仿佛”可用来表示比喻关系有明确的语感，是自觉地使用“仿佛”。

[5] ……看见一节奇文，略谓有一种人，不知好坏，不辨善恶，仿佛色盲者的不分青红皂白，可以说是害着价值盲的病。当时就觉得这个比喻的巧妙新鲜，想不到今天会引到它。

作为读者对他人的比喻句有明确的语感和认识。例中比喻正是通过“仿佛”将本体和喻体联系起来的。

1.1.2 从词义的历时发展看作为比喻词的“仿佛”的固定义

从现代汉语语料和使用者语感看：“仿佛”可表示比喻关系，有相应的句法功能和修辞功能。这种用法，不是偶一用之，不是临时用法。“仿佛”表示比喻关系，这种含义，跟现代汉语里其他比喻词一样，都表现为固定的词义，而不是临时产生的含义。这种含义，也不是仅限于修辞学的术语义，而是存在于普通使用者共有的语感中。（此处所说的“表示比喻关系”，更不是指一个词在言语表达过程中“临时产生的比喻义”。）

从词义的历时发展看，“仿佛”表示比喻关系并不是现代汉语阶段才产生的。近代汉语中这个义项即已成熟稳定。如元代王实甫《西厢记》“柳丝长咫尺情牵惹，水声幽仿佛人呜咽”中的“仿佛”就是表示“像”。这类用法中的“仿佛”在表示比喻关系时可能还带有“好像”“似乎”等语义成分，而清代的运用情况则更为明确地表现为比喻，如：

[6] 竟有一等人，无故一心私念，闹的他自己亡魂失魄，仿佛热地蚂蚁一般，行踪无定，居止不安。（清·石玉昆《七侠五义》）

如果说“‘仿佛’+喻体+‘一般’”结构中，表示比喻关系不是由“仿佛”独立承担，其作为像义动词可能还不够典型，而在“仿佛+体词性宾语（喻体）”结构中，“仿佛”则完全独立承担了表示比喻关系。比如下列清代用例：

[7] 瞧见那蒙茸细草，都变成满目凄迷，听见那碧水潺湲，竟仿佛人声哽咽。再看那些红桃绿柳，宝马香车，无一不是助他的咨嗟，伤他的怀抱。（清·李百川《绿野仙踪》）

[8] 再往西走，见一个山峰，仿佛劈开的半个馒头，正面磨出几丈长一块平面，刻了许多八分书。（清·刘鹗《老残游记》）

可以说，“表示比喻关系”，是“仿佛”从近代汉语到现代汉语阶段较为稳固的主要义项和用法，可看作其固定义和固定用法。

1.1.3 从修辞关系看“仿佛”

此类“仿佛”是将本体与喻体连接起来。下面我们重点说说“仿佛”所带宾语作为喻体的临时性和固定性问题。

（1）喻体由说写者临时组合而成

大多数情况如此。上述各例即是。再如：

[9] 中国江苏省北部的农村被一片油菜花的艳黄色所淹没，这明亮的风景仿佛农户敞亮的心情。

“这明亮的风景”是本体，“农户敞亮的心情”是喻体，是临时组合而成的短语，“仿佛”是把本体和喻体联系起来的比喻词。

（2）喻体是具有一定凝固性的短语

表示比喻关系的动词“仿佛”与现成的较为定型的常用喻体形成句法上的动宾关系，二者“语义和谐”（陆俭明，2010），共同强化，使全句的比喻性更加突出。如：

[10] 他忽然听说母亲因心脏病去世了，他仿佛五雷轰顶。

喻体“五雷轰顶”，是一个主谓短语，成语，结构凝固性强。《现代汉语词典》释义：“比喻遭到巨大的打击”。这个成语的含义就是一个比喻义。

[11] 刘燕看完传真，淡淡一笑，心中却仿佛打翻了五味瓶。

[12] 消息传出，大上海仿佛炸开了锅，成千上万的影迷和市民隔夜就潮水般涌向火车站……

上述二例中的喻体“打翻了五味瓶”、“炸开了锅”，都是动宾短语，惯用语，结构凝固性较强，都是整体比喻表义，熟知度高。大多数惯用语如此。

[13] 刘禹锡仿佛一只破皮球，被踢来踢去——却依然达观。

喻体“一只破皮球”及承前省略主语的后续句“被踢来踢去”是具有一定凝固性的比喻表达形式。

[14] 仿佛落水者抓住了救命稻草，迈尔斯以最快的速度找出了那本书……

上例喻体“落水者抓住了救命稻草”，有一定凝固性，是现成的、常用的喻体。汉语中有不少这类常用喻体（有的结构凝固性强，比喻义明确稳定，已收入惯用语等熟语词典），使用时一般由比喻词将其与本体联系起来。

从句法关系看，此类“仿佛”，做谓语中心语。作为动词，不可重叠，一般只用肯定式而不用否定式。一般来说，本体是主语，喻体是宾语。宾语的句法性质和句法功能，较为复杂（下文详论）。

从语义关系看，此类“仿佛”属“断事动词”，与所带宾语之间没有施事、受事、用事等关系。（邢福义先生《汉语语法三百问》（商务印书馆2002年第73—75页）曾将“表示是非、有无、像似等意义的动词”看作“断事动词”，包括三小类：（1）是非类。现代汉语里只有一个“是”。（2）有无类。包括“有”和“没有”。（3）像似类。包括“像、似、如”和双音节的“好像、犹如、比如”等。“断事动词的重要特点，是带名词宾语，动宾之间只有断事关系，没有施事、受事、用事等关系。”）

1.2 作副词：“仿佛”充当其他比喻词的修饰成分

1.2.1 副词“仿佛”的句法位置和搭配情况

从语料看，“仿佛”主要修饰表示比喻关系的动词“是”，有时也修饰“成”、“像”、“变成”、“变作”等。

[15] 庐山的繁荣与凋敝，仿佛是一支中国历史发展的晴雨表。

这是“仿佛+是”。

[16] 这一段时间，岛内民众仿佛都成了“福尔摩斯”，人人对“陈水扁的伤口”、“子弹会转弯”、“保安人员当时举止违反常规”等议论纷纷，都自有一套说法。

[17] 袁世凯觉得自己仿佛成了一只过街老鼠，人人喊打了。（该例来自百度）

上述二例是“仿佛+成”。例中“福尔摩斯”、“过街老鼠”，都是熟知度较高的常用喻体。

[18] 海浪席卷而来，我看到轮船迅速沉入海中。刹那间，整个世界仿佛像黑暗的地狱一般。到处是尖叫声、呼喊声。

[19] 沙滩虽然很小，沙却又白又细又软，阳光照在上面，仿佛像雪一样。

上述二例是“仿佛+像+喻体+一般/一样”格式。再看“仿佛”修饰其他比喻词（下例是“仿佛+变作”）的情况：

[20] 瞧着那窗外的一丛迎春花，你自己也仿佛变作了它的一枝。

此类“仿佛”，不是把本体与喻体连接起来，不是比喻词，而是表示“似乎”，表示不确定判断，修饰句中“是”“成”“像”等表示比喻关系的动词，是副词，充当状语。

有的学者将“仿佛”所在的句子一律看作比喻，把不同义项和用法的“仿佛”都看作表示比喻关系的动词，欠妥。如：“他对她，对自己，对现在与将来，都没办法，仿佛是碰在蛛网上的一个小虫，想挣扎已来不及了。”例中“仿佛”被看作是明喻词，是动词，所连接的主语和宾语是谓词性的。其实，稍加分析，我们不难发现，例中“仿佛”是修饰“是”的副词，表示不确定判断，而“是”才是表示比喻关系的动词，“碰在蛛网上的一个小虫”是“是”的宾语，是喻体。

1.2.2 副词“仿佛”在比喻句中的修辞功能

副词“仿佛”虽然不直接表示比喻关系，但与全句的比喻表达密切相关。

一方面，由“是”充当比喻词的比喻，是一种特殊的判断，将两个被判断的对象联系起来时，主观性强，口气硬，而表示不确定判断的副词“仿佛”的修饰，使整个比喻带有一定的主观猜测或估计的意味，可缓和比喻词“是”的强硬和生硬的程度。“是”“成”这类侧重客观事实的判断词与“仿佛”侧重主观推测的副词相组合，二者相互补充，增强了句子语义表达的可接受性。如：

[21] 这种建筑一问世，仿佛成了中国的“金字塔”，引起了人们的好奇和关注。

若直接说“这种建筑……成了中国的‘金字塔’”，成为一个判断句，口气武断。而“成”之前加“仿佛”修饰，全句由判断句变为比喻句（即陈望道先生所论“譬喻”之一种：“暗喻”），同时其口气武断程度也相应减弱。

从“仿佛”的词义发展看，表示不确定判断（可解释为“好像，似乎”）与表示比喻关系（可解释为“像”）这两个义项之间有密切的联系（“像”义动词，多为多义词，其多个义项之间有发展演变关系）。“‘仿佛’+是/成/像”结构中，从句法位置看，“仿佛”用作表示不确定判断的副词，但是与之相关的表示比喻关系这个语义也在一定程度上参与了比喻句的构建，辅助像义动词“是/成/像”，使语义表达更细致准确。

另一方面，此类“仿佛”有时可促进词语搭配得以成立，使句子既合乎句法结构要求，又符合语义表达要求。如：

[22] 漓江的水真绿啊，绿得仿佛是一块无瑕的翡翠。

例中“仿佛”若删去，词语之间的句法搭配不合适，句法合格程度受到影响，句子结构难以成立。再如：

[23] 立冬小雪，正是渔民拉干贝的季节。渔船都扬起白帆，往来拉网，仿佛是成群结队翩翩飞舞的白蝴蛛。（杨朔《海市》）

[24] 湖中的岛屿三块石清晰可见，整个轮廓仿佛是一艘白色巨轮，漂泊在蓝蓝的海面上。

虽然“是”也可以表达比喻关系，所构成的比喻句一般看作“暗喻”的一种，但“是”毕竟主要用于表达判断（而表示比喻关系并不是“是”的主要义项和功能），上述二例若仅用“是”连接本体和喻体，“是”前没有一定修饰限定，那么“渔船……是成群结队翩翩飞舞的白蝴蛛”这样的表达，句子的语义合适性会受到影响。换句话说，若删去“仿佛”，句子的语义表达、词语之间的语义搭配都难以成立。

“是”字比喻句，受到语义和语体的限制，对搭配和上下文有一定的条件要求。“是”前有时需要加“仿佛”“像”“似乎”等副词修饰，就是搭配条件之一。此处不详论。

1.2.3 “‘仿佛’+是/成/像”结构在语篇中同其他比喻词共现

[25] 自从在破窑旧房里出生，穷苦就像影子一样缠住了我们，而今“山里娃”的春天走来了，命运仿佛是一个漫不经心的播种机，将我们漫不经心地播撒在山旮旯里，并且让我们在那荒芜、偏僻、风雨无常的土坡和沟岔里深深地扎下了根。

[26] 巴西队的球，仿佛是诗，浪漫而优美；意大利的球，宛若散文，潇洒而有

风度；德国队的……

上述二例，都是前后出现两个比喻。例[25]中，上一个用的比喻词是“像”，下一个是由“仿佛”修饰的“是”，例[26]上一个是由“仿佛”修饰的“是”，下一个是“宛若”，它们出现在上下句相同的句法位置上、相同的修辞结构成分的位置上，形成语篇中临时性的同义形式（李胜梅，2007），前后相互“浸染”，共同强化，突出了它们对比喻关系的表达，突出了语篇中上下句的比喻强度。

[27] 如果说特区仿佛是一排葡萄架，那么一幢幢大楼像是一串串葡萄，均匀地分布在绿色的长廊里。组团间隔有一条条绿化带，各组团的功能和人口分布合理。

上句的“仿佛是”，下句的“像是”，二者出现在相同语义位置、相同句法位置、相同修辞结构成分位置上，同义呼应，一方面共同强化，一方面使上下文用词体现活泼变化不雷同不呆板。例中“仿佛”与“像”都用来修饰表示比喻关系的动词“是”，这种上下文用法也可以部分地体现“仿佛”与“像”在语义和功能上的一致性：都可以表示不确定判断，这种情况下都是副词。

1.2.4 “‘仿佛’+是/成/像”结构的存在价值和分析意义

状中结构“‘仿佛’+是/成/像”表示比喻关系，有其独特的存在价值：（一）“仿佛”与“是/成/像”等的组合，性质上有别于单个比喻词，也不是两个比喻词的连用。它既不同于可直接表示比喻关系的比喻词“像”（构成陈望道先生所称明喻），也不同于可表比喻关系的动词“是”、“成”以及“变成”“成为”“变作”等（构成陈望道先生所称“暗喻”），也不同于可表比喻关系的动词“仿佛”。（二）保证句法搭配(“‘仿佛’+是/成/像”与宾语之间的搭配)的合格性；（三）增强语义搭配的和谐程度和表达的可接受性。

区分比喻表达中作为副词的“仿佛”与作为动词的“仿佛”，并对“‘仿佛’+是/成/像”结构同时进行句法分析、修辞分析和语篇分析，有利于我们考察并辨析一些似是而非的相关修辞现象。比如“像是”的明喻暗喻归属问题（张帅旗、孟昭泉，1998）。其实“是”前的“像”只是充当修饰成分的副词，并非比喻词，由副词“像”修饰的“是”充当比喻词，其结构和语义都有一定的特殊性，尚需进一步分析。明喻与暗喻的这种纠结，说明修辞现象本身存在复杂性，需要具体分析而不是笼统地强行归类，也说明学界明喻暗喻的分类依据和分类方法尚存在一定缺陷，需要重新探讨。

二、表比喻的“仿佛”句

2.1 “仿佛”的宾语

此处重点说说“仿佛”所带宾语的内部结构和句法功能。宾语的句法性质，有两种情况：NP；VP。

2.1.1 宾语是NP

宾语NP是名词，或是体词性偏正短语，有定语修饰限定。换个角度，从语义内容看，“仿佛”所连接的喻体是形象具体的“事物”。如：

[28] 各路军阀在帝国主义主子的直接插手下赤膊上阵，主政者仿佛走马灯一样一晃而过，迅速浮沉。

[29] 三位男性端坐在高高的木凳上，脸对着正前方，仿佛三尊石佛。除了左边那位偶与话机对讲，其余两人一言不发。

喻体“走马灯”是一个名词，喻体“三尊石佛”是一个体词性偏正短语，语义上都是形象具体的事物。

2.1.2 宾语是VP

从内部结构看，“仿佛”的宾语VP，有主谓结构、动宾结构、以动词为中心语的偏正结构等。换个角度，从语义内容看，“仿佛”所连接的喻体是对形象具体的“事件”的指称或陈述。从比喻关系看，“仿佛”所引导的VP，有的是对本体（全句大主语）自身的假设性陈述，有的是引出另外一个形象具体的“事件”对本体加以说明。

（1）宾语是以动词为中心的状中式偏正结构

[30] 照片上的史枯，脸颊仿佛刀劈斧砍一般，线条甚是苦难，眉头总是锁着……

“刀劈”和“斧砍”分别是以动词为中心的状中式偏正结构，“刀劈斧砍”虽然内部构成并列结构关系，但作为整体从功能看仍是动词性，共同充当“仿佛”的宾语。它与出现在宾语位置上的其他动词一样，从认知语义看，也是对“事件”的指称。

（2）宾语是动词或动宾结构

[31] 每周上音乐课时，全班同学个个都乐得手舞足蹈，仿佛过节一般。

[32] 走在幽深的小巷，仿佛在诵读着一部古老的史书。

前一例，宾语有后置的比拟助词“一般”；后一例“仿佛”直接带宾语。

（3）宾语是主谓结构

主谓结构，若从整体的句法功能看，有的是谓词性的，有的是体词性的，但从认知语义看，一般都是对“事件”的指称和陈述。所以本文将其放在VP里加以阐述。值得注意的是，作宾语的主谓结构，其小主语与全句大主语之间的关系，有下列两种情形（领属和不领属）：

[33] 他听到这个消息，仿佛心里放下了一块石头。

例中“仿佛”所带宾语（加点部分）是一个主谓结构，其小主语（“心里”）领属于全句的大主语(“他”)，这个主谓结构是对大主语加以形象的说明。

这种情况下的“仿佛”也可以出现在“小主语”与“小谓语”之间，比较下例：

[34] 听说自己以后可以不必再去和李士群周旋了，顿感一阵轻松，心头仿佛卸去了一块重压的石头。

此时从表面看，“仿佛”之后是一个动宾结构而不是主谓结构，但句中比喻关系和表义情况与例[35]基本相同，都是直接对本体（大主语）自身加以假设性的想象性的陈述，这是“喻体的假设性”的一种（李胜梅，1997）。

与之情况不同的则是：有的“仿佛”后的主谓结构的“小主语”与全句的“大主语”并不一致，并无领属关系。此类喻体是通过陈述另外一个形象的事件来说明本体(大主语)。如前文例[3]（仿佛婴儿出生后……）。再如：

[35] 昏明交割时分，草原上亮起了点点灯光，仿佛千百颗明珠滚落到丝绒地毯上。

[36] 小墩子却突然不再说什么，只是两手紧紧张张地在自己的一个人造革挎包里掏腾什么，后来，掏出来一样东西，仿佛贼娃子被迫交出赃物似的，颤抖着举给他看。

两例的喻体（加点部分），都是主谓短语，其小主语都不领属于大主语，例[35]“千百颗明珠”不领属于“草原上”，例[36]“贼娃子”不领属于“小墩子”。例[35]“仿佛”直接带宾语，例[36]宾语有后置的比拟助词“似的”。

2.1.3 “仿佛”的词义与“仿佛”宾语的句法性质之间密切相关

比较上述“仿佛”宾语的几类情形，“仿佛”后接名词、体词性偏正结构以及整体功能为体词的主谓结构时，其表示比喻关系的语义和功能，明确、显强；而后接谓词性的主谓结构、动宾结构、偏正结构时，“仿佛”虽然是表示比喻关系的动词，但是表示不确定判断这个语义也在一定程度上略有存留；而在“‘仿佛’+喻体+‘一般/一样/似的’”格式中，“仿佛”稍多地存留了表示不确定判断这个语义。

2.2 “‘仿佛’+宾语”结构的类型

2.2.1 “仿佛”+喻体（NP/VP）

上述例[2]~[5]、[7]~[14]、[29]、[32]~[35]即是，“仿佛”直接带宾语，动宾关系明确。

2.2.2 “仿佛”+喻体（NP/VP）+“一般/一样/似的”

上述例[1]、[6]、[28]、[30]、[31]、[36]即是。再如：

[37] 她的脸色苍白而带光泽，仿佛大理石似的；一双眼睛又黑又大，在黯淡的囚房中，宝石似的闪着晶莹的光。

例中喻体“大理石”是一个名词，“仿佛……似的”框式结构引出喻体并由此将本体与喻体联系起来。

[38] 这个亭踞在突出的一角的岩石上，上下都空空儿的；仿佛一只苍鹰展着翼翅浮在天宇中一般。

例中喻体“一只苍鹰展着翼翅浮在天宇中”是一个主谓结构，“仿佛……一般”框式结构引出喻体并由此将本体与喻体联系起来。

此处说说助词“一般/一样/似的”的词义和用法。江蓝生（1999）指出，从先秦到唐宋，汉语的比拟式基本上都是全式（引者注：即前面有像义动词的“D+X+Z”式，即“像义动词+喻体+比拟助词”式）”而简式（引者注：即“X+Z”，即“喻体+比拟助词”）很少见。唐宋时期出现了新的比拟助词“相似”和“一般”。“一般”本是形容词，进入比拟结构后词义虚化，用如比拟助词。我们看到，现代汉语阶段，比拟助词“相似”已不用，“一般”继续使用，但“词义并未消失净尽”。“是的”和“似的”是来源不同的两个比拟助词。现代汉语北方话中念作shì·de（是的）的比拟助词不是来自“似/也似/→/似的/也似的（sì·de）”系统，而是来自明代表示判断语气的句末助词“是的”（江蓝生，1992）。至明代，比拟助词“似、也似”后面加上结构助词“的”，使得比拟助词“似的”增加了结构助词的功能（江蓝生，1999）。

如此看来，“仿佛”+喻体（NP/VP）+“一般/一样/似的”，是近代汉语阶段比拟式在现代汉语的沿用和发展。该格式表示比喻关系不完全由“仿佛”独立承担，后置的“一般”“一样”“似的”这样的助词还残存其源头和发展过程中表示比拟和判断的词义。“仿佛”在表示比喻关系的同时，也存留一定的表示不确定判断的词义。作为动词的比喻词“仿佛”与比拟助词“一般/一样/似的”配合使用，构成现代汉语中一种较为稳定成熟的表示比喻关系的格式，从结构形式上强化了句子的比喻特征，从语义上细化了这一类比喻的表达。

2.3 “‘仿佛’+宾语”结构的组合能力和句法功能

表比喻关系的动词“仿佛”与其所支配的宾语所形成的结构一般在句中做谓语而不是做定语、状语，所以，我们可把由“仿佛”充当比喻词和谓语中心语的句子称为“表比喻的‘仿佛’句”或“‘仿佛’比喻句”。

江蓝生（1999）指出，从先秦到唐宋，汉语比拟式的语法功能都是在句中做谓语。现代汉语的比拟式“像+X（引者注：即喻体）似的（+NP/VP）”，从形式上可以分解为：a“像+X似的”和b“X似的+NP/VP”两式。其中，a式是汉语固有的“D+X·Z”式，b式来自阿尔泰语的“X似+NP/VP”的变体（变在“似”后加了结构助词“的”）。从功能上看，汉语的比拟式主要做谓语，阿尔泰语的比拟式主要做修饰语（定语、状语）。

现代汉语中，“仿佛”是一个常用的像义动词，既可进入江蓝生先生所说的a式，构成“仿佛+X似的”，也可直接带宾语，构成“仿佛+X”。这两种由“仿佛”

构成的动宾结构，都在句中充当谓语，是汉语固有的比拟式的沿用。

“‘仿佛’+宾语”，在句中作谓语的情况：（一）大多数情况是独立做谓语。上述例[1]~[14]、[28]~[38]都是。（二）有时则做连动结构的前项。如：

[39] 东京地下交通十分发达。12条地下铁路总长近200公里，仿佛经络一般将偌大的城市有机地连为一体。

喻体“经络”是名词，“仿佛……一般”将本体与喻体联系起来。“‘仿佛’+喻体+‘一般’”结构(VP1)，与后接动词性短语“将偌大的城市有机地连为一体”(VP2)构成连动结构，共同充当谓语，如此通过对喻体的陈述去进一步陈述本体。从比喻的结构成分看，VP1中提供形象的喻体，VP2可看作本体和喻体的相似点（这种相似点与那种表示性质状态的形容词性的典型相似点不同），VP1与VP2在语义上相互配合。

2.4“仿佛”比喻句的语篇环境

2.4.1“仿佛”比喻句的后续句

从句子的组织和延展看，从上下句的语篇衔接看，下文是否对由“仿佛”所支配的宾语即所引导的喻体所指称的“事物”和“事件”加以进一步描写，有如下两种情形：

（1）下文有承前省略主语的后续句对喻体加以进一步描写

先看“仿佛”+NP：

[40] 由县妇联组织青年妇女营造的3.9万亩绿色工程，仿佛一顶巨大的绿色斗篷，把这座昔日的荒山遮盖得严严实实。

“一顶巨大的绿色斗篷”，从句法上看，是“仿佛”的宾语，也是下一句陈述的对象；从修辞关系看，是喻体，后续句（“（主语承前省略）把这座昔日的荒山遮盖得严严实实”）对其展开了进一步的描述。

[41] 南方的河总是温情脉脉，一年四季水总是盈盈的，仿佛体态丰腴的少女，风姿绰约，袅袅娜娜地轻移莲步，曳动长裙。

“仿佛”将本体“南方的河”与喻体“体态丰腴的少女”联系起来。喻体是一个体词性偏正短语，后续句进一步顺势描写这一喻体的特点，由此更形象地说明上一句的“总是温情脉脉，一年四季水总是盈盈的”。下面两例亦如此：

[42] 这里的一切都是新的，仿佛一本刚刚打开的书，等待我们重新认识和解读。

[43] 这么些年来，他们的评论一直是我业务上的一个参照点，仿佛一把尺子，总是在帮我丈量着我的度。

再看“仿佛”+VP：

[44] 无数的诱惑仿佛已经编织成一张巨网，随时都会把人网住。

[45] 他紧张地怀抱方向盘，仿佛抱着个聚宝盆，入定般的沉默着。

“仿佛”后都是动宾结构，后续句对喻体的“事件”作进一步陈述。

上述[40] ~ [45]各例都是通过后续句进一步描写喻体而去描写本体的。此类比喻句中的“仿佛”，除了在句内联系本体和喻体，还直接影响了下文的句子结构，对后续句有启引作用，因而还表现为语篇现象，促进了语篇的衔接与连贯。

（2）下文不再顺势描写

此类比喻句中的“仿佛”，表现为句内现象。后续句所陈述的仍是全句的大主语，上下文保持视角一致和陈述对象的一致。

[46] 他只是摇头，眼睛死盯着炉火，一动不动地坐在那里，仿佛一尊石像。也许，对于难言的痛苦，一时难于说出，他沉默了一阵。

“仿佛”将本体“他”与喻体“一尊石像”联系起来，喻体是体词性偏正短语。下文并没有对喻体展开进一步的描述，而是继续陈述上句的“他”。

2.4.2 上下文中与其他比喻词和比喻句构成同义强化

[47] 青山绿水环绕中的古城集安，仿佛湖水中一片静立的荷叶，而城中伫立了1500多年的好太王碑则似荷叶上的一滴露珠，璀璨夺目。

从作者的语感看，显然是把“仿佛”与下文的“似”看作同义词来造句的。

[48] 叶子和花仿佛在牛乳中洗过一样，又像笼着轻纱的梦。

设喻者把上句的“仿佛”与下文相同句法位置上的“像”看作同义词。

不仅上下句相同句法位置上的比喻词之间构成同义强化，而且上下句都是比喻句，句际之间也有共同强化比喻的作用。

我们在前文描写过“‘仿佛’+是/成/像”结构在语篇中同其他比喻词共现的情形。此处描写的则是“仿佛”同其他比喻词的共现。这两种共现的修辞功能基本相同，都是同义强化；突出比喻词对比喻关系的表达，突出比喻句的比喻强度；体现用词活泼变化。

2.4.3. 上下文中出现比喻自述强化比喻特征

人们在言语表达过程中陈述自己正在说写的行为和方式，或正在说写的话语单元，可称为“言语自述”（李胜梅，2004）。有时，说写者运用“仿佛”来组织比喻句时，也会直接点明自己的表达方式或所说写的句子是比喻。如例[3]上文先出现“比喻说”，下文再出现由“仿佛”充当比喻词的比喻句（“勇气”号伸开“两腿”就仿佛婴儿……）；例[4]上文先出现“硬作比喻”，下文出现由“仿佛”充当比喻词的比喻句（她倒仿佛南唐）。

语篇中，比喻句与比喻自述这样前后配合，可以构成更大的语篇单位，形成语篇中的“比喻自述言语块”（李胜梅，2012）。其主要作用：突出“仿佛”表示比喻关系的表达作用，体现修辞功能；强化所在句子的比喻特征；促进上下句形式衔接、语义连贯，体现语篇功能。

2.4.4 “仿佛”比喻句多用于书面语

从附属色彩看，“仿佛”一般用于书面语，“仿佛”所在的句子一般具有一定文学色彩，主要用于散文或小说中作家的叙述语言而不是人物对白。与之不同，“像”作为现代汉语中的一个典型比喻词，则通用于口语和书面语。

3. 余论：“仿佛”词、“仿佛”结构、“仿佛”句之间的关系

比喻词的含义和用法与所构成的比喻句的特点密切相关。我们把作为比喻词的“仿佛”与“‘仿佛’+喻体”结构与表比喻的“仿佛”句三者联系起来并且放在语篇中考察，有助于我们尽可能充分地全面地认识“仿佛”词和“仿佛”句。

词的语体特征与所在句的语体特征密切相关。“仿佛”是一个“语体词”，无论是作为动词还是作为副词，都体现出较为鲜明的书面语特征，若是口语中使用，则会在一定程度上体现其口语的文雅和书面色彩。相应地，“仿佛”所在句也体现出一定的书面语特征。

此项研究对“仿佛”一词及其他比喻词的全面探讨（词汇意义、句法功能、修辞意义、篇章功能等）、词典释义、对外汉语词语教学等具有理论意义和应用价值，限于篇幅，另文阐述。

参考文献

[1] 江蓝生.助词“似的”的语法意义及其来源[J].中国语文，1992年第6期.

[2] 江蓝生.从语言渗透看汉语比拟式的发展[J].中国社会科学，1999年第4期.

[3] 李胜梅.喻体的假设性[J].修辞学习，1997年第4期.

[4] 李胜梅.“话说回来”的语用分析[J].修辞学习，2004年第3期.

[5] 李胜梅.语篇中的同义形式[J].南昌大学学报，2007年第4期.

[6] 李胜梅.比喻词的含义与词典释义问题[Z].中国修辞学会2011年学术研讨会暨吴士文先生诞辰85周年纪念会论文，2011.

[7] 李胜梅.“语篇言语块”的理论位置及研究路径[J].阜阳师范学院学报，2012年第3期.

[8] 陆俭明.修辞的基础——语义和谐律[J].当代修辞学，2010年第1期.

[9] 张帅旗、孟昭泉.论“像是”“是像”的明喻暗喻归属问题[J].中州大学学报，1998年第2期.

论中国判词语体的产生与演变

田荔枝
（[中国]　山东大学）

摘　要： 语体是适应不同交际功能、不同题旨情景需要，经过抽象而形成的语言运用特点的综合体。每一种语体均系适应人类社会交际需要而产生，都有着表现自己语体特点的不同的语言材料、语言手段。它们实际上是各种修辞现象所组成的一个抽象综合体。判词因其重要的社会价值而为世人所重视并成为法律语体中最具代表性的下位语体，其语体特色足以代表法律书面语体特征。中国判词从其产生历经数千年的发展变化，不同历史阶段呈现出不同的语体特色。判词语体作为汉语语体体系中的一个独立的语体样式，是语言运用在司法判决领域所形成的功能变体，是为适应司法判决领域需要，运用全民语言形成的语言特点体系。

关键词： 判词语体；产生；演变；原因

一、判词语体的产生

语言与语体的关系，实际上是语言与言语关系的具体反映，因为言语总是以具体的言语事件为表征而显现出来，而具体的言语事件又确实都归属于特定的语体。[1]

1. 语判先于书判

语判即以口语形式表达的口头语体判词，书判则是以书面语形式表达的书面语体判词。判词产生于诉讼之事，因为有诉讼才有判案，然而最早的判案却不一定诉诸于文字，孔子曾称赞子路“片言可以折狱”[2]，说明早期的判词可以是以口头语体形式出现。“言语的先在性，即意味着语体的先在性，因为语言产生的伊始，就是借助于语体才得以生成、存在。”[3] 但是判词特定的交际任务和功能的实质，决定了口头语体形式的判词与后来书面语体形式的判词除了语言风格的不同，在内容要素上应该是一致的。

“判词是应司法的需要而产生的，它的出现应有一定的文化基础和背景，那就是法律制度的相对完善和健全，使判词成为司法制度的形式之一，并具有相对的稳

1　丁金国：《社会语文形态与语体的演变》，《修辞学习》2009年第5期第1页。

2　《论语·颜渊篇第十二》。

3　丁金国：《社会语文形态与语体的演变》，《修辞学习》2009年第5期第2页。

定性和规范性，其次是整个社会的文字表达达到一定的水平。”[4] 只有当案判的内容和处理情况诉诸书面语言，以一种比较固定的格式和规范表现出来之后，真正具有书面语体意义的判词才得以形成。

中国夏代的法律史称“禹刑”，当时已有了初步形成的刑书。《尚书·大传》有“夏刑三千条”的记述。《左传·昭公十四年》引《夏书》说：“昏、墨、贼，杀。皋陶之刑也。”又说：“已恶而掠美为昏，贪以败官为墨，杀人不忌为贼。”殷代甲骨文字印证了《礼记·王制》中有关殷代诉讼程序、审判制度、执行刑杀、监禁羁押等的记载。

古代中国自春秋战国兴起封建法典化运动以来，经历了秦朝的进一步发展，到汉代，其法律体系日益庞大，就法律形式而言，已有律、令、格、式四种。从律文来看，共有四类，即《九章律》、《傍章律》、《越宫律》、《朝律》，总计有60篇之多。据《汉书·刑法志》载，当时共有律令359章，大辟（死刑）409条182事，死刑决事比13472事。因此，“文书盈于几阁，典者不能遍睹”。与前相比，法典化的进步是显而易见的，但同时，也带来了体系庞杂、内容重复、语焉不详的缺陷。自魏晋南北朝到隋唐，经过400多年的改革，法典化运动有了新的发展，其总趋势是精简或合并律文，变汉律60篇为唐律的12篇；变律令359章为唐律的502条。无论从律文本身，还是法律内容、法律语言，都进行了改革，法律语言也变得更加精练。[5]“中国古代判词产生的时间，当在殷周时代。因为，一方面中国古代在殷代即产生了中国最早的文字甲骨文，为判词的产生创造了条件；另一方面，中国古代法律早熟，根据古籍记载、最晚在舜时代，产生了对判词的社会需要。”[6]

《尚书·舜典》：“舜圣德聪明，建法曰：象以典刑，流宥五刑，鞭作官刑，扑作教刑，金作赎刑，眚灾肆赦，怙终贼刑。钦哉钦哉，惟刑之恤哉？于是流共工于幽州，放驩兜于崇山，窜三苗于三危，殛鲧于羽山，四罪而天下成服。又五流有宅，五宅三居。惟明克允。”

《周礼·秋官·司寇》：“以两造禁人讼，入束矢于朝然后听之；以两剂禁入狱，入钧金三日致于朝，然后听之。以三刺断庶人狱讼之中，一曰讯群臣，二曰讯群吏，三曰讯万民。听人之所刺宥以施上服下服之刑。又以五声听狱讼求民情，一曰辞听，二曰色听，三曰气听，四曰耳听，五曰目听。凡听五刑之讼必原父子之亲，君臣之义以权之。意论轻重之序，慎测浅深之量以别之。悉其聪明，致其忠爱以尽之。疑狱泛与众共之。众疑则疑之，必察小大之比以成之。成狱辞，吏以狱成告于正。正听之。正以狱成告于大司寇，大司寇听之棘木之下。大司寇以狱之成告于王，王命三公参听之。三公以狱之成告于王，王三宥然后制刑。”穆王作《吕刑》，曰：“两造俱备，师听五辞；五辞简孚，正于五刑；五刑弗简，正于五罚；五罚弗服，正于五过。五过之疵，惟官，惟反，惟内，惟货，惟来。”此外，《礼

4 苗怀明：《中国古代判词的文学化进程及其文学品格》，《江海学刊》2000年第5期第156页。
5 郭成伟：《唐律与〈龙筋风髓判〉体现的中国传统法律语言特色》，《法学家》2006年第5期第55页。
6 汪世荣：《中国古代判词研究》，中国政法大学出版社1997年，第25页。

记·月令·孟秋之月》："是月也，有司修法制，缮囹圄，具桎梏，禁止奸慎罪邪务博执。命理瞻伤、察创、视折、审断。决狱讼必端平。"

上述记载说明，判词的产生有其社会需要和相应的法律制度背景。

关于理狱断案的记载，在先秦史籍中已有之，如《左传·昭公十四年》：

晋邢侯与雍子争鄐田，久而无成。士景伯如楚，叔鱼摄理。韩宣子命断旧狱，罪在雍子。雍子纳其女于叔鱼，叔鱼蔽罪邢侯。邢侯怒，杀叔鱼与雍子于朝。宣子问其罪于叔向。叔向曰："三人同罪，施生戮死可也。雍子自知其罪而赂以买直，鲋也鬻狱，邢侯专杀，其罪一也。已恶而掠美为昏，贪以败官为墨，杀人不忌为贼。《夏书》曰：'昏、墨、贼、杀，皋陶之刑也。'请从之。"乃施邢侯而尸雍子与叔鱼于市。

叔向把行贿的雍子、枉法的法官叔鱼、杀人的邢侯都判了死刑。"曰"，即为判词。然而这种判词在以后的秦汉至六朝这几代正史中，甚少记载。仅在《魏书·窦瑗传》中见有三公郎封君义的一席判词。南朝（梁）萧统编的总集《昭明文选》中，不见收有判词。"体大思精"的文体论专著《文心雕龙》，也没有论及"判"这种文体。其原因在于"判"在这一历史阶段尚未发展成为一种公认的文体。

然而，文体不同于语体，语体可以表现为口头的形式，亦可表现为书面形式，判词语体的产生应该是在判词文体被公认之前，正如索绪尔《普通语言学教程》中提出："要言语为人所理解，并产生它的一切效果，必须有语言；但要使语言能够建立，也必须有言语。从历史上看，言语的事实总是在前的。"判词语体作为司法裁判事件的体现，理应成为后来判词文体的先行。

因此，古代判词语体主要表现在口头和书面两个方面，它随着法律制度的产生、沿革而形成和发展，同时伴随我国文体理论产生和不断细化，加之其司法功能的需要，判词书面语体不断完善并渐趋稳定，口头判词语体则逐渐消失。但从现有的资料来看，难以断定先秦以前是否有书面语体意义的判词出现。

就在这种演变过程中古代判词语体大致经过了萌芽阶段（夏、商至春秋后期）、雏形阶段（秦汉时期）、繁荣阶段（唐、宋两代）、成熟阶段（明、清两代）四个历史时期，最后发展为近代、现代判词语体。

2. 散体判词先于韵体判词

以表达意义为主的语体是散体判词，与之相对应的，以表情为主的语体是韵体判词。尽管在语言产生之初，韵散相杂，但语用中最基本核心的成分，还是散体。散语体对于韵语体来说是基础，是"原型"。人们在运用语言进行交际时，无论何种体，都要以表达意义为前提。达意是交际的第一要义，这点无论从儿童的语言习得，还是从聋哑人的习语过程都可证实。现存古老文献所提供的事实亦可支持这一点。如果说语言是处在不断地发展变化之中，那是因为人们对语言的运用始终是处在"变"的运动状态，所以说散体判词所代表的是判词的原型范畴，是各类判词语体的核心。之所以称其为原型，是因为其本质特征与人们大脑中的经验最接近、最匹配，因而也最容易被感知和记忆。需要说明的是原型与隶属之间虽是等级关系，但其边缘并不是清晰的，而是经常处在模糊状态，甚至会相互重叠，互相渗透。

二、判词语体的稳定与变化

“语体是语言运用的‘先导’，人们每一次的语言运用，都自觉或不自觉地在遵从着一定的语用模式运作，都受着一定的语体规约。因为任何一种独立的语体，都以其相对封闭的构成成分作为其存在的根据。”[7] 语体的这种客观性、社会性决定了判词语体存在的相对稳定性。然而，作为司法裁决的载体，判词与司法制度、社会文化环境以及语文政策有着密切关联，后者的变迁直接影响到判词语体的规范，由此也就决定了判词语体在任何意义上的稳定都是相对的，而其变化却是绝对的。“语体的浸润与演变主要采取两种形式：一是渐变，一是突变。渐变是常态，是语体自然的演化过程；突变是偶发态，是超出常规的演变，当然突变中也隐含着渐变的事实。”[8] 无论渐变或突变，都存在着一个正负方向问题。正向演变既有利于社会语言生活的稳定，也利于判词语体体系的严整化、科学化，更好地发挥其对社会的服务功能。负向演变则不然，其本质上是对判词语体功能的偏离甚至损毁，如古代“世俗喜道琐细遗事，参以滑稽”[9] 的花判和当代史上文革时期的政治化判词就是例证。

语体的渐变是由语体的稳定性特征所决定的，因为任何一种语体都是历史发展的产物，一经定型，对社会的语言生活来讲，就具有一种无形的规范作用。判词语体从产生之日起，就以系统的形态处于言语社群之中，从而使判词语体得以保持有序的状态服务于社会。但判词语体的司法属性决定了它不是一成不变的。常态的渐变是在人们在不知不觉之中发生的，如古代判词语体从商、周至明清的演变，三千年来一直是处在渐变的常态之中。无论是散判还是骈判，实判还是拟判，在语体风格上大体呈现伦理化、文学化、情感化与典雅化的倾向，在行文程式语言上，由原始的“曰”“断曰”“议曰”“论曰”到后来的“查”“讯得”“审得”等基本程式。

正如胡明扬在《现代汉语和现代汉语规范化》[10] 中指出，一般认为，先秦古文是和当时的口语基本一致的，到汉代就开始和口语脱节，到隋唐之际，这种脱节现象已经十分严重，因此就出现了最早的白话作品。这些作品反映的语言已经和古代汉语大不相同，我们称之为近代汉语。唐宋以后的文言文直到五四以前，基本上没有重大变化，但人民群众口头的语言一直在发生变化，和文言文的距离越来越远，几乎成了两种完全不同的语言。五四以后，白话文逐步取代了文言文，但是在各个领域全面取代文言文还是解放以后的事。如果说在《尚书》时代，判词语体还属当时的典型口语白话，那么到了秦汉则以书面语为主要特征。自古至清，三千年来的

7 丁金国：《语体风格分析纲要》，暨南大学出版社出版2009年，第128页。
8 丁金国：《语体风格分析纲要》，暨南大学出版社出版2009年，第128页。
9 [宋]洪迈：《容斋随笔》。
10 胡明扬：《现代汉语和现代汉语规范化》，载《现代汉语讲座》，知识出版社1983年，第2页。

判词语体发展的基本轨迹脉络清晰，除唐代盛行的骈体判词及风格滑稽的“花判”外，古代判词在语体规范上没有特别大的改变。

“突变”不是某一语体的个别成分的改变，或某种语体的消长，而是特定语言的语体系统发生整体性的变化。在汉语语体风格演进史上，这种体系性的变化，唯辛亥革命及五四“白话文运动”，在革除旧体倡明新体中来得彻底，其促发语体在语言生活中的变化最为典型。辛亥革命对帝制文牍语体的革除，五四“白话文运动”对文言文的扫荡，其结果是造成了汉语语体内部构成要素的骤变，从而引起汉语语体体系的整体性嬗变。由于旧语体赖以存在的功能域的消失，引发了体系性的置换，随着新的功能域的形成，与之相应的新语类也相继而生。由此可见，一切突变都是“人为性”的，其突变的因由和轨迹都清晰可见。辛亥革命成功伊始，其第二号公告就是《公文程式令》，在废止帝制时代的文牍语类同时，新式的公文程式也届时产生。这一改变是本质性的，其所创制的公牍语类，当是汉语现代公牍语类的发端，加之白话文运动的推波助澜，从而使现代公牍语类终于在汉语语言生活中站稳了脚跟。此后的变化，都是沿着渐变的规律运行。即使有象“文革语类”那样的冲撞，也未能伤及自民国、五四以来所奠立的根基。这种体系性的变化，可总括为：废止了帝制时代公牍语类的整个体系，在革除沿用两千多年的制、诰、誓、敕、诏、谕、册、奏、章、本、表、疏、等四十余种文牍语类的同时，创制了呈、令、谕、批、示、公布、状、咨、公函、照会等新语类；在程式和体制上新旧迥然，突出表现于称谓、开头语、收尾语等方面。旧时的称谓，上下、尊卑、贵贱等级森严，称谓出错，轻则杖罚，重则丧命。文牍的开头、结尾专有一套陈腐的套语。诸如“奉天承运，皇帝诏曰”、“臣某言”、“稽首上书”；结尾语用“钦此”、“特谕”、“诚惶诚恐”等不一。这一切统统予以废除，公务以官职相称，民间则以“先生”、“君”等相呼。文牍的内部结构，也都重新作了规定。其他类型的语体，虽无法定格式，但在白话语类及翻译语体的影响下，也发生了很大的变化；在语言的语义品级、词语节律、句读结构、表达方式等方面都发生了变化，与此前比较，发生了体系性的置换，瞬时的骤变，竟然超越几千年的演化。

在这种体系性变化的前提下，判词语体亦随之发生变化。古代判词发展到近代，在其由简到繁、由初级到高级的演化中，从文言到文白间杂经历了个质变过程，不论在语词、结构、表达方式等方面均出现了重大转型，而这种转型正是在社会制度重大变迁的背景下发生的，是一种正向的突变，出现了判词语体的近代化转型，也正是到了清末“判词”开始被称为“判决书”，其意义不仅在于单纯的名称变化，而在于判词语言载体背后社会的变迁。

在很长一个时期里，由于历次政治运动的影响，司法工作受到严重破坏，现代判词语体随之出现了负向突变，以至完全背离判词的法律语体特性，背离判词语体规范，以政治话语取代法言法语，使判词语体彻底丧失了应有的司法功能，成为政治话语霸权操纵下的服务于政治的工具，这就是“文革”时期出现的政治化判词，姑且称之为“文革判”。

作为共时态的语体，从其产生起就处在变化状态，都是历时发展的产物，在其共时的构成成分中，均可寻觅到历时演变的痕迹。而演变则是语体存在的常态，是语体的生命源泉，汉语语体史上那些凝滞僵化的语体，如骈体文和八股文的消亡，是最好的例证。可见，一切演变都是历时语体的自然延续，旧的结构在演变中并没有全然消逝，而是潜隐在新的结构之中。语体演变的表现方式有：交叉渗透、消失、蘖生、融合。

而判词语体的演变主要表现为交叉渗透和消失两种情形。

判词语体的交叉渗透是演变的主要方式，也是判词语体生存的主要形态。通常交叉渗透并不改变语体的性质，只是在语言运用中的自然流动。交叉渗透作为一种演变方式，演变的结果，可能是"正向"演变，即向着优化方向变，也可能是"负向"演变，如"花判"、"文革判"等。"花判"是文学语体向判词语体的渗透，"文革判"则是政论语体向判词语体的渗透，这种渗透均是对判词语体司法理性的消解，或者说是判词语体功能偏离、受损的退化过程。

判词语体的消失，是指某一判词语体从有到无的语用现象而言。这一现象在语体的突变时，表现最为明显，当然消失的程度不一，有的完全消亡，如花判、杂判；有的则是"转生"，借助于新的躯壳而复萌。如拟判转化为公案小说。无论判词演变成为纯文学文体还是融入叙事文学，判词的文学化倾向都消解了判词作为实用性文体的文体意义，开拓扩展了判词的文学价值。这种趋势从文学的方面来看，无疑是一件幸事，而从判词实用和法律的角度来看则应当受到批评，历史上曾有徐师曾《文体明辨序说》批评唐代判词"其文堆垛故事，不切于弊醉；拈弄辞华，不归于律格，为可惜耳。"以维护判词的实用性。

由上可知，判词语体演变的规律呈常态与变异相协、规范与反规范互动。语体的共时结构，就是一种常态，是一种约定俗成的模型，本质上是一种规范格式，而其变化形态则是一定背景下发生的阶段性现象，对语体的稳定有着或正或负的作用。

三、判词语体演变的原因

"语言的生命在于运用，而语言运用却必定诉诸于语体，任何脱离语体的语言运用是根本不存在的，所以说语言的变化，都必定植根于语体之中。但是，语言的变化常始于个别、局部，而语体的变化则是语言变化的积淀，也就是说，语言中个别成分的改变，并不一定都立即引起语体的变化，因为语体的变化，并不仅限于语言要素，还包括非语言要素的改变。"[11] 如汉语词汇的双音节化，最先出现在公牍语体中，双音节化的结果，是汉语在发展中的重要演变，而恰恰这种演变最先显现在语体上。可见，"语言的演变必然寓于语体，而语体的演变却并不一定都蕴涵着语言的演变。"[12] 语体演变的动因可总括为外部原因和内部原因。

11 丁金国：《语体风格分析纲要》，暨南大学出版社出版 2009年，第134页。

12 丁金国：《语体风格分析纲要》，暨南大学出版社出版 2009年，第134页。

1. 判词语体演变的外部原因

主要涉及社会物质文化、语言政策以及制作者个体文化素养三方面原因。

社会物质文化的发展，必然要求与之相应的语言形式来表现，这是由语言与社会的共存关系所决定。对此，刘勰《文心雕龙·时序》论到："文变乎世情，兴废系乎时序"。语体发展史上所出现的语体生发、消亡、兴衰、更替现象，都直接、间接与社会经济、政治、文化的兴盛、消长息息相关。判词语体的演变与法律制度及其变迁具有直接的关系。

中国古代"法自君出"，君主掌握国家最高立法权，一切法典、法规皆以君主名义颁行。中国古代法律不受宗教影响，而强调遵循礼教，强调维护纲纪伦常。经过汉儒改造，礼融进了诸子中的可取成分，又成为"礼教"，成为指导立法、司法的原则和理论依据。法律以刑法为主刑始终是中国古代法律的主题。古代没有部门法的划分，历代法典、法律通称刑律，实体法与程序法也不区分，民事诉讼程序与刑事诉讼程序混一。另一方面，专制君主无视下民的主体权利，平民百姓更无权利意识，以讼为耻为累等等，致使中国古代民事立法偏枯，与刑法畸重形成强烈反差。司法从属于行政，在地方，一地行政长官即兼理同级司法审判。这些古代法制特点对古代判词语体的发展变化具有根本性的制约作用。

另外，语言文化政策的推行，所触发的语体演变，则是以行政手段有意而为之，这在历史上不乏其例。仅以公牍语体而论，从秦汉到民国，历代历朝均有明文规定，对公牍语类的选取和格式的要求。民国以降，国共两个政权，各自都曾多次发布过有关公牍语体的政策。1949年以来，中央政府曾四度修订公牍语类的制作及处理办法，由此可见某些语体的人为性特征。社团和名人的感召力，也是一种有意推动演变的行为，五四白话文运动当属此类。其结果是彻底推翻了文言古体，代之以现代口语为特征的各种语体的新生。判词语体由文言转而为文白间杂以至现代白话文、当代普通话的运用，均说明是语言文化政策的直接推动。

另外，制判者个体文化教育程度和社会的审美取向也是语体演变的一个重要因素。从语体发生学的角度看，任何一种新语体的产生，都始于个体，都是先由个体所创造，进而经言语社群无数次的运用，最终为言语社群接受或扬弃。例如中国古代的文学化的判词，以及近代民国时期大理院精美的判词、马锡五审判方式下通俗化的判词等等均与制判者个体素质有密切关系，当然不同个体素质的出现也是不同时代司法理念选择的结果，反过来个体素质下产出的判词又作用于所在时代的司法理念，如是，汉语判词语体在历史的流变中得以不断地丰富和发展。

2. 判词语体演变的内部原因

主要是判词语体内部构成成分的消长更替、判词语体与语体体系中其他个体语体的交叉渗透、体系内部进行功能的再分配问题。

个别语体内部构成成分的消长、更替，最初不会发生体系性的变动，只有当特定语体本身发生消长时，才会引起体系性的连锁反应。如古代判词语体中的“拟判”，其在古代中国曾极盛一时。然而后来，这种形象化判词由于其内部构成成分的逐步改变，文学叙事成分的介入，一种新的语体形式“公案小说”应运而生。实际上“公案小说”只是“拟判”的拓展，判词在唐代“发展完备并完成其文学化的转型过程，形成了自身特有的文学品格，成为一种新的文学体裁。”[13] 虽然这是从文体角度阐释，但实际上同时也说明判词语体引起内部文艺语体因素的不断增长，最终由断案释明为主旨的判词分蘖为叙说故事的公案小说，其内部的基本构成和其功能，均发生了质的改变，由判词语体转化为纯粹的文艺语体。

各语体间相互交叉与渗透是不同语体间相互作用，相互感应的一种现象，是语体存在的普遍事实，严格讲，纯之又纯的语体并不多见，且不说开放的文艺语体，即使相对独立、封闭的法律语体等也难免其他体语体的渗入。也许“交叉与渗透是语体本身的一种运作机制，是发展的重要内在动力，是语体自身生命力的表现。……社会才呈现出绚烂丰繁的语言生活。”[14] 然而，从判词语体流变的历史过程中我们可以看到，不论是发生在古代的文学语体向判词语体的渗透，还是发生在现代的政论语体对判词语体的冲击，都是一种负向的演变，因为文学语体的形象性和政论语体的政治功利性都在消解判词语体的司法理性，由此，可以断言：判词语体只有在相对封闭的语体规范下才能更好地实现其交际职能，语体交叉渗透理论的积极价值在判词语体这里很难得到体现。

“只要文学语体与大众语体的对立保持着适当的关系，对立的双方就可以成为两个相互补充的源泉，向语言供输力量并确保语言的纯洁性。”[15] 此言虽然是在论及文学语体和大众语体即高雅语体与通俗语体问题，实际上关系到高低语体的对立的问题，我们也可以由此推及判词语体与大众语体之间的关系，在正常的语言生活中，只有保持高雅语体与大众语体对立，是维系语言社会的基本条件之一，正是这种对立，才使言语交际得以有序地进行。有人曾提出判词语体的大众化、通俗化要求，实际上这是在模糊这两种语体间的界限和功能，是一种有悖语体交际职能的极端论点。当然，这种对立的距间比例必须合适。

概而言之，目前有关判词语体形成问题，一般认为是人类社会交际多方面的需要为判词语体形成和存在提供了社会基础，语言材料、表现手段在功能上的分化是判词语体存在的物质基础。由于语言外部因素与语言自身因素的相互结合才形成语体。随着客观环境的变化，人类认知能力的进化和发展，对于正在形成中的语体范畴来说，出现消长龃龉的情况是一个历史地逐步形成的过程，并且在语体形成之后，仍随着社会发展而发展变化着。

---

13 苗怀明：《论中国古代公案小说与古代判词的文体融合及其美学品格》，《齐鲁学刊》2001年第1期第109页。

14 丁金国：《语体风格分析纲要》，暨南大学出版社出版，2009年，第136页。

15 [德]威廉·冯·洪堡特：《论人类语言结构的差异及其对人类精神发展的影响》，姚小平译，商务印书馆2004年。

三、结 语

语体是适应不同交际功能、不同题旨情景需要，经过抽象而形成的语言运用特点的综合体。每一种语体均系适应人类社会交际需要而产生，都有着表现自己语体特点的不同的语言材料、语言手段。它们实际上是各种修辞现象所组成的一个抽象综合体。判词因其重要的社会价值而为世人所重视并成为法律语体中最具代表性的下位语体，其语体特色足以代表法律书面语体特征。我国判词从其产生历经数千年的发展变化，形成独具的语体特色。判词语体作为汉语语体体系中的一个独立的语体样式，是语言运用在司法判决领域时所形成的功能变体，是为适应司法裁判领域需要，运用全民语言形成的语言特点体系。其语体规范特点表现为：理性化、专业化、书面化、中性化。

判词作为司法公正的最终载体，是连接公众与司法的纽带，公众对司法的直接评价，往往并不是来源于对审判工作的全面分析，而是来源于对个案处理结果的观察和感受，判词语体规范是公众感受司法理念最直接的路径，叙述、说理、引用法律条文等做到无懈可击，才能使判词成为司法公正的载体，产生切实的司法公信力。

参考文献

[1] 陈汝东.当代汉语修辞学[M].北京:北京大学出版社，2005年.

[2] 丁金国.语体风格分析纲要[M].广州:暨南大学出版社，2009年.

[3] 苗怀明.论中国古代公案小说与古代判词的文体融合及其美学品格[J].齐鲁学刊，2001年第1期.

[4] 苗怀明.中国古代判词的文学化进程及其文学品格[J].江海学刊，2000年第5期.

[5] 陶东风.文体演变及其文化意味[M].昆明:云南人民出版社，1994年.

[6] 田荔枝.从《折狱新语》看判词语言风格的变化[J].语言文字应用，1996年第4期.

[7] 汪世荣.中国古代判词研究[M].北京:中国政法大学出版社，1997年.

[8] 吴承学.中国古代文体形态研究[M].广州:中山大学出版社，2000年.

[9] 吴承学.唐代判文文体及源流研究[J].文学遗产，1999年第6期.

[10] 熊先觉.司法文书研究[M].北京:人民法院出版社，2003年.

[11] 杨育棠.中国古代判词语体风格变迁——从唐代的骈判到宋代的散判[A].周庆生 王洁 苏金智，语言与法律研究的新视野[Z].北京:法律出版社，2003年.

[12] 姚小平.洪堡特——人文研究和语言研究[M].北京:外语教学与研究出版社，1995年.

[13] 中国华东修辞学会，复旦大学语言文学研究所. 语体论[M].合肥:安徽教育出版社，1987年.

The Emergence and Evolution of China's Verdict Style

Tian Lizhi
(Shandong University, China)

Abstract: In pragmatics, style is a system which is consistent with each communication function and context. Those features formed from abstract progress make up a complex which becomes a style. Each style comes into being as a result of social intercourse needs and each one has its own material and skill to represent its features. Actually, it is an abstract complex of various figures of speech. Verdicts are to be valued by people for its important social value and are the most representative type among legal documents. Its style features are enough to represent judicial written style. China's verdicts enjoy a long history and have experienced thousands years of changes, and now it possesses its special character. As an independent style sample, verdict style is a functional variant when language is applied in the judicial verdicts and is created to fit in the judicial judgment and objectives.

Keywords: verdict style; emergence of style; evolution of style; causes

国际汉语教材编写与国家形象修辞策略

秦惠兰

（[中国] 上海师范大学）

摘　要： 中国“国家形象”的传播与构筑有各种各样的形式、层次、途径，其中最直接、有效、亲和、畅通的路径是汉语国际传播，包括“对内”的对外汉语教学和现在正在“对外”进行的汉语国际推广。汉语传播既是一种语言的传播，也是一种话语的传播，它们在共同构成的“中国式话语”中塑造着一个中国“国家形象”。而提供这种话语的基础文本就是汉语教材，中国“国家形象”的塑造也因教材文本语料的优劣而受到影响，因此，编写对外汉语教材时必须考虑文本的话语策略。

关键词： 汉语国际传播；“国家形象”；对外汉语教材；话语策略

关于中国“国家形象”的讨论，近年来颇受关注。面向全球的中国“国家形象”传播，最直接、最有效、最畅通、最亲和、最平民化的路径，就是汉语国际传播，包括“对内”的对外汉语教学和现在正在“对外”进行的汉语国际推广。[1] 两者都在传播汉语的过程中通过“中国话”共同构建着中国的“国家形象”，形成一个特殊的国际话语权空间。这种构建中国“国家形象”的主要载体来自于汉语教材所提供的课文文本，因此，对外汉语教材文本“话语”的优劣，直接关系到中国“国家形象”的输出，关系到中国在世界和平崛起过程中所要塑造的一个良好的“国家形象”。本文拟对对外汉语教材编写中的国家形象传播策略作一探讨。

一、国家形象构建与教材编写原则

许多专家学者都指出，汉语国际推广目前面临着两大瓶颈：一是教材，二是教师。但讨论多局限在语言教学的角度，如在《世界汉语教学》杂志创刊20周年之际，有学者曾对教材问题提出了16条意见（李晓琪，2007）。但是其中只有“结构、功能、文化因素在新时代教材中的定位与体现”一条，是和我们讨论的教材文本中的国家形象问题有些关系，但是其在整个教材建设中也并不显得突出。其实，汉语国际推广也好，在国内展开的对外汉语教学也好，教材与教师的瓶颈问题始终没有得到真正意义上的解决。

笔者以为，当前形势下，缺乏主动传播中国优秀的传统文化的责任意识，缺

1　“对内”指在中国境内进行的对外汉语教学，“对外”指在境外进行的汉语教学。

少正确传播中国国家形象的清醒意识，恐怕是除上述两个瓶颈之外汉语国际推广目前面临着的另一个更为迫切需要解决的重大问题，虽然它们不是同一个层面上的问题，前者是一个学科策略问题，后者是一个国家策略问题，[2] 但它们却又是互相关联的。因此，很有必要在16条意见之外再加上1条：在教材编写中要有构建良好的中国“国家形象”之意识。因为每一位从事对外汉语的教师乃至每一册教材的编者也都可能成为一个国家形象的叙述者。[3]

汉语传播既是一种语言的传播，也是一种话语的传播。语言的传播是指作为一种语言知识、技能的传授，传播对象即作为受众的学习者是学习一门语言。同时也是学习民族文化，以及历史、宗教、政治、经济、乃至日常生活。外国人在学习汉语这种语言时，必定也会感受到与其深深交融在一起的中国文化、民族感情、生活习俗等，体会到“中国式话语”的特殊性。因此，汉语传播也是一种话语的传播，外国学生在学汉语的过程中，透过“中国式话语”，也在学习、了解中国人的思维方式、情感模式，了解中国与西方世界的种种不同，并试着理解这个给他们带来或神秘、或恐惧的东方大国。

然而，汉语国际教育者大都忽略了汉语作为一种话语的传播，人们总是把汉语仅仅作为一种语言加以研究，教材编写也只是关心甲级词、乙级词的编排率、复现率，语法点的难易先后顺序，人们并不太关心这种话语所会传达的文化价值与国家利益诉求。因此，应走出对外汉语教学的传统误区，不要将汉语国际推广仅仅视为语言或文化传播，而应将其看作阐释中国价值观及树立中国良好国际形象的外交努力的一部分。[4] 上述意见是正确的。如果说三十年前、二十年前，甚至是十年前，我们的汉语传播方式主要还是“开门迎客”式的对外汉语教学，我们走向世界的意识、条件、环境都还不够成熟，那么今天“主动出击”式的汉语国际推广，就完全应该把传播汉语当作传播“中国式话语”的最好时机，利用好这个特殊的国际话语权空间，将我们中国的“话语”心平气和地、从容不迫地缓缓道出，大范围地培养来自不同国家、群体、阶层倾听“中国话”的友好受众。

我们应该充分意识到，在国际社会对中国还持有种种怀疑、不信任，某些西方国家对中国还充满种种敌意的情况下，来自不同领域、不同身份的外国学生恰恰为我们开通了一条民间通话的渠道，切莫轻视这种民间通话的影响和力量，汇聚起来，传播出去，就能达到我们政府想做却轻易达不到的目的。而且，这些学生若干年以后可能就是教育界的精英、商界的大亨、某国政界的要员，在学习汉语期间获得的对中国的良好印象，对中国民情的了解，将直接影响到他们将来对中国的政策。

我们认为，一方面我们确实应该重视传播优秀的中华文化，改变以往那种在教材中只重语言的结构与功能，忽视教学内容文化性的倾向，把中华优秀传统文化

2 金立鑫：《试论汉语国际推广的国家策略和学科策略》，《华东师范大学学报》，2006年第4期。

3 胡范铸、薛笙：《作为修辞问题的国家形象传播》，《华东师范大学学报》，2010年第6期。

4 冯凌宇：《汉语国际推广与中国公共外交》，《长江论坛》，2010年第6期。

中所蕴含着的思想传播出去，让西方人了解并理解这是中国两千多年来一以贯之的“处世哲学”。另一方面，我们也必须防止“厚古薄今”的倾向，防止传统文化遮蔽了当今中国的文化创造力和文化软实力的展示，从而影响世界各国对当今真实中国的了解和理解。

一位外国记者在谈到孔子学院时说，“和平与和谐是中国目前一直宣称的价值观，中国希望以此来消除别的国家对中国迅速崛起的担忧。”[5] 正因为对外汉语教材文本所提供的“话语”，能反映出中国在世界和平崛起过程中所要塑造的“国家形象”，能相当程度上承担起向世界释放中国渴望和平、和谐的信息。因此，我们认为教材编写应重视中国“国家形象”的内容，对涉及国家形象的内容应遵守“友好、亲善”“和平、正义”“开放、进步”“文明、健康”的编写原则。

二、既有教材中国家形象构建的弊端

然而遗憾的是，检点我们已往的汉语教材，我们确实发现有做得很不够的方面，给中国“国家形象”造成了负面影响。

例如，在一本总共只有十五篇课文的速成教材里，并且是“入门篇”里，出现了一篇名为《钱包被小偷偷走了》的课文（苏英霞、翟艳，2005），[2]这会给不少是第一次来华的留学生们留下怎样的“中国印象”呢？由于使用该教材的教学对象，绝大多数都是利用假期来华做短期修学旅游的外国留学生，他们的汉语水平处于初级阶段（同时也决定了他们对中国的了解一般不会太多），修学时间一般不会超过一个月，通常也就占2～3个星期。在这么短的时间里，他们无暇对中国有比较细致、全面的观察和了解，基本上是我们给他们什么他们就学什么，“拿到篮里都是菜”，结果是拿到了一个“中国有小偷”，“小偷偷我钱包”，“在中国小心倒霉事”，“中国脏、乱、差”的印象回去。因为学生初次习得“被”字句，就是和“钱包被小偷偷走了”，“新自行车被偷了”，“护照被小偷偷走了”，“我被一辆三轮车撞倒了”，“胳膊和腿都被撞青了”，“一下楼就被（西瓜皮）滑倒了”，“他的胳膊被摔伤了”，“B先生被这人撞倒了”，“他的腿被摔青了”，“自行车也被摔坏了”等句子所共有的语义指向紧密联系在一起的，在这些具体句子意义的基础上就会形成一个语篇命题：一个由“钱包被小偷偷走了”而引发的不良之“中国印象”。[3]

类似这样的课文例子还有很多。甚至在一些教材的练习中，也因编写者的随意性出现了很不恰当的例句，特殊情况下有可能会引起一些国家学生的疑虑，例如：“根据情报提供的线索，敌军已经入侵我国边境。我们准备彻底消灭入侵之敌。”[6] 此处，我国俨然与某国已经交战，硝烟味十足。在当前我国与某些邻国海洋权之争极度敏感的情况下，作为具有特殊“话语权”的汉语教材课本，尤其应该注意输出话语时的分寸，避免因教材的不慎影响到中国在国际上作为一个负责任的大国形

5　张西平：《汉语国际推广中的两个重要问题》，《长江学术》，2008年第1期。
6　邓小宁：《高级汉语精读教程 Ⅱ》，北京大学出版社，2007年。

象。再如“历史证明，我们两国之间的友谊具有坚实的基础，在新的国际形势下一定会得到进一步加强。”[7] 而事实上，历史不仅从来没有证实中国与任何其他国家之间的友谊永远坚实，而且这样的句子出现非常容易引起有些国家的反感。

因此，很有必要对我们以往的教材进行一番梳理，将那些负面的、消极的、有损中国“国家形象”，或容易给人留下不良之“中国印象”的课文、例句等剔除出去，重新建立一个汉语国际传播背景下的汉语教材评价体系，努力传递出中国正面的、积极的、恰如其分的信息，杜绝暴力、愚昧、丑陋的内容。

三、国家形象传播的教材话语策略

汉语国际传播追求的最高利益是国家利益，输出的正面形象是“国家形象”，展示给世界的是和平崛起的中国模式，播撒的是交流、合作、友谊的种子正因为此，我们更应该重视并认真研究在教材文本中构建中国“国家形象”时的话语策略。

所谓话语策略，是指人们在运用语言交际时为使交际意图实现而对话语资源采取的一套修辞措施，话语资源的良好运作是有效地达到交际意图的重要方法。由于对外汉语教材的受众通常是以第二语言学习为目标、母语为非汉语的外国学生，其庞大的话语资源使得我们编写人员不得不慎重考虑应采取何种话语策略来实现中国作为文本输出方的交际意图与终极目标。

1. 处理好“高调与低调”的关系

处理好“高调与低调”的关系本身就是一个策略问题。拿“汉语国际传播”来说，开始时我们用的是“汉语国际推广”，与汉语国际推广配套施行的具体行动就是国家拿出财政拨款在世界各地建孔子学院，但是孔子学院并不是处处都受欢迎，一些国家颇有非议，许多外国人不理解中国政府为什么花费如此巨资来推广语言，于是产生了恐惧和抵触心理。（魏崇新，2010）如美国哈西恩德海茨地区的一所学校，因免费从孔子课堂获得课本、手提电脑和扑克牌卡片等教学用品，批评者将其视为一个宣传工具。该行政区的前教育主管克雷默说，我不反对教外国语言，但这是来自中国的一个宣传机器，在美国绝对行不通。（陈一，2010）

由此可见，汉语和中国文化的海外传播并非一帆风顺。所以早就有一些学者建议，“汉语国际推广”不宜以政府出面，“推广”二字宜改为“传播”。同理，构建教材文本中的中国“国家形象”，我们也首先要处理好“高调与低调”的关系。过去由于我们的国家宣传过于片面，注重意识形态的说教，政治色彩浓，造成世界上诸多国家对中国的不理解与不信任感，尤其是在西方国家逆反心理颇为严重。巡检我们的一些汉语课本，我们也发现了一些类似政治宣传的语言。例如：

中国统一既是全世界炎黄子孙的共同愿望，也是中国政治之必需，更是21世纪

7　邓小宁：《高级汉语精读教程 Ⅱ》，北京大学出版社，2007年。

中国和世界历史之必然。（邓小宁，2007）

中国对统一问题的渴望与执着是毋庸置疑的，但如何才能将这种一贯的坚定信念传达给世界呢？相对于上述“义正词严”的表述，我们完全可以另一种方式传达出“要求统一”的呼声：

…………

B: 中国的功夫片拍得真好，在韩国都有很多观众。

A: 功夫片中，你最喜欢谁的电影？

B: 我最喜欢看香港演员成龙的电影，真打真摔，不用替身，都是真功夫。

A: 哎，说到香港，你知道吗？香港已经在97年回归中国了。

B: 知道，这就是有名的“一国两制”，对吗？

A: 对，我们也衷心祝愿朝鲜半岛早日统一。

B: 谢谢你。我也祝中国海峡两岸早日统一。（秦惠兰、黄意明，2004）

上面的这段对话就涉及“统一国家”的敏感话题，但话题却是从“功夫片——香港——‘一国两制’”开始再逐渐进入到“半岛统一——两岸统一”的，由于代表中方的A首先表达了我们中国对朝鲜半岛统一问题的态度，自然也就赢得韩国学生B对我国海峡两岸统一问题的支持，用“将心比心”的办法巧妙地把我们对统一的呼声表达了出来。

有学者指出：我们主张在对外汉语教学中必须坚持民族立场，在关涉国家利益的大是大非问题上——如国家主权、领土完整、民族团结等问题上决不能含糊，要态度鲜明，立场坚定。这是跨文化互动的前提。在以往的教学中为了避免矛盾和冲突，对外汉语教师大都会回避观念文化、特别是意识形态观念文化冲突的话题，容忍和原谅学生“严重的文化上的不妥行为”。[8] 笔者完全赞同上述主张，但认为就如何恰到好处地表明我们的立场和态度，心平气和地、有理有据地阐释我们的观念，游刃有余而又智慧地说服别人，却是一个关涉到话语策略的问题。

2. 有效利用直接与间接两种方式

在汉语教材中构建中国“国家形象”的元素很多，上文提到的几点编写原则，有的可以直接出现，也有的可以用间接委婉的话语修辞方法出现，例如：介绍我国的长城，这几乎是所有教材都会出现的内容，但绝大多数教材都偏重于其历史、构造和传说，或是偏重于言说者的自豪感和满足感，忽略了长城之于中国人的历史文化意义，之于世界人民的“中国印象”，而在一本观光汉语教材中，我们看到了这样一场对话：

A. 小时候，我在影片中看到过长城，这次来北京，我一定要去长城。

8　亓华：《汉语国际推广与文化观念的转型》，《北京师范大学学报》，2007年第4期。

B. 对，长城是世界八大奇迹之一，中国十大名胜之首。最早的长城已有两千多年历史了。

A. 好像中国有一句话，叫“不到长城非好汉”。这是什么意思？

B. 就是说，一个人只有到过长城，才能算作好汉。可见长城在中国人心中的地位。

A. 那我也要做一回好汉，体会一下古代将军的感觉。

B. 那很好，不过长城是以防御为主的，这说明中国人民是一个热爱和平的民族。[9]

对话的结尾一转，很好地托起了一个爱好和平的“中国形象”，甚至是自古以来即如此的中华民族形象。由于“长城”代表着中国，编著者突出了其“防御”性，也就意味深长地向世人宣告着中国人民从来就不是一个主动好战的民族，这对世界上某些国家近年来不断宣扬着的“中国威胁论”，绝对是一个非常有力的回击。类似这种“润物细无声”式地客观塑造中国良好形象的片段在该教材中还有很多，我们认为，这是编著者在编写教材时使用的一种间接委婉的话语策略。

再比如我们的课本中常常有介绍中国菜、中国建筑的内容，从菜名、建筑名到实际的制作或建筑，都体现了中国人的“和合思想”，我们可以充分利用讲究五味调和的中国菜和注重对称的建筑物来巧妙地告诉外国学生，让他们感性地体会到中国今天的“和平崛起”和建设“和谐社会”是一种优秀传统文化的继续，“和为贵”思想指导下的中国文化原本就不具有侵略性。

3. 正确处理认同与求同的关系

“认同与求同”也是我们认为应该把握的一项话语策略。这里所谓的“认同”有多重含义，可以是指凡具有人类普世价值的精神也是我们认同的价值，也可以是指崇尚现代科学精神的理性追求；可以是指以“汉字文化圈”为范围的对优秀的中华传统文化的认同，也可以是指全球华人的文化认同、民族认同。而“求同”则是指我们希望别人认同的价值观，如果求同不行，则可存异。

事实上，由于世界上各个国家各个民族大都或多或少地存在一些文化差异，并导致不同的价值观和意识形态，因此彼此的交流沟通才显得格外地重要。有学者指出：早在1993年Kramsch就提出利用“文化冲突”，可以创造一种语言文化教学的新策略。文化冲突并不可怕，它是教师、学生和教材内容在教室里发生的文化价值的互动，有利于培养学生化解冲突和解决实际问题的综合能力。国外的汉语教学，特别是美国大学汉语教学从来不回避文化冲突和文化批评，相反还以此作为中高年级汉语教材和教学的主要内容和观念，我们的回避却意味着主动放弃话语权和引导权，客观上造成了“文化失语”和“文化沉默”。[10]

---

9 秦惠兰、黄意明：《观光汉语（下）》，北京大学出版社，2004年。

10 亓华：《汉语国际推广与文化观念的转型》，《北京师范大学学报》，2007年第4期。

又比如很多汉语教材都会有介绍春节的内容，中国周边不少国家也同样有过春节的习俗，这是历史上形成并延续至今的一种文化认同，然而通过教材也使世界上很多其他国家的人民更加了解并理解了中国这一重要民俗。我们欣喜地看到，现今欧美一些国家在中国传统节日春节到来之际也纷纷推出了新年贺礼——属相纪念邮票，有的地方政府如纽约州甚至还把大年初一定为了该州的法定假日，还有一些外国学生饶有兴趣地主动参与春节活动。2013年初，在美国白宫回应华人留学生关于春节放假的请愿时还表示：尽管将春节定为联邦法定假日还需要国会采取行动，但我们乐于作出保证，确保这个重要的庆祝活动得到广泛的认可和尊重。类似这样的从了解到理解到认可的事情，我们的教材其实还可以发挥很多很多的作用。

综上所述，我们认为，应全面评估对外汉语教材文本，剔除那些明显有损中国“国家形象”或易造成学习者不良印象的内容，运用修辞智慧，重新审视、谨慎修改那些明显带有政治宣传色彩的内容；应大力加强教材编写人员对汉语国际传播重要性的认识，采取多种有效的话语修辞策略；不仅在介绍中国的文化类教材中传播我国优秀的传统文化，展示现代中国尤其是改革开放三十多年来的中国形象，让世界各国的人民尽可能地了解中国的历史文化、理解中国的改革发展；同时还应采用“分散”的话语策略，将中国元素灵活巧妙地组嵌到其他类型的教材中，向世人展示一个“友好、亲善”、“和平、正义”的中国“国家形象”，也向世人展示一个“开放、进步”、“文明、健康”的中国“国家形象”。

参考文献：

[1] 陈一. 孔子课堂在美引起争议[J].环球时报，2010年4月6日.
[2] 邓小宁.高级汉语精读教程 Ⅱ[Z].北京:北京大学出版社，2007年.
[3] 李晓琪. 汉语国际推广事业中的教材建设[J].世界汉语教学，2007年第3期.
[4] 秦惠兰. 对外汉语教材中的“中国印象”与修辞策略——从《钱包被小偷偷走了》谈起[J].云南师范大学学报，2012年第2期.
[5] 秦惠兰、黄意明.观光汉语（下）[Z]. 北京:北京大学出版社，2004年.
[6] 苏英霞、翟艳.汉语口语速成（入门篇 · 下）[Z]. 北京:北京语言大学出版社，2005年.
[7] 魏崇新.对外汉语教学思考(上、下) [J]. 人民日报，2010年7月28 日，7月29日.

Rhetoric Strategies of China's Image in Editing Chinese Textbook

Qin Huilan
(Shanghai Normal University, China)

Abstract: The communications and construction of China's image of nation have various forms, levels and means, in which the international communications of Chinese, including the "internal" teaching of Chinese as a foreign language and the "external" international promotion of Chinese, proves to be the most direct, effective, cordial and smooth way. The communications of Chinese is communications of language as well as discourse, and they are forming China's image of nation in the "Chinese discourse" they construct. What provide the fundamental texts of the discourse are the teaching materials of Chinese, by whose quality the construction of China's image of nation is affected. As a result, the discourse rhetoric strategies of the text must be considered carefully when teaching materials of Chinese as a foreign language are compiled.

Keywords: international communications of Chinese; image of nation; teaching materials of Chinese as a foreign language; discourse strategy

学会介绍

世界汉语修辞学会

世界汉语修辞学会，是汉语修辞学研究的国际学术组织，由世界各国从事汉语修辞学及相关研究的学者组成。2007年7月于国际修辞学史学会（ISHR）第16届年会上成立于法国斯特拉斯堡市帕莱斯大学，学会注册地韩国，秘书处所在地为中国北京大学。

本会宗旨为团结世界各国和各地区从事修辞学、汉语修辞学以及相邻学科研究的专家学者，积极开展国际修辞学特别是汉语修辞学研究，促进世界各国和各地区汉语修辞学及相邻学科学者之间的交流与合作，推动汉语、汉语修辞、文化及其教学的发展、繁荣。该会工作语言为汉语，辅助工作语言为英语。

世界汉语修辞学会创会会长为中国北京大学陈汝东教授。现任会长为韩国外国语大学罗敏球教授。世界汉语修辞学会成立以来，积极开展国际学术活动，加强与世界各国学者的联系与合作。已先后于中国的曲阜师范大学（2008年7月）、香港香港教育学院（2010年7月）、韩国仁川大学（2012年10月）成功召开了三届年会，第四届年会将于2014年10月在韩国首尔大学召开。世界汉语修辞学会是一个开放的国际学术组织，欢迎有志于修辞学特别是汉语修辞学研究的学者加入学会。

The Chinese Rhetoric Society of the World (CRSW)

The Chinese Rhetoric Society of the World（CRSW）is an international academic organization of Chinese Rhetoric Studies. Its members consist of scholars from around the world engaged in Chinese Rhetoric and related research. The society was founded in the 16th Annual Meeting of the International Society for the History of Rhetoric (ISHR) at Palestrina University of Strasbourg, France, in July 2007. This organization registered in Korea, Its secretary is located in Peking University, China.

The aim of the organization is to unite experts and scholars from the different countries and regions engaged in the study of rhetoric, Chinese rhetoric and relevant disciplines, carry out studies on international rhetoric, especially Chinese rhetoric studies actively, to promote exchanges and cooperation between scholars engaged in Chinese rhetoric and adjacent discipline studies from the world's countries and regions, to promote the prosperity of the study and teaching of Chinese language, Chinese rhetoric and culture development. The working language of The Chinese Rhetoric

Society of the World is Chinese, auxiliary working language is English.

The founding President of the Chinese Rhetoric Society of the World (CRSW) is Chen Rudong, professor of Peking University in China. The current President of the society is Na Mingu, professor from Hankuk University of Foreign Studies in Korea. Since its establishment, the society carried out international academic activities actively, strengthened the contact and cooperation with scholars from all over the world, has held three annual meeting successively in Qufu Normal University (July 2008,China), the Hong Kong Institute of Education (July 2010, Hong Kong), University of Incheon (October 2012, Korea). The fourth annual meeting will be held in Seoul University in October 2014. The Chinese Rhetoric Society of the World (CRSW) is an open international academic organizations, welcome scholars who are interested in rhetoric, especially Chinese rhetoric studies to join the society.

全球修辞学会

全球修辞学会于2012年10月成立于在韩国仁川大学召开的世界汉语修辞学会第三届年会暨国际修辞学研讨会。

全球修辞学会为国际非营利性公共学术与业务组织，由世界各国从事新闻学、传播学、语言学、文学、伦理学、法学等领域研究和教学特别是从事修辞学研究或教学的学者、研究人员、爱好者，以及媒体及其从业人员、媒体经营与管理人员等组成。学会目前由来自中国、美国、法国、意大利、德国、英国、南非、墨西哥、澳大利亚、阿根廷、埃及、保加利亚、丹麦、芬兰、韩国、日本、加拿大等国家和地区的数百名学者组成。

全球修辞学会的宗旨是团结世界各国的学者，从普世视角研究人类各种文化、文明、宗教、国家、民族背景下的修辞现象和修辞规律，促进修辞学与哲学、文学、语言学、传播学、社会学、心理学等的多学科交叉与融合，促进世界各国、各学科之间学者的交流与合作，为人类所面临的全球问题的解决提供创造性的修辞学理论和思想。全球修辞学会积极开展与相关国际学术组织的交流与合作，共同推动全球修辞学的发展与繁荣。

全球修辞学会下辖世界汉语修辞学会、全球传媒伦理与法制联合会、全球语言与文化教育学会、国际修辞传播学会、国际语言传播学会等分会。全球修辞学会秘书处设在北京大学。该会工作语言为汉语和英语。全球修辞学会创会会长为北京大学陈汝东教授。

The Global Rhetoric Society

The Global Rhetoric Society was founded at the Third Annual Conference of The Chinese Rhetoric Society of the World (CRSW) & International Conference on Rhetoric Studies which was held at Incheon University of Korea in October, 2012.

The Global Rhetoric Society is a non-profit international public academic organization. Its members consist of scholars, researchers and enthusiasts engaged in research and teaching of journalism, communication, linguistics, literature, ethics, law, particularly those who engaged in research or teaching of rhetoric from around the world. Its members also include journalists, media marketers and media managers.

The purpose of The Global Rhetoric Society is to unite the world scholars, study the rhetoric phenomenon and law in the background of all kinds of cultures, civilizations, religions, nations and ethnicities from the universal perspective, to promote integration and intersection of rhetoric and philosophy, literature, linguistics, communication, sociology, psychology etc, to promote exchanges and cooperation between the countries all over the world and scholars from various disciplines, to provide creative rhetoric theories and ideas to solve the global problems of mankind. The Global Rhetoric Society conducts exchanges and cooperation with relevant international organizations actively, to jointly promote the development and prosperity of the study of global rhetoric.

The Global Rhetoric Society has the following branches: the Chinese Rhetoric Society of the World, the Global Alliance of Media Ethics and Law, the World Association of Language & Culture Education, the International society for rhetorical communication Studies, the International Society for Linguistic and Rhetorical Communication Studies. the secretary of the Global Rhetoric Society is located in Peking University, China. The working languages of the Society are Chinese and English. The founding President of the society is Chen Rudong, professor of Peking University in China.

学者介绍

陈汝东，博士，现任北京大学新闻与传播学院传播学系教授、博士生导师，1995年于上海外国语大学获文学博士学位后，一直在北京大学任教，曾任中文系讲师、副教授、新闻与传播学院副教授、教授；现兼任全球修辞学会会长、全球传媒伦理与法制联合会会长、世界汉语修辞学会与全球语言与文化教育学会名誉会长、美国卡耐基委员会全球伦理联盟委员会委员等。

主要学术兴趣为修辞学、新闻传播学、语言学等领域的新兴交叉学科，近年兴趣主要为传媒史、传媒制度与政策、传媒话语、国家修辞、比较修辞、修辞传播学教育等；著有《社会心理修辞学导论》、《对外汉语修辞学》、《认知修辞学》、《当代汉语修辞学》、《语言伦理学》、《传播伦理学》、《新兴修辞传播学理论》等；在国内外重要期刊发表论文百余篇，主持了"新兴修辞学交叉学科前沿理论研究"、"受众伦理研究"等国家和教育部基金项目。

他先后创建了全球修辞学会、世界汉语修辞学会等多个国际学术组织，并多次应邀到英国牛津大学、日本早稻田大学以及美国、韩国、瑞士、保加利亚等国的大学讲学、研修，并多次应邀在国际修辞学史学会等国际学术组织的年会上做大会主旨演讲，其学术成就具有广泛的国际影响；兼任《国际修辞学研究》主编以及《当代中国话语研究》、《韩中语言文化研究》（韩）、《修辞学》（韩）、《非洲修辞学年鉴》（南非）、《新闻大众传播研究》（美）等多家期刊的编委，《北京大学学报》的《北大学人》、《江淮论坛》的《学者风采》以及新华网、人民网等对其做过报道。

Chen Rudong is a professor of School of Journalism and Communication of Peking University of P. R. China. He is now the presidents of the Global Rhetoric Society and the Global Alliance of Media Ethics and Law, honored presidents of the Chinese Rhetoric Society of the World and the World Association of Language & Culture Education, Council member of Global Ethics Network of the Carnegie Council and etc.

Prof. Chen got his Ph.D in linguistics and applied linguistics from Shanghai International Studies University in 1995. He has been teaching at Peking University since 1995 up to now. He has taught and done researches at the universities in the

United Kingdom, the United States, Korea, Japan, Bulgaria and etc. Prof. Chen founded the Global Rhetoric Society, the Chinese Rhetoric Society of the World, the Global Alliance of Media Ethics and Law, and other international academic organizations. He was invited to give keynote speeches at conferences of ISHR and other international academic organizations many times. He is well-known worldwidely in the field of rhetoric studies.

His research interests cover studies on rhetoric, journalism, communication and language especially interdisciplinary subjects such as socio-psychological rhetoric, cognitive rhetoric, ethics of language, ethics of communication and rhetorical communication. He has published 8 books on rhetoric and communication studies, such as *An Introduction to Socio-psychological Rhetoric*, *Chinese Rhetoric for Foreigners*, *Cognitive Rhetoric*, *The Contemporary Rhetoric of China*, *The Ethics of Language*, *Ethics of Communication*, *New Theories on Rhetorical Communication Studies* and etc. In addition, Prof. Chen has published more than 100 papers in the journals around the world. He has chaired and undertook two national programs of the Chinese Government as a chief researcher. His story was reported by *Xinhuanet*, *People's Daily Online*, *Journal of Peking University*, *The Journal of Jianghuai Tribune* and etc.